W9-CMK-785

# CURRENT PERSPECTIVES
## *on the*
# Culture
# *of* Schools

## NANCY B. WYNER

Brookline Books

**Library of Congress Cataloging-in-Publication Data**

Current perspectives on the culture of schools / Nancy B. Wyner, editor.
    p.    cm.
  Includes bibliographical references (p.  ) and index
  ISBN 0-914797-61-1
  1. Educational anthropology—United States.  2. School enviornment—United States.  3. Intercultural educational— United States.  4. Educational change—United States.
5. Education—United States—Aims and objectives.
I. Wyner, Nancy B., 1931-
LB45.C86   1991
370.19'0973—dc20

                    91-7219
                    CIP

*The following chapters were reprinted with permission of the publisher unless otherwise noted:*

Chapter 1: Erickson, F. (1987) 'Conception of School Culture: An Overview' *Educational Administration Quarterly* 23, #4, pp. 11-24. ©1987. Reprinted by permission of Sage Publications, Inc.

Chapter 2: The Superintendency and Politics from A. Blumberg with Phyllis Blumberg. (1985) *The School Superintendent: Living with Conflict* (N.Y.: Teachers College Press, ©1985) pp. 45-71.

Chapter 5: Stanlaw, J. & Peshkin, A. Black Visibility in a Multi-ethnic High School — Abridged version from *Class, Race & Gender in American Education*. Lois Weis, Ed. Permission requested from State University of New York Press, Albany, N.Y.

Chapter 6: Ost, David H., The Culture of Teaching: Stability and Change. Reprinted from *Educational Forum* by permission of Kappa Delta Pi, an International Honor Society in Education.

Chapter 11: Lieberman, Ann, Saxl, Ellen R., & Miles, Matthew B. (1988) 'Teacher Leadership: Ideology and Practice' in Lieberman, Ann, ed. *Building a Professional Culture in Schools*. (New York: Teachers College Press, ©1988). pp. 148-166.

Chapter 12: Fullan, Michael (1990) Staff Development, Innovation, and Institutional Development. In *Changing School Culture through Staff Development*. ASCD 1990 Yearbook. Reprinted with permission of the Association for Supervision and Curriculum Development, ©1990.

*To the loving memory*
*of my mother Ceil Hauptman Braverman,*
*and for my children, Cassia, Adam Zachary and his wife Katya,*
*and Isaiah who continue to enrich my heart.*

# Acknowledgements

Special thanks are due to my students, particularly those who participated in *The Culture of the School*, a course I have taught at the college for several semesters. Each semester bilingual, ESL and mainstream teachers talked together as colleagues. We gathered stories, shared anecdotes, and reflected on meanings woven into the regularities and interactions of school cultures. Their stories were eloquent and thoughtful. Some were angered to recall their experiences. Others were embarrassed to talk about their disappointments and the frustrations of inequity and exclusion. And yet they were joyful when things went well in their relationships with students and colleagues. These teachers cared about teaching and the students they taught. Their stories brought us together and strengthened our collective understanding of why changes are imperative in the culture of the school to enable teachers and children to work and learn together.

My own teachers continue to be important to me: I was an apprentice teacher to Lucille Ezekiel at the Overseas School in Rome, Italy. Her passion for teaching and sensitivity to the aesthetic and social context for teaching young children created a garden of ideas and interests in my teaching career. Others continue to influence my thinking — Barbara Biber, Margaret Yonemura, A. Harry Passow, M. Virginia Biggy, and many others who helped along the way, each in their own way.

I am especially indebted to Seymour B. Sarason who visited our campus as Scholar in Residence. He met with my class and his visit was memorable. His intense interest, thoughtful questioning, and responses to student concerns were lessons of humaneness and caring. He listened to their stories, valued and affirmed each for their diversity, sensitivity and sense of responsibility. He championed their efforts to change the way things worked in their schools — on behalf of the children, the profession of teaching and their own dignity as persons. He gave new dimension to their struggle. He is a *melamed*, a wise man, who opened the way to ideas and possibilities, as he has done throughout his career.

This book is a response to his strong encouragement, and to the vitality of his contributions to school improvement. This collaborative endeavor was shaped by the thoughtful contributions of chapter authors and Dr. Milton Budoff, publisher.

*Nancy Wyner*

# Table of Contents

**INTRODUCTION**  *Seymour B. Sarason* ............................................................. xi

**PREFACE**  *Nancy B. Wyner* .................................................................. xiii

**CONTRIBUTORS** ............................................................................ xvii


## THE CONTEXT

**CHAPTER 1**  *Frederick Erickson*
Conceptions of School Culture: An Overview ................................................ 1


## CONTESTED VALUES IN THE CULTURE OF THE SCHOOL

### Leadership and politics

**CHAPTER 2**  *Arthur Blumberg*
The Superintendency and Politics ................................................................. 13

**CHAPTER 3**  *Flora Ida Ortiz*
An Hispanic Female Superintendent's
Leadership and School District Culture .......................................................... 29


### Diversity in Student Cultures

**CHAPTER 4**  *Nancy Lesko*
Implausible Endings: Teenage Mothers and Fictions of School Success .... 45

**CHAPTER 5**  *James Stanlaw & Alan Peshkin*
Black Visibility in a Multi-Ethnic High School .............................................. 65


## CULTURES OF TEACHING IN A TIME OF CHANGE

**CHAPTER 6**  *David H. Ost*
The Culture of Teaching: Stability and Change ............................................. 79

**CHAPTER 7**  *Nancy B. Wyner*
Unlocking Cultures of Teaching: Working with Diversity ......................... 95

**CHAPTER 8**  *Jacqueline F. Moloney*
Changing Faculty Beliefs About the Underprepared Student .................. 109

**CHAPTER 9**  *Leonard C. Beckum with Arlene Zimney*
School Culture in Multicultural Settings ...................................................... 123

## CULTURE BUILDING FOR DIVERSITY AND EXCELLENCE: CHANGING INSTRUCTIONAL METHODS, ROLES, REGULARITIES, AND RELATIONSHIPS

**CHAPTER 10**   *Shlomo Sharan &Yael Sharan*
Cooperative Learning: Changing
Teachers' Instructional Methods ....................................................................143

**CHAPTER 11**   *Ann Lieberman, Ellen R. Saxl, &Matthew B. Miles*
Teacher Leadership: Ideology and Practice ....................................................165

**CHAPTER 12**   *Michael G. Fullan*
Staff Development, Innovation and Institutional Development ...............181

**CHAPTER 13**   *Richard I. Arends*
Challenging the Regularities of Teaching
Through Teacher Education ........................................................................203

## REFLECTIONS ON CULTURES IN POSTMODERNISM

**CHAPTER 14**   *Peter McLaren*
Decentering Cultures: Postmodernism,
Resistance, and Critical Pedagogy ................................................................231


**INDEX** .........................................................................................................259

# Introduction

If you are the kind of person who tries to remain optimistic about educational reform, you obviously do not have an easy time of it. You are, if you read the literature, whether professional and popular, you are quite aware that all sorts of efforts are being made to improve our schools. However, if you are a practitioner on the firing line, you probably find yourself reacting by saying "Here we go again" or "I'll take this new nostrum with more than a few grains of salt." Those are justifiable reactions, given the record over the past decade of failure. This is in no way to impugn the seriousness of most of these efforts or to deny that they have had no positive outcomes whatsoever. The fact remains that, overall, our schools have been intractable to change. It is that intractability that caused me to write my recent book *The Predictable Failure of Educational Reform* (1990). I did not write it to reinforce my image as a wet blanket, ready to give up on our schools but to emphasize the fact of intractability and to explore its significances.

The one source of optimism in this otherwise sad picture is that in the past decade or so there has been an increasing recognition that we have not taken seriously that the culture of schools, unwittingly but effectively, is the major obstacle to the initiation and maintenance of reform efforts. Reform, we have learned, is not an exercise in engineering or dependent upon increased resources, or an effort whose outcomes require heroic degrees of motivation. What we have learned is that the way schools are organized, the behavioral and programmatic regularities which characterize them, the undergirding axioms that remain silent and go unchallenged — these are the factors which are beginning to be confronted with all the turmoil and conflict one should expect from the dynamics of cultural change.

We should not overestimate what we know about the culture of schools and we certainly not expect that as our knowledge broadens it will be obvious what our options for change are. If I am right that we are at the beginning of a more realistic confronting of what we are up against, the future will be a difficult one. We've learned a lot but not enough to assume that we will not make a lot of errors in using what we have and will learn.

In this book Dr. Wyner has brought together a number of perspectives on school culture. I believe this book reflects a trend to move away from bandaids to a more penetrating analysis of how we have to think. Cultural change does not cause new ways of thinking, it is a consequence of those ways. The contents of this book are a contribution to altered ways of thinking. There is much to provoke new thinking in this book. There are no polemics in this book, no scapegoating, no panaceas. It contains chapters by people who are no longer willing or able to accept the school culture as we traditionally have understood and accepted it.

*April, 1991*

Seymour Sarason, Professor of Psychology Emeritus, Yale University

---

Sarason, S.B. (1990) *The Predictable Failure of Educational Reform* (1990). San Francisco, CA:Jossey Bass.

# Preface

> ...all games are conventions, all cities are conventions, ultimately all culture is a convention, particularly if we remember that culture means tilling the soil in patterns and with purpose, making, as Thoreau said, the earth say beans instead of grass, that is, putting design and shape into a common environment, beginning in the mind whence all design flows.
>
> A. Bartlett Giamatti, *Take Time for Paradise*

In the recent restoration of Michaelangelo frescos in the Sistine Chapel ceiling it was determined that pseudo-restorers, using *velature*, or glazes containing binder, obscured Michelangelo's original frescos. These "pseudo" images, coated with glaze, stuck firmly in the imagination of millions.

Most of us will find it incredulous that our images of Michaelangelo's frescos have been obscured and changed by the work of later "restorers." Fortunately, the technical competence and integrity of modern restorers has made it possible to see the works as the artist intended.

To believe in what we see as the "truths," to grow accustomed to the way things are so that we scarcely hear, see or feel the familiar is characteristic in our lives. Educators who have studied life in schools have come to recognize that a certain intellectual effort is required to see how such phenomena can pose serious problems or call for intricate explanatory theories. One is inclined to regard them as necessary or somehow "natural[1]." Wittgenstein pointed out that "the aspects of things that are most important for us are hidden because of their simplicity and familiarity (one is unable to notice something—because it is always before one's eyes)." It is as though we must make the familiar strange to understand the complexity of our experiences.

In his study of the everyday realities and complexities of school life, Sarason (1971, 1982) concluded that teachers and administrators were unaware of the cultural and organizational regularities of their school and were not oriented toward using this information to examine organizational and professional realities.

*Current Perspectives on School Culture* brings together a wide range of perspectives to indicate the complexity of how schools operate and how complex it is to alter their current function. My intention is to provide practitioners and graduate students with theories, ideas and reflections on life in schools that will help them to look at the complex organization of their school, and to see beneath the glaze of routine and regularity, as a necessary step toward planning and implementing school improvement and change.

---

[1] Ludwig Wittgenstein, Philosophical Investigations (New York: Oxford University Press, 1953), Section 129, cited in Noam Chomsky (1972) *Language and Mind*, New York: Harcourt Brace. 24-25

Research on schools has expanded beyond earlier theories focussed mainly on implementing an innovation, the role of change agents and users of innovations, to in-depth ethnographies and case studies of the realities of school life. Goodlad, Lightfoot, McLaren, Sarason, Sizer, and others have developed rich, detailed descriptions of what goes on in schools, and how new ideas are managed—the myths, rituals, regularities, the nature of discourse and experiences of teachers, students and administrators in school cultures. These portraits have helped educators to plumb beneath the daily events of schooling; to reflect on the tenacious grip of myth, tradition and power on teaching and learning; and, to question the tensions between the changing needs of students and society and the unchanging regularities of schooling.

Contemporary perspectives reflect a shift in focus to dynamic social interactions and their symbolic meanings, changes in viewing social phenomena as objectified, and social knowledge as a source for reporting regularities in society—a view that contributes to reproduction of existing institutions. Critical pedagogy has broadened our understanding of political and social influences and challenged the reader to understand powerful influences that impede or promote forces of change in the interests of instruction and learning. Educators are urged to question social behavior as intentional and meaning as problematic (McLaren, 1989,1991). Critical awareness of the social phenomena of schooling promises to provide an important source for understanding how schools work, how the change process evolves; what structures, experiences, requirements and supports it requires for a desired implementation, and institutionalization over time, Fullan, 1991; Lieberman, 1991)

As these perspectives are further developed, reflections on the processes that operate within teacher education, staff development and teacher-student interactions are increasingly important sources for conceptualizing the culture of the school and understanding how members of the school culture choose to enact their values, social relationships and authority.

Many of the chapters in this book, *Current Perspectives on School Culture*, were commissioned for this publication. In addition, articles in the journal literature are reprinted since they deserve to become part of a composite sourcebook for the study of the culture of the school. Several chapters focus on cultural analysis of values in school cultures and reflect on the interrelationships of values among diverse social groups—of teachers, students and university faculties. New demands to change school culture require careful study and reflection on all moments of the school day, every facet of the social interplay, and all elements that influence life in school—the external and internal influences on resistance and creation of cultures of school. In this book we have tried to reach out to describe and understand what we perceive today.

Writers of these chapters describe the complexities and tensions of the social context of school culture, and they express concern about cultural differences of teachers and students, the needs of linguistic minorities, and the underprepared student, policies and practices in teacher education, staff development and programs for teenage mothers, the work of a superintendent in change efforts to bring a whole district toward equity and excellence. Diverse approaches help the reader to grasp the dynamics, problems and strengths of school and university cultures. Regularities and rules, symbols and discourse, myth and meanings are used to interpret a world bounded by a sense of place called school. In the view presented here, social structure and culture are intertwined. Cultural differences are seen as lines tracing status, power, and political interest within and across institutional boundaries (Erickson, 1987).

There are as many school cultures as there are schools. And within each school culture, subcultures proliferate—cultures of collaboration, and cultures of change, cultures of teaching and cultures of resistance. The grammars created in the culture of the school must be listened to and understood if we are to interpret and improve schools. Within the culture of any particular school, persons work amidst complex and interconnected relations, rooted in language, tradition, custom, history and perceived social status — a complex equation of possibilities, disappointments, implications and meanings concealed or conveyed, depending on the values and attitudes of participants. In some of these cultures, people work in isolation, and in other settings collegiality is evident. The plurality of perspectives brought together in this publication will help the reader to understand the multidimensionality of school culture from the viewpoint of practitioners, teacher educators, planners and policymakers.

Significant attention will be given to the personal, to the clash of values and expectations that erupt among professional and personal traditions and histories, between established subgroups and "newcomers," the unempowered majority. Readers will be encouraged to question whether we are paying attention to the wrong things, sifting out behaviors we should observe, question and challenge as potential impediments to changing school cultures, overlooking strengths, positive interactions and relationships that nurture effective schools. Changing school cultures to meet the needs of community, staff and students is the challenge of the decade. Several of the authors propose alternatives for staff development and teacher education that offer hopeful new directions.

This approach to the study of schools is not neat or methodical. It does not propose logical constructs. But from its thrust toward validating experiences, perceptions and attitudes, the social realities and aspirations of students, teachers and parents who believe in public education can be shared, studied, changed and celebrated. The true purpose of efforts to study school cultures is to push awareness of the present, to change the realities and possibilities of diversity within these settings.

*Nancy B. Wyner, Editor*

# Contributors

**Richard I. Arends** is Professor of Education, University of Maryland. His works include *Learning to Teach* and, "Connecting the university and the schools" in *The 1990 ASCD Handbook on Staff Development.*

**Leonard C. Beckum** is University Vice-President and Vice Provost, Duke University. From 1985-1990, Dr. Beckum was Dean, College of Education, The City College of The City University of New York. Prior to that time he was Director of the Race Desegregation Center at The Far West Regional Laboratory. He is a member of the Board of Directors, AACTE.

**Arthur Blumberg** is Professor of Education at Syracuse University. He received his Ed.D. from Teachers College, Columbia University and has served on the faculties of Springfield College and Temple University. Dr. Blumberg has authored or coauthored several books including *Supervisors and Teachers: A Private Cold War* and *The Effective Principal.*

**Phyllis Blumberg** is Associate Dean, College for Human Development, Syracuse University. She received her doctorate from Syracuse University in counseling and guidance.

**Frederick Erickson** is Professor of Education, Chair of the Educational Leadership Division of the Graduate School of Education, and Director, Center for Urban Ethnography, University of Pennsylvania.

**Michael G. Fullan** is Dean, Faculty of Education, University of Toronto, Ontario, Canada. He is primarily concerned with change processes in education.

**Nancy Lesko** is Assistant Professor, Department of Curriculum and Teacher Education, Indiana University. Lesko is author of *Symbolizing Society.*

**Ann Lieberman** is Visiting Professor of Education at Teachers College, Columbia University. Her publications include *Rethinking School Improvement: Research, Craft, and Concept; Building a Professional Culture in Schools;* and, *Teachers, Their World and Their Work.*

**Jacqueline Fidler Maloney**, is a licensed social worker. She is Director of The Centers of Learning and the Freshman Center, University of Lowell.

**Peter McLaren,** Scholar-in-Residence, Associate Professor,and Associate Director, Center for Education and Cultural Studies, Miami University, Oxford, Ohio. His works include *Schooling as a Ritual Performance; Life in*

*Schools;* and *Critical Pedagogy, the State, and Cultural Struggle* (Co-editor Henry A. Giroux).

**Matthew B. Miles** is senior research associate at the Center for Policy Research, New York City.

**Flora Ida Ortiz** is Professor of Educational Administration, School of Education, University of California, Riverside. Recent books include *Career Patterns in Education,* and *The Superintendent's Leadership in School Reform.*

**David Ost is** Professor, Department of Biology, California State University, Bakersfield, California.

**Alan Peshkin** is Professor of Education at the University of Illinois, Urbana-Champaign.

**Ellen Saxl** is on the faculty of Teachers' College, Columbia University.

**Shlomo Sharan, Ph.D.,** Professor of Educational Psychology, Tel-Aviv University, Israel, is author of numerous books on cooperative learning, including (H. Shachar, co-author) *Language and learning in the cooperative classroom* and, *Cooperative Learning: Theory and Research.*

**Yael Sharan** is on the staff at The Israel Educational Television Center, Tel-Aviv, Israel.

**James Stanlaw** is a Research Associate, Bureau of Educational Research, University of Illinois, Urbana-Champaign.

**Nancy B. Wyner, Ed.D., J.D.** Associate Professor, *Leadership in Schooling,* College of Education, University of Lowell. Publications include "Educating linguistic minorities: Public education and the search for unity" In *Educational Horizons.* (1989); and, "Cognitive, Emotional, and Social Development: Early Childhood Social Studies" (co-author Elizabeth Farquhar). In *The Handbook of Research on Social Studies Teaching and Learning,* sponsored by the National Council for the Social Studies.

**Arlene Zimney** was special assistant to Dean Leonard C. Beckum at the City College of New York, 1987-1990.

# The Context

# Chapter 1
# Conceptions of School Culture: An Overview[1]

*by Frederick Erickson, University of Pennsylvania*

It is not clear what the term culture means in current discussion of school culture. Is it to refer globally to everything that happens routinely in schools, or are there more precise definitions that can be useful? This article reviews a range of definitions of culture. Three main conceptions of culture are discussed; a culture as bits of information, culture as conceptual structure and symbols, and culture as meanings generated in political struggle. Through examples and commentary the author considers the relative utility of the different conceptions of culture for helping one think about the diverse and systematically patterned ways of making sense that students, teachers, and administrators bring to their everyday encounters with one another in schools.

When you walk into a school you may get a global impression of the school's distinctive tone or character. What cues led to that impression? The walls and their decorations, the floors and the way they are polished, the demeanor of students and staff walking through the halls, the nature of the instruction that takes place in classrooms, the relationships between staff and administration? Behind or beneath the cues, some social scientists assume, lies a shared set of organizing principles called culture. Is school culture something more than just another word for school climate? Are there some aspects of culture that you do not get a sense of at first glance, that are not shared by everyone in the setting? How, in other words, might we think of culture? Where is it in the school? What is its specific content? How would we find it if we went looking for it? And why bother?

*Culture* is a term that presents difficulties as well as interesting possibilities when we try to apply it to a school as a whole. Writing on educational issues, Sarason (1971) and Feiman-Nemser and Floden (1986) have used the term *culture* to refer to an undifferentiated entity; the overall character or ethos of an educational setting, such as a school, or of an educational role, such as that of teacher. A problem with such usage is that it leaves the term without distinct content and leaves the phenomenon of culture in the school invisible and tacit—it's somehow in the air and all around us but we can't see it or talk about it. This essay attempts to make the notion of culture more explicit and visible in order that it can become a more usable construct within current discourse concerning educational reform.

The use of *culture* as a formal, scientific term originated within the field of anthropology. Even anthropologists have widely disagreed over how to conceive of culture, leaving us with a fuzzy understanding of the concept. Anthropologists Kroeber and Kluckhohn (1952) attempted unsuccessfully to resolve these debates through a book-length review of variations in the uses of the term. Their monograph identified hundreds of different shadings of the meaning for the word *culture*. Since then no scholar has attempted to claim sole possession of the correct definition, but many working definitions have been proposed. Each of the major definitions entails a differing theory of the nature of culture. We will review here only a few of these main conceptions of the phenomenon.

Culture in the social scientific sense does not, of course, mean "high culture." Usually anthropologists have thought of culture as a system of ordinary, taken-for-granted meanings and symbols with both explicit and implicit content that is, deliberately and nondeliberately, learned and shared among members of a naturally bounded social group. Typically the groups studied by anthropologists have been hunting and gathering bands or residents of small villages. These are the basic social units of premodern societies.

But schools are not primitive villages. Who should we expect to see culture in schools? Considerable debate continues over how much culture there is to be learned even within a small-scale social unit, and whether everyone in the group learns it or whether it is differentially learned. Large, complex, modern societies fundamentally differ in some ways from smaller societies. In modern societies some crucial social relations take place indirectly and anonymously, while in traditional societies decision making and the exercise of power are less anonymous. In complex modern societies social divisions and differential access to power run along lines of class and race and across major social institutions such as those of commerce, law, and education. Serious questions have been raised about whether or not the anthropological conception of culture is applicable at all to modern societies. Some sociologists and others concerned with social theory have argued that the notions of social structure or of political economy explain more adequately the observable variations in the actions, beliefs, and sentiments of individuals and groups than does the anthropological notion of culture.

In spite of these difficulties the concept of culture can be helpful as one tries to gain new and deeper understanding about the nature of daily life and instruction in schools. In thinking about the role of culture in schools, three main conceptions of culture seem most relevant. All three presume that culture is essentially ideational—not behavior itself but a set of interpretive frames for making sense of behavior. Each conception presumes a way in which cultural knowledge is shared within a social group. (The following discussion draws upon that of D'Andrade, 1984.)

One of the conceptions of culture defines it by analogy to information bits in a computer or to genetic information in a breeding population. According to this interpretation, culture consists of many small chunks of knowledge that are stored as a large pool of information within the bounded social group. No single member of the group has learned all of the knowledge that is possessed within the group as a whole. The amounts and kinds of information known are seen as varying widely across individuals and subgroups within the total population. (For more discussion of this conception, see Goodenough, 1981.)

Another conception sees culture as a more limited set of large chunks of knowledge—conceptual structures that frame or constitute what is taken as "reality" by members of a group. These central organizing constructs—core symbols—are seen as being shared widely throughout the bounded social group. Within the group routine ways of acting and making sense repeat the major framing patterns again and again, as within a musical composition many variations can be written on a few underlying thematic elements. This concept emphasizes relatively tight organization of patterns, coherence in the meaning system, and identical (or at least closely shared) understanding of symbols across diverse members of the social group. (For more discussion of this view of culture, see Geertz, 1973.)

A third conception treats social structure and culture as intertwined, identifying strong patterns of differential sharing of cultural knowledge in the social unit. Cultural difference is seen as tracing lines of status, power, and political interest within and across institutional boundaries found in the total social unit, by analogy with the ways in which differences in air pressure or temperature are displayed as isobars on a weather map.

One stream of work in this third mode sees culture as arising through social conflict, with the possibility of differing interest groups becoming progressively more culturally different across time even though the groups may be in continual contact. From this perspective the central interest is not the nature of cultural knowledge itself, but the relationship between the content of cultural knowledge and the specific life situation of the persons and groups in which the knowledge is held. A key question is, "Given certain kinds of daily experience, what kinds of sense do people make of it, and how does this sense-making influence their usual actions?" This position assumes that new cultural knowledge—whether in small information bits or in larger conceptual structures—is being created continually in daily social life. This new culture is accepted, learned, and remembered, or rejected, ignored, and forgotten, depending upon where one sits in the social order. This definition of culture emphasizes (1) the systematic nature of variation in cultural knowledge within a population, and (2) social conflict as a fundamental process by which that variation is organized. (For more discussion of this conception, see Giroux, 1981; and McDermott and Goldman, 1983; Willis, 1977.)

In the first two conceptions, and especially in the second, cultural learning is seen as primarily intergenerational; culture is conceived as tradition that is transmitted across generations through socialization. The third conception accounts for cultural learning and change within a single generation and also considers cultural transmission and continuity across generations.

In terms of social theory, the second concept of culture views social processes as fundamentally homeostatic, with tendencies toward equilibrium providing orderliness in social life. Also from the perspective of social theory, the third conception of culture views conflict as the fundamental social process, from which arises the regularity that can be seen in society. It is apparent that the three different notions of culture involve differing basic assumptions about the nature of people, institutions, and social relations. It should come as no surprise, then, that the three conceptions of culture might illuminate different aspects of daily life and everyday sense-making in the school as a formal organization.

Much of our cultural knowledge is implicit, consisting of overlearned ways of thinking and acting that, once mastered, are held outside conscious awareness. Consequently we are too close to our own cultural patterns to see them without making a deliberate attempt to break our learning set—to introduce a bit of distance between ourselves and our taken-for-granted "reality." To render our transparent assumptions visible it is necessary to cultivate deliberately the ethnographic stance of moderate alienation. When ethnographers go to an exotic setting they try to get close to the way the "natives" understand things, but they try to maintain distance as well. The opposite problem arises in domestic ethnography. One's energy need not go mainly into developing insight into strange customs as comprehensible and, so to speak, familiar. Rather, as I have noted elsewhere (Erickson, 1984), when we try to make new sense of the settings in which we live routinely, the initial task is to make the familiar strange.

One way of cultivating an alienated perspective—a way that is heuristically strategic for considering our own lives—is to imagine a different possible way in which a routine activity could be organized. One continually can ask, "Why is the X way not done in the Y way?" and "What are all the different possible ways of perceiving/believing/doing/evaluating X?" Knowledge of a wide range of the ways humans have used to organize the routine tasks of everyday life helps one imagine these alternative possibilities; this knowledge leads also to the realization of how arbitrary is the culturally framed choice of one of those possibilities.

When we wish to escape the limitations of our own cultural lenses it helps to entertain deliberately an awareness that human choice is part of the backstage machinery that stands behind the routine conduct that presents itself before our eyes. Hymes (1980) puts this point more formally in saying that for us to apply educational ethnography in our own cultural situation requires that we do educational ethnology at the same time. (Ethnography can be defined briefly as the description and analysis of customary action and sense-making found in a particular human group. Ethnology is the comparative study of ethnographic case studies and historical evidence that takes into account the full range of variation in human lifeways in contemporary times and in the past.) For our purposes here, the ethnological perspective on education can be thought of as a metaphor for consciously recalling a wide range of variation in ways of enacting an educational activity or of holding a given educational aim or belief. In considering this wide range of options, all of which have been regarded as normal and reasonable by some human groups, we can, in addition, imagine new possible options beyond those we know to have already existed.

## Examples of Culture in Schools

The following discussion of examples of cultural patterns in educational settings considers phenomena at the level of the school classroom, at the level of the whole school, and at the level of the school district. From district to district and from building to building one sees reading instruction led by a teacher working with a small group of children around a table. The children take turns reading aloud from a basal reader while the remainder of the class does other work. Usually this consists of filling in the blanks on printed workbook pages or dittoed work sheets that accompany the reading or arithmetic text. Usually the teacher assigns the children to one of three or four reading groups; the children are placed homogeneously by "ability," according to a combination of criteria—the child's tested reading level and the teacher's judgment about the appropriateness of the test scores in indicating the child's ability (and, in the case of kindergarten and first grade, the child's "readiness").

This is a typical pedagogical configuration. It can be thought of as an academic task structure consisting of a particular kind of social organization and a particular kind of cognitive organization. The social organization reflects a pattern of role and status allocations among members of the interacting group. That social organization frames (and is reflexively framed by) a cognitive organization of certain kinds of attention and information processing that go to make up the intellectual activity of reading, done in a certain way.

Not all ways of interacting in teaching/learning reading are appropriate within this task structure, nor are all ways of thinking. Thus pedagogical choice dictates the academic task structure, which has powerful implications for the kinds of reading that can occur. These are arbitrary selections of some social organizational and cognitive options from among the many that are possible. The particular combination of pedagogical options selected by a given teacher may make sense, given certain pedagogical assumptions, but the combination chosen is neither necessary nor absolute. The structure is not inherent in the fundamental nature of tasks, as we are so apt to believe of our most customary actions and assumptions. Rather, this customary pedagogical arrangement is the result of implicit and explicit human choice, just as monogamy or polygyny are choices that have been made alternatively in human groups for the social organization of marriage.

The ubiquity of this arrangement of pedagogical task structure in teaching reading (basal readers and workbooks used in ability groups) can be explained along lines other than cultural. We might attribute the omnipresence to the workings of market influences in the general society. Textbook publishers sell a reading series, which includes workbooks, sets of ditto masters, and sets of unit-by-unit tests. School systems compete, and are enjoined by state government to improve reading performance as measured by the tests. Thus district personnel are willing to buy a reading series as a curriculum package and then mandate its use in a uniform manner by teachers. Through various formal and informal means of influence those central office mandates are complied with (and/or passively resisted) at the classroom level of the school system.

Another line of explanation is that of teacher convenience and the triage press of a school day that is overburdened for both children and teachers. Using the basal reader and seatwork could be easier than using literature to teach reading or constructing one's own reading materials. Teachers, it could be argued, seek to "satisfice"—they might wish to provide a more thorough and creative kind of reading instruction but that would take more time and energy than are available, and so they settle for the basal, the dittos, and, perhaps, try some "enrichment" that goes beyond the mandated material.

A related explanation concerns the pedagogical capacity of the average elementary teacher. Most elementary teachers, it has been argued, are not able to construct their own reading programs. They need and want the basal series, with its prepared materials and its prescriptions for social and cognitive arrangements of reading task structure.

Market influences, time press, and lack of deep pedagogical understanding on the part of teachers may or may not be plausible explanations for the absence of teacher-constructed curricula in reading and writing in the early grades. But these are all general explanations. They do not account for the particular choices that have been made regarding pedagogical task structure—the use of "ability groups" accompanied by seatwork, the emphasis on reading aloud as a source of evidence for the teacher's assessment of the students' skills acquisition, the emphasis on sequential, "bottom-up" presentation of isolated skills in the reading and writing curriculum.

Certain specific characteristics of the typical sociocognitive task structure for reading recur so often within and across American school systems that it seems reasonable to assume that the specific options often are grounded— they make sense—in terms of certain core pedagogical beliefs within a professional culture that is broadly shared. These beliefs can be thought of as culture in the sense of conceptual structures—constitutive frames for reality. Among the beliefs seem to be the following:

(1) Ability, which varies widely in students, is a trait that resides within the individual and is, at least in the school-age child, relatively fixed.

(2) Hierarchies of skills (e.g., Bloom's taxonomy) make intuitive sense as ladders of stepwise acquisition. Lower order skills (e.g., decoding, spelling) must be mastered before higher order skills (reading for comprehension, writing texts consisting of multiple sentences). Lower ability students have trouble with lower order skills and must practice them before moving on to higher order skills. Among high ability students, practice on higher order skills may enhance their lower order skills (i.e., if they can write meaningful texts they probably have mastered spelling) but this is not true for lower ability students.

(3) Reading and writing are separate and distinct processes.

(4) The acquisition of reading and writing requires strong intervention and assistance on the part of the teacher, especially for low ability students.

It is unlike learning to speak, which children learn to do without nearly so much formal assistance or adult-designed practice as the need in learning to read and write.

In the field of reading and writing instruction, bitter controversy surrounds all of the statements above. There is no clear empirical warrant for or against these assumptions. Proponents of the "skills" approach (bottom-up ladder of acquisition) and of the "process" approach (nonhierarchical, not isolating separate skills) each claim empirical evidence for their position and accuse members of the opposite camp of ignoring contradictory evidence. Yet despite this bimodal distribution of belief among specialists in the field, common practice by classroom teachers is unimodally distributed toward the skills approach. When framed by the underlying cultural postulates sketched above, the skills approach (and the currently fashionable emphasis on "direct instruction") makes intuitive sense.

This brings us to a crucial point in understanding the nature of cultural knowledge. It is precisely that which makes intuitive sense to someone that is evidence of some aspect of the individual's cultural system. As professional educators we can think: Of course it is difficult to learn to read, so strong instructional interventions are necessary in classrooms if children are to have a fair chance at learning to read. Of course students vary widely in "ability." Of course Bloom's taxonomy can be considered as a ladder of skills to be acquired sequentially. Of course teachers save comprehension discussion for the "high ability" reading group. Of course children from "father-absent" families are expected to do less well in school than children from "father-present" families. All of these propositions, which when viewed critically might seem highly debatable, make obvious sense—they go without saying—within a professional perspective. That professional perspective is a cultural one—specific to some sets of humans and not to others.

In Japan, for example, many teachers and administrators believe that it is not necessary to spend time teaching reading in early elementary school. It is assumed that learning to read is easy, and that it will be learned at home and in the community. To reason judiciously is what is difficult. Strong pedagogical intervention by teachers is required for children to learn to think well and to develop their character and interests. How different this is from the professional cultural assumptions of American educators, given the current emphasis on stepwise and painstaking acquisition of isolated basic reading skills!

Cultural frames define for us the range of available and desirable options. The wholesale and successively brief adoption of educational fads that range in their content across diverse educational philosophies can be seen as evidence of the existence of conceptual structures that are culturally learned and shared by school professionals. Look at the range of fads: teacher effectiveness research and training, school effectiveness training, instructional management by behavioral objectives, human relations training, teaching the whole child, learning for living, back to the basics. We can ask, "What is it that is culturally shared—what, specifically, is the content of the implicit assumptions and knowledge that make some deliberate practices and explicit beliefs seem obviously right, while other seem obviously wrong?" We can also ask how such frames for making sense are invented and how they are learned.

Culture, considered as bits of knowledge and as conceptual structures, defines options because it shapes what we think is possible. Most fundamentally it is ontological—it defines what is in the world, what exists and what does not. This has been obvious in controversies over textbook content. Clearly the current debates over secular humanism in the schools have to do with ontological propositions contained in teaching materials. Does the book say that family arrangements involve life-style choices that are morally neutral, or, at least, are up to individual choice? What about single-parent families? What about families in which both the adult caretakers are lesbians? What is there in the world and what is not?

In current middle school and high school social studies texts we see not only little of religion mentioned, but little detail devoted to such topics as the reconstruction period or labor strife. The description of how a bill becomes a law leaves out the role of lobbyists in the process.

Eisner (1985) has called this nonrandom absence of information the null curriculum, as distinguished from the explicit curriculum and the hidden (latent) curriculum (p. 107). The null curriculum can be seen as a special case of a more general phenomenon in schools and society, that of nonrandomly structured absence. This is a key aspect of the cultural organization of routine experience in social life. It is a means by which ideological content is enacted in society; certain voices and perspectives of participants in daily life are made legitimate and salient or are systematically silenced.

Cultural knowledge, frames of interpretation, and standards of appropriateness also obtain outside the classroom and the textbook. In most school faculty meetings, although never stated in so many words, an informal order of precedence in speaking is taken for granted. The order differs subculturally from school to school. In a faculty, rights to sequencing and to numbers of turns at talk may be allocated along the lines of seniority of service, or across key departments, or by ideological position of the person speaking. The new administrator or teacher needs to learn the unspoken order or change it deliberately or inadvertently.

Consider a different kind of example. Central office administrators and school boards emphasize the statistical mean when preparing and studying quantitative reports. In educational institutions the mean is a ubiquitous measure of what happened. Yet statisticians know that measures of central tendency obscure certain interesting kinds of variation. The school board may ask for a ten-year tabulation of mean scores for the Scholastic Aptitude Test as a measure of the effectiveness of instruction in the high schools. Looking at the year-by-year variance in test scores rather than looking at the mean might yield much more information. Yet it does not occur to the board members, to central administrators, to principals, or to teachers to consider the variance. This can be seen as a matter of cultural expectation, not simply as a matter of the presence or absence of knowledge of statistical technique.

A few final examples can illustrate the notion of oppositional culture that was discussed in connection with the third conception of culture. From that perspective, when conflicting interests arise between social aggregates, one will find members of the various groupings developing culturally learned badges of social identity. These are status markers in styles of action and in patterns of value and belief. During the course of interaction among groups in conflict, the cultural differences among them will increase over time rather than decrease. Bateson (1975) called this process of progressive differentiation across time complementary schizogenesis (pp. 107-127). Sometimes in a schizogenetic sequence of intergroup contact, slight cultural differences will be accentuated because they have assumed powerful symbolic weighting.

For example, Fanon (1970) has reported that in the years shortly before the culmination of the anticolonial revolution in Algeria, the Parisian French accent of the (Algerian) announcers on Radio Algiers was strongly criticized as a symbol of colonial oppression. The day after the revolution, people stopped complaining about the accents of the announcers. Even though the announcers' speech had not changed in its behavioral form, the symbolic meaning of their speech style had changed as the political conflict was resolved (pp. 53-54, 67).

The point is that when reasons for conflict already exist between groups in society, cultural differences between them, whether the differences are large or small, become an excellent resource (and medium) for engaging in and escalating the conflict. From the point of view of the third conception of culture it is not the presence of cultural difference between groups that causes trouble, rather, it seems as if trouble goes looking for culture as an excuse to start a fight and to keep it going.

Turning to examples from a high school, think of the disagreements among students who differ in ethnicity, race, and social class about which band should play at a major school dance. Consider as well the interactional display of badges of disaffiliation from school by the educationally alienated high school students described in Britain by Willis (1977) and in the United States by Cusick (1973 ), among others. Willis's and Cusick's students do not seem to be following only culturally learned rules to govern their behavior. Rather the actions appear to be deliberately or nondeliberately strategic; they work hard on an improvisatory way of *not doing school*. This puts them in a schizogenetic relationship with school authorities and with nonalienated students. They become more culturally different as time goes on.

The actions of the alienated students can be seen as manifesting a cultural politics of resistance that is invented (at least in part) in their own generation as well as partaking of the cultural resources of previous generations. (See Giroux, 1981, for a review of resistance theory as applied to educational settings.) In a later study of school faculties, Cusick (1983) found that working hard at not doing school characterized the activity of teachers who were alienated from their professional work. We might speculate that, as with high school students, the teachers' badges of disaffiliation were in part invented in the current moment (i.e., the teachers were not simply following learned traditions). The teachers might also have been influenced by the actions and beliefs of previous cohorts of alienated teachers, some of whom became role models for the next professional generation of alienated teachers.

## Conclusion

Table 1 displays the relationships between the three conceptions of culture and the examples of school cultural actions. The three concepts of culture can be seen to apply somewhat differently to the examples that were presented (although it should be noted that the assignment of these examples to the conceptions is a bit arbitrary and should not be taken too literally).

Of the three conceptions of culture that were reviewed, the third one is the most comprehensive, in that it can encompass both the notion of culture as bits of information differentially distributed among subgroups of society and the notion of culture as a set of root symbols shared widely in a particular society. The third conception is also more dynamic than the other two, in that

### Table 1-1

*Varying Conceptions of Culture as Applied to the Examples Discussed*

| Examples | CONCEPTION I Culture as Knowledge Bits | CONCEPTION II Culture as Conceptual Structure | CONCEPTION III Culture as Political Struggle |
|---|---|---|---|
| Reading pedagogy in the classroom using ability groups and basal textbooks | • | • | |
| Debate over secular humanism in the curriculum | | • | • |
| Turn-taking order in faculty meeting by seniority, department andpedagogical philosophies of education | | • | • |
| Use of the mean to summarize frequency distributions | • | • | |
| Conflict over what band should play at the school dance | | • | • |
| Alienated high school students and teachers working at not doing school | | • | • |

it accounts for sociocultural change and conflict as well as for certain kinds of stability and homeostasis. A major difference between the third view of culture and the previous two concerns the role of tradition in the processes by which cultural knowledge becomes shared among individuals. In the first two conceptions tradition is seen as central to culture sharing. Shared culture is the result of explicit and implicit teaching and learning across generations. In the third conception, intergenerational cultural transmission is taken into account, but in addition there is strong emphasis on the invention and diffusion of new cultural patterns within a single generation, for reasons of oppositional display and resistance.

In all of these conceptions, culture is seen as knowledge and as framing for meaning, rather than as social behavior or its artifacts. In that regard these definitions differ from some of those used by other authors on the issue of school culture. One's sense of the role of culture in the schools will differ depending upon what conception of culture one adopts, or what eclectic mix among them one develops.

Why bother with the notion of culture when thinking about schools? One main reason is that the notion of culture as shared ways of making sense reveals the action patterns and underlying assumptions in the conduct of educational practice that otherwise might go unnoticed, or they might be dismissed as trivial because they are so commonplace. Another reason is that when one sees professional sense-making by educators as learned and as involving arbitrary choices from a range of alternative possibilities one gains a sense of a broadened range of policy options. A final reason is that by seeing patterns of social organization as grounded in culture and in human agency we identify a reasoned basis for hope in the possibility of educational reform. When we make visible the ways in which humans form the distinctive shapes of their lived history through implicit and explicit choices, we see that what people have made they can change.

## NOTES

[1.] Frederick Erickson, "Conceptions of School Culture," *Educational Administrative Quarterly* (November 1987): 11-24

## REFERENCES

Bateson, G. (1975). *Steps to an ecology of mind.* New York: Ballantine.

Cusick, P.A. (1973). *Inside high school: The student's world.* New York: Holt, Rinehart & Winston.

Cusick, P.A. (1983). *The egalitarian ideal and the American high school.* New York: Longman.

D'Andrade, R.G. (1984). Cultural meaning systems. In R.A. Schweder & R.A. Levine (eds.) *Culture theory: Essays on mind, self, and motion.* Cambridge, MA: Cambridge University Press.

Eisner, E. W. (1985). *The educational imagination: On the design and evaluation of school programs* (2nd ed.). New York: Macmillan.

Erickson, F. (1984). What makes school ethnography "ethnographic"? *Anthropology and Education Quarterly, 15*(1), 51-66.

Fanon, F. (1970). *A dying colonialism.* Harmonsworth, England: Penguin.

Feiman-Nemser, S., & Floden, R. (1986). The cultures of teaching. In Wittrock (Ed.), *Handbook of research on teaching* (3rd ed.; pp. 505-526). New York: Macmillan.

Geertz, C. (1973). *The interpretation of cultures.* New York: Basic Books.

Giroux, H. (1981). *Ideology, culture, and the process of schooling.* Philadelphia: Temple University Press.

Goodenough, W. H. (1981). *Culture, language, and society.* Menlo Park, CA: Benjamin/Cummings.

Hymes, D. H. (1980). Educational ethnology. *Anthropology and Education Quarterly, 11*(1), 3-8.

Kroeber, A. L., & Kluckhohn, C. (1952). *Culture: A critical review of concepts and definitions.* Cambridge, MA: Papers of the Peabody Museum, Harvard University, Vol.47, No.1.

McDermott, R.,& Goldman, S. (1983). *Teaching in multicultural setting.* In L. Van Der Berg, S. de Rijke, & L. Zuck (Eds.), Multicultural education. Dordrecht, The Netherlands: Faris.

Sarason, Seymour B. (1971, 1982). *The culture of the school and the problem of change.* Boston: Allyn & Bacon.

Willis, P. (1977). *Learning to labour: How working class kids get working class jobs.* London: Saxon House.

# Contested Values in the Culture of the School

# Leadership and Politics

# Chapter 2
# The Superintendency and Politics[1]

*by Arthur Blumberg and Phyllis Blumberg*

There are, of course, countless numbers of nonelected executives of focal public enterprises. Each one of them must, from time to time, and some more than others, engage in the political processes that are necessary to the functioning of the organization. School superintendents, though, seem to constitute a set within this broader whole that is somehow different from the whole in important ways. For example, they have responsibility for an enterprise to which some of the most deeply held values in the American tradition are attached. The same cannot be said for the municipal director of public works or the executive in charge of parks and recreation. superintendents assume their positions as supposed experts, yet their expertise becomes useless unless they are able to develop a supportive constituency among the school board, community, and professional staff. The organization that they are to lead and manage is composed of people who often have equal or more expertise in education than the superintendent. Because of this fact, they must deal with a lay policy board and with community groups in ways that don't apply, for example, to a director of public health or even of public welfare. The list of points of difference that separate the superintendency, conceptually and functionally, from the vast array of other public executives could go on and on.

The import of these differences in the superintendency as a public office for the work life of a superintendent has been nicely put by Boyd (1974). He notes, first, "the development of the role of the chief school officer as an *educational statesman*, a professional administrator who exerts extraordinary leadership and influence in policy-making primarily as a result of the weight his recommendations carry with nonpartisan lay boards which are pursuing the public interest" (p.1). Boyd then goes on to highlight the conflict, perhaps the most important one as far as the person of the superintendent is concerned. Starting out with a comment that echoes Iannaccone's comment about the preferred politics of pedagogues, Boyd writes:

> However much the role of the educational statesman has become central to the ideology of school administrators, and however much schoolmen would prefer to play that role, it is obvious that they sometimes face situations in which the role is not a viable one. Since the reform era, as well as before it, school superintendents have had to contend at times with boards which interfere in administrative matters and are reluctant to defer to expertise and delegate authority. Moreover, superintendents sometimes must deal with school boards and communities which are torn with factions and evince partisanship despite a

nominally nonpartisan system. In such situations, superintendents find that circumstances seem to demand that, rather than the role of the educational statesman, they must adopt the more hazardous role of the political strategist, i.e.. a leader who, because he cannot generally count on being given support, must instead win support through adroit maneuvering and persuasion based upon careful analysis of existing and potential coalitions on the school board and within the community. (p .1)

The rose garden inherent in the concept of the educational statesman becomes, more frequently than Boyd suggests, a lawn full of weeds for the superintendent. Further, to continue the metaphor, the weeds are not all of the same species. The metaphor, of course, breaks down. Expert lawn care, using a variety of procedures, requires the eradication of all weeds. Expert "superintending," using any of a variety of procedures, requires the cultivation of many "weeds," helping them change form, and only occasionally if ever requires their outright eradication. There are superintendents for whom playing the political strategist constitutes the job's joy, excitement, and challenge. It almost presents them with their raison d'etre. For others, however, the role is distasteful, uncomfortable, and to be avoided whenever possible. Hess suggests the reason for this discomfort, commenting that when he engages in the political side of his job, "the superintendent is a power-broker, a dealer in influence" (1981). Shades of Watergate and Abscam! Further, one can hear some superintendents reacting negatively to this description with "That's not the way it's supposed to be! The purity of what we're about is being contaminated, and me along with it." But that's the way it is.

## The Politics of Survival

All of the superintendent's educational expertise—curriculum development skills, knowledge of the problems of teaching and learning, for example—comes to naught if the superintendent does not survive in his position. *Survival* may seem like too strong a term to use, implying as it does life and death. Its aptness, however, comes from its common use by superintendents themselves. The very term and its frequent employment convey an image of the superintendency that is a curious one, setting it apart from other positions of executives in the public sector. One rarely hears, for example. overt concern expressed about the survival of district attorneys, police chiefs. or directors of social welfare. There clearly are such concerns among superintendents, however, and they are not only of recent vantage. Testimony to this can be found in both chapters 1 and 2 of this book. Recall, for instance, the somewhat humorous letter from the country superintendent to his daughter in which he said he was still leading the district, but he wasn't sure by how much.

Survival can be of many types, however. There is a wide range of conditions within which a person might survive in the superintendency, and certainly some of them are definitely preferable to others. The condition that is of interest to us here involves the variables of potency and activity.

It is not news to anyone in the field of education, lay or professional, that there are some superintendents who have survived for a very long time, the primary tools of their extended tenure being a lack of potency and activity. They have simply kept the system functioning through routine administration, kept the tax rate within acceptable limits, and have avoided irritating anyone in any but rather inconsequential ways. They are not bad people, of course, and the fact of their survival is probably indicative, more than anything else, of a good match having been made between them as individuals and the needs and desires of the communities in which they serve.

At the other end of the continuum are the superintendents who have survived for a long time, have retained their potency and activity, and are, in short, able to be the educational statesmen to whom we have referred. Not infrequently they are involved in controversy from which they seemingly emerge in a stronger position than they were previously. They have retained and enhanced their power. They have done more than just kept the system running. The politics of their survival has been less concerned with surviving per se and more with behaving in ways that permit them to have a continuing productive impact on the system, thus ensuring their survival and power. That is, they become a commodity that is valued because it is potent and active, and not because it is impotent and inactive.

Burlingame (1981) deals implicitly with the survival issue in a paper entitled "Superintendent Power Retention." The casual and naive reader may be shocked and repelled by his first sentence: "I seriously doubt that honesty is the best policy for superintendents who wish to retain power" (p. 429). Burlingame is not, of course, proposing a recipe for an immoral code of behavior for superintendents. Rather, what is at issue is that the schools, by both their organizational and technological character, are systems that elude an operational goal orientation, inspection, and control. Superintendents are caught in a dilemma. They

> must diligently seek to control both the internal reality and public image of the schools. In a very real sense, however, superintendents can control neither the internal reality of what goes on in the schools nor the public image of the schools. Under these conditions of relative powerlessness, superintendents become not only involved in processes of mystification or cover-up, but also become practitioners of tactical rules of survival. (p. 433)

These tactical rules of survival are

1.  Act like a Superintendent so that others can know how to act.

2.  Anticipate that ignorance will produce more positive than negative results.1

3.  Stifle conflict by denial, bolstering, and differentiation.

4.  Provide simple solutions for human problems, complex solutions for technical problems.

5.  Don't decide; help or hinder others to decide.

6.  If you must decide, make the second best decision. (p. 438)

Again, the casual reader may be repelled by all this. Certainly, such a set of rules is not congruent with the values that our schools espouse. On the other hand, maybe they are, if one takes the position that the schools not only espouse the value of "honesty is the best policy," but implicitly one of "Let us try and understand how the world works." But my purpose here is not to argue the rightness or wrongness of Burlingame's point of view nor whether his analysis, though it is based on a deep and sensitive understanding of school organization life, is the most appropriate one. What is important for our purposes here is to understand that there *is* a politics of superintendent survival. It is real, and just how a superintendent chooses to make it function for himself will affect the character of his position and his ability to exercise leadership.

## The Politics of State and Federal Relationships

The need for superintendents to be involved politically with both state and federal decision making and regulatory bodies is a relatively recent one. Prior to the late 1950's, such involvement was infrequent, certainly as far as the federal government was concerned. Things changed, and radically, with the entrance—some could say intrusion—of the federal government into the field through federal monies for education and their accompanying regulations. And, of course, court decisions, starting with those concerned with racial segregation in the public schools, represented an additional force that influenced the ways a superintendent might see his job. A third factor was the growing militancy and political strength of the teachers' unions. Teachers' unions are not only concerned with local issues. They are concerned and active, as they legitimately should be, with trying to influence decisions affecting education, particularly. on the state level.

The interaction of these factors has had two major effects on the working life of school superintendents. First, and obviously, it has made their work much more complex. They perform their jobs under constraints few would have imagined three decades ago. The sources of conflict were introduced into their lives. Second, these circumstances meant a new form of political involvement for superintendents. They could no longer tend to their local business with occasional goodwill visits to the state education commissioner's office. If they wanted to affect things, they had to become involved in the politics of poker and influence, especially at the state level.

A superintendent's involvement in state and federal politics is less well defined and pervasive than the other parts of a superintendent's life that we have mentioned previously. A few superintendents are actively engaged in such politics. But most seem to limit their involvement to complaining about state and federal mandates that are handed down without accompanying fiscal support. The issue is raised here, however, not for intensive discussion but to indicate that the situation exists and that it will continue to play a part in determining how the superintendency gets enacted. An important effect of these circumstances is that the superintendency is inevitably inserted in one fashion or another into partisan politics. The teachers' unions, often opposed to the prerogatives claimed by superintendents, obviously don't share these feelings about inappropriateness. So it is probably true, then, that to the extent that superintendents avoid such a political role, they will probably lose control over their domain.

This somewhat extended introduction to the "total immersion in politics" concept of the superintendency was not intended to be an in-depth discussion of the "politics" of education, however that term is defined. It was designed to provide a backdrop against which the reader might think about the several comments that the superintendency in this study made about what they considered to be the "political strategist" focus of their role. The day-to-day meaning of the backdrop seems well summed up in the words of one superintendent, who said, "It doesn't make any difference what the decision is you have to make. When you make it, you are impinging on somebody else's territory." This comment is perhaps a bit too broad. There are certainly decisions that superintendents make that involve trivia or are encapsulated and that don't intrude on the territorial prerogative of other individuals or groups. But it is undoubtedly true, and this is our point of departure, that few, if any, of the decisions that confront a superintendent that have to do with the substance of education or the governance of the system can be dealt with on the merits of the arguments alone. Matters of whose territory is whose are almost always involved and must be taken into consideration.

## The Superintendents Comment on the Politicalness of Their Jobs

The superintendents in this study, though they tended to describe the politics of their office in somewhat different terms, had no difficulty at all in relating to the concept. Here is a sample of the range of their responses:

> It's political, highly political. It's political because it's a human enterprise. I do things politically, yes. I am politically motivated. More in the sense of trying to get ahead of somebody. Sometimes I'll say to the administrative staff, I don't want to be pressured into this, and, therefore, let's decide now whether it's a good direction to take, and if it's a good direction, let's beat them to the punch."

* * * * *

> It's a terribly political job. And I think it's increasingly becoming a measure of the superintendent of schools. In graduate school we took a course in the politics of education. What a joke! The whole damn thing is political. You always have to behave politically with the board. You can't ever believe you're going to have an off-the-cuff conversation. There's no such thing in my experience. And I think one of the unfortu-

nate parts of it is that you hear of certain superintendents being put down as being really, really political. I guess the way I have always interpreted that is that these are people who are solely concerned about the image of the district, the job, the decision. They very seldom, if ever, will make a decision that costs them their chips.

\* \* \* \* \*

This is a very political situation. There's almost a Tammany Hall syndrome operating. People in the community, for example, think there's always someone "on the take." Or people get jobs because of someone they know. The president of the board happens to be chairman of the Republican Party. He's a very powerful political figure. At our first meeting I said, "Are there any sacred cows? You people want changes. You want all sorts of things. Are you aware of the implications of change? Are there any sacred cows?" And that's a way of saying, of course, "If you want changes, whom do you want to cover, protect?" And, of course, there are absolutely none. And I know that will be the response. But that's my way of paving the way.

\* \* \* \* \*

Here's how my job is political. What I do is to create demands and achieve solutions in meetings. The solution involves a constant set of trade-offs. I just went through one. We are going to reorganize our elementary schools. I had a solution which I think was probably the best one. Why wouldn't I think so? It was mine! The solution that evolved was, let's say, 35 percent different than mine. But it was still a good one. So the trade-off I made is okay because we built in a support system and are more likely to achieve it. So that you're constantly assessing what's achievable and what you can do. You are constantly trying to assess what are the community norms and the staff norms and how far beyond them you can go and still be within a workable acceptable framework of achievability. So you make trade-offs. You say, "What do I give up in order to get what I can get?"

\* \* \* \* \*

I guess I've been active in the political sense in the community. I touch base with the power people. The county legislators the state assembly-man, the village officials, the mayor, a couple of manufacturers, big property owners. I meet them in business situations and socially. The result is that people say you're doing your job, you've been accepted, and you get support.

The images of the politics of the superintendency conveyed in these comments carry elements of sameness as well as difference. Without doubt. there is agreement that effective performance, and probably survival, requires of the superintendent a shrewd sense of political imperatives. This involves first, the need to keep one's personal or institutional "radar" continually scanning both the school and political community. One scans for both friends and foes. One also scans both for potential opportunities to achieve something and for potential sources of conflict. A superintendent said, for example,

> Being political means having a real sense of the workings of groups—power groups, pressure groups decision-making processes. You're dealing with different constituencies; with people interacting with each other with their own special interests. And you really have to have that all sorted out so that you can anticipate their reactions. You have to be political!

What happens as a result of the scanning operation, it seems, tends to become a matter of one's own motivation and interactive style preferences. We have one person, for example, whose concern is "beat them to the punch." Don't let yourself be 'one-upped' by the community," seems to be the message here. But there is another message that suggests that this is a strategy aimed at maintaining control and relative freedom of action. Further. if you can continually "beat them to the punch" you don't get pressured into doing things at a time and under circumstances not of your own choosing, a hallmark of an effective politician. Another superintendent tends to think of the politics of his job as putting behavioral constraints on him. In effect, when he said, "You can't ever believe you're having an off-the-cuff conversation," he was saying that he has to operate, at times, in an atmosphere of distrust; that he has to be careful not to say anything that he wouldn't want quoted. The waters in which the superintendent swims are occasionally dangerous ones, and he must be careful not to get caught in the undertow—or at least circumspect enough to avoid getting his big toe nipped by the fiddler crabs that abound in every school district.

For another superintendent, politics in his district exhibits "almost a Tammany Hall syndrome." The community is a distrustful one, and public officials are suspect merely because they are public officials. Behavior must be adjusted to meet the situation, and so, in his first meeting with his school board president, he raises the question of "sacred cows" that should be left alone, knowing full well what the answer will be. But the political game needs to be played out, and it is. Each takes the measure of the other, thereby enabling both of them to establish a satisfactory way of working together. And for yet another superintendent, the words with which he describes the political focus of his job might well have been spoken by the majority leader of either legislative house in Washington. The emphasis is on "what's achievable" and not on what should exist in the best of all educational worlds. Further, "what's achievable" is measured not by how much power can be mustered to force through a particular decision, but by whether or not the decision will be supported by the community.

The superintendency as a political office is revealed a bit differently by the comment "I touch base with the power people." But notice that this superintendent, too, is responding to community norms. His reading of the local situation told him that it was important in that community simply to be known as a person to the people in the community power structure. His willingness to be known and to reach out in order for others to know him was sufficient to garner community support. It was what was expected. His example presents a bland view of the politics of the superintendency. But an extremely important point is hidden behind the blandness. The community in which this superintendent works is, in itself, a rather bland one. An important point is at issue here: It is impossible to understand the politics of the superintendency simply in terms of the personal predisposition of any particular superintendent. Superintendents interact with change, and are changed by the communities in which they serve. The political world view that a superintendent brings to one community, which serves him well there, may be counterproductive in the next. What is required perhaps, is a statesman's view of politics, if the two terms, which Boyd viewed as opposites, can be joined. Such a view (though he did not use the term statesman) was voiced by one interviewee in the following way:

> So the superintendent must be totally aware of the changing pressure groups, and the changing potency of different pressure groups. That's the backdrop, and obviously that backdrop produces tremendous pressure and tremendous tension, in particular to those who have not been able to intellectualize it. They can't tell where all the pressure's coming from, and they're not sure why everything that is happening to them is happening the way it is. They are sitting in a pile of paperwork, yelling about it and criticizing it instead of trying to understand what it means.

Being "political," then, involves more than possessing personalized strategies and tactics for playing the politician's role. It also involves the ability to take a broad and (curiously) an almost disinterested view of the kaleidoscope of interacting forces that impinge on school system problem-solving and decision-making processes. First, one must have a comprehensive understanding of what is going on. It is not sufficient, for example, to sense that a particular group is mobilizing to defeat a school budget; that another group is organizing to protest a sex education program; that the community is in conflict over a prospective busing program; or that competing pressure groups are trying to influence a decision about integrating special education students into regular classrooms. One must understand the possible relationships that these groups may have with one another, their sources of power, and their potential influence. Only with these types of understandings can a superintendent think through appropriate strategies for action. But that is rather obvious. What is not obvious is the need to consciously conceptualize one's awareness of these various forces.

Conceptualizing the politics of conflicting forces in a school community is not merely an academic exercise for a superintendent. It is very closely related to his ability to create some sense of order in his work world. Unless this can be done, the superintendency becomes a hodgepodge of seemingly unrelated, distracting demands for action. Superintendents can become overwhelmed with what they interpret to be meaningless paperwork. They can also become organizational "firemen" and engage predominantly in management by crisis. In short, they can lose control of their work lives as they respond to situations randomly. It doesn't take much imagination to picture such a superintendent becoming angry and frustrated, losing his sense of perspective, and perceiving himself as victimized by the ignorance of others.

The need for order in one's work life also requires a superintendent to maintain a sort of detached sense of distance from the fray. This may appear to be a curious statement. Certainly superintendents are involved in what they do. Certainly they have an emotional stake in their plans, their budgets, and so forth. But they are also human beings, with wives, families, and very personalized needs. Just like everyone else, they have a personal world that makes demands on their intellectual and emotional energy. To prevent their work lives from consuming their personal lives, they must be able to stand back, intellectualize what is going on, and perhaps conceive of daily circumstances as some sort of drama that is being played out. They are involved in the drama, but they are also part of the audience. Thus they are able to maintain a sense of their own integrity and—if this is not too bold a statement—their sanity, in situations that some superintendents will tell you are absolutely insane.

To sum up: The highly political and conflictual world of the superintendency appears to be randomized, irrational, and uncontrollable. To the extent that a superintendent can understand the complex web of events that he confronts and subject that understanding to his own intellectual analysis, he is better able to order the world, control it, and maintain his own sense of self.

The imperative of "superintendent as politician," no matter how good a case can be made for it, does not sit well with all superintendents, however. In reacting to discussion about the superintendency placing strong demands for skilled political behavior on the person who occupies that position, one superintendent, a woman, said:

> I think it's important, but I'm not a very good politician. I am not a person who is inherently political, and perhaps that may be one of my weaknesses. I feel I am in this as an educational leader and to deal with what's right. If I were strictly a political type, I could come in here and do nothing. I could take my salary. I would just do what the board wants me to do. And there would not be the conflicts I have. So some people tell me that I should be more of a political animal than I am; that I should appease this group and that group. I've worked with people like that, and I'm sure it's a lot easier. I often say that people want a big fat marshmallow as a superintendent and not a big fat witch.

Another person, commenting that he finally found out what the politics of education was all about when he became a superintendent, said:

> Well, I discovered what I'm sure many superintendents discover. A lot of time is spent satisfying idiot board members and teachers. You have to do some of that, of course, but if you were to set your own priorities

it would be awful low on the scale. Most of it deals with petty issues. For example, we have some board members who are highly Title IX-oriented: no "his" or "her." I must have wasted several days rewriting policy to take out "his" or "her." It's garbage. It's pathetic. It's pathetic. And they're paying me thirty some odd thousand dollars a year to do that. Or, there are instances of an eighth grader playing JV soccer. Who the hell cares, if he's capable? Or, is it true that such and such teacher is being indiscreet? You trace that kind of garbage down in order to keep them happy. It all takes time, and it's petty.

I've had a couple of sessions with them about all that stuff because it makes me angry. I asked them where the hell they were. I'm becoming more of a risk taker. I guess I've discovered the more conflicts I have, the more I'm willing to do it. It's not that bad.

One thing becomes immediately obvious when these two comments are compared with those that preceded them. It is that the word *politics*, as it applies to the superintendency, triggers responses that seem to vary with the individual and with the perceptions they hold of themselves in their position. The earlier remarks seemed to be somewhat detached and analytical. They conveyed an image of a person engaged in an intellectual game—almost a chess game where one's moves depend not only on one's perception of the current situation but also on one's view of the future. The object of it all, of course, is to win.

This stance was clearly not foremost in the minds of the two superintendents whose comments were just quoted. Rather, they say the "politics" of superintendency in negative terms. "Being political," in the first case, seemed to mean kowtowing to the board and placing the smoothness of that relationship ahead of the demands of educational *leadership*—whatever that term may connote. In the second case, the superintendent as politician seemed to mean engaging in educationally meaningless tasks that took a great deal of time, simply to avoid ruffling the feelings of one constituent or another.

It has to be true, of course, that both of these people also enacted behaviors that would be congruent with the broader political view of the superintendency that was expressed in remarks of their colleagues. But they did not see their role centrally in those terms. Both of them, in fact, perceived of themselves primarily as educators whose major thrust was affecting the quality of curriculum and instruction. The broader system view, although they functioned within it, seemed not to be a focal guide for their action.

Two other bits of information about these two interviewees reinforce the idea that the political focus of the superintendency was not central to the thinking of these two people. The superintendent we quoted first, indicated elsewhere in the interview that being a superintendent for the rest of her professional life was not necessarily a goal, either in the district in which she was currently employed or in another one. It would depend on how things worked out. In point of fact, she did not rule out returning to the classroom if the superintendency turned out to be a less than desirable circumstance for her. She would continue doing what she was doing as long as she could be an "educational leader"—or until she simply got tired of it. The second superintendent we quoted, I learned, was abruptly terminated by the school about a year after our interview for refusing to make an administrative personnel change that the board had demanded but that he disapproved of. Not sensing the potential fallout of his decision, he had taken one risk too many. He had thrown down the gauntlet and lost.

In addition to describing their general concept of the politicalness of their position, the superintendents also expressed some of the perspectives they held of themselves relative to the politics of their work world. Specifically, they discussed the topics of their own power, the notion of winning and losing, the balancing acts they perform, and their need to protect themselves.

## The Power of the Superintendency

To speak of the power inherent in the office of superintendent of schools as if it was a one-dimensional concept is to oversimplify an extremely complex set of circumstances. Are we talking about the relationships the superintendent has to the school board, the community's political officeholders, teachers as individuals, principals, teachers' unions, pupils, the community at large? All of these, separately or in interaction with one another? Are we talking about legal power to make decisions, organizational power to allocate resources or reward and punish, the power that is inherent in the ability to control sources of information, or what? It becomes glaringly obvious that when the global concept of power gets broken down in relation to the settings in which it may be exercised, questions related to power and the superintendency become both elusive ones to ask and almost unanswerable.

It also is true, of course, that questions related to the superintendent's power cannot be dealt with ahistorically. We have referred several times to the highly emotional conflicts that were waged almost a century ago between school boards and superintendents over the issue—baldly stated—of who should run things. Though those battles yielded no clear-cut victor—an impossible outcome in any case, given the American pattern of local control of schools and the idiosyncratic conditions existing in each school district— it is clear that over the years the balance of power has shifted from the school board to the superintendent. This shift was reflected in the graduate education of school administrators. Two of the superintendents interviewed, for example, somewhat older than the others, commented that their doctoral work in the 1950s clearly contained the message that (1) they were the experts, and (2) it was their job to run things, even if they became bullies in the process.

Pendulums swing both ways, however, and events in our society since the mid-1960s seem to have engendered a movement in the direction of diminished power of the superintendent. The growth of strong teachers' unions, community concern about costs and school effectiveness, and the focus on the legal rights of students are among the major factors that have contributed to a lessening of the prerogatives of the superintendent's office. This trend has, of course, been described in the professional literature. We noted earlier, for example, Burlingame's paper entitled "Superintendent Power Retention," as well as Campbell's expression of concern about the possibility of superintendents becoming obsolete. Another example, very directly to the point, is Nolte's article entitled, "How Fast Is the Power of the Superintendent Slipping?" (1974). Using biblical imagery, he writes, "School superintendents today, many complain, are like shorn Samsons whose source of power has been snipped away by numerous Delilahs" (p. 42).

What appears to be the situation, then, is that a state of flux currently exists with regard to the power prerogatives of superintendents. Indeed, the fluidity of the situation was testified to as the superintendents in this study reflected on the question of their power. They were asked to respond to the very general question of whether or not they felt powerful. Their reactions were varied:

> Yes, I feel powerful. Just consider it from the economic perspective alone. We have a multimillion-dollar budget, and it has to be administered in some way. The money brings people to you in terms of purchasing. And I'm powerful in terms of being able to solve tax propositions for better education.

* * * * *

> I think I exercise power over curriculum development. I can get things going. I can and do mandate that my principals give consideration to certain programs. And I can and do see to it that they stay on top of things in that area.

* * * * *

> I don't feel powerful. The question of power is a joke, because you're responsible to the board of education. That's where the power really is. The last thing I do is tell Mrs. Jones, "You gotta do it this way."

* * * * *

> Sure, I feel powerful. Especially in terms of dealing with the school system and even with the community. Yeah, I feel that power; the power to change things, the power to change lives and to know that people react to that. There are times I certainly feel good about that, to have the opportunity to say yes or no, and they've got to do it. But that same feeling doesn't always carry over to the school board. Legally they call the shots. Sometimes I feel a little vulnerable with them.

* * * * *

> I don't really feel powerful. In some situations I guess that if I said something it would mean something. I know some people say my job is very powerful. I'm the head of the whole thing. It makes me smile. I can't change a teacher, really. If you look at what you can change, I don't think you can say you have a lot of power.

* * * * *

> You have power if your timing is right. You keep people talking, and then, when you sense the situation has come as close as it can come you move. You've got to make sure that everything has been played out so

there's nowhere else to go, and then you gotta move.

\* \* \* \* \*

Mostly I'm powerful in terms of personnel. Probably the strongest handle on that is through the power of appointment. The board cannot appoint someone without my say-so. The same thing goes for tenure. There can be no reorganization in the district staff without my approval. But I can't make that happen by myself either.

\* \* \* \* \*

I don't really feel powerful. I know it's there. I can move teachers around, and there's nothing they can do about it, but that would be wrong. The hardest thing I have to do is to avoid the use of power in this office. Sometimes I see something that is so stupid and so outrageous that I really want to react to the SOB with the power of my office. I have to stop myself.

It's hard to say, of course what the reactions of superintendents to the question of how powerful they felt would have been had they been queried in the mid-1950s. Quite possibly the responses would have been different, reflecting the differences in American society between then and now. "Power to the people" has made an impact, even if in a somewhat diffuse manner. At this time, though, the reactions seem to be "Yes," "No," and "It depends." If there ever has been such a thing as the "Imperial Superintendent," the comments alone indicate that that concept is no longer in vogue. Rather, even though there were affirmative responses to the question concerning feeling powerful, a pervasive tone throughout was one of a sense of limit, both personally and organizationally. Further, it seems as though this sense of limit is related to the territory in which the superintendent is operating. For example, a working hypothesis about the power of the superintendency might go something like this: To the extent that a superintendent's managerial duties (home territory) are involved, he is apt to feel powerful. When he moves outside the managerial part of his job, his power becomes diluted. That is, as he tries to exert influence across organizational and community boundaries, the question of having the power to get his way gets transformed into the question of having political acumen. He can recommend, set things in motion, and try to mobilize support. But as one superintendent said, "I can't change a teacher, really." Nor indeed, or so it seems, are superintendents able, for the most part, to propose decisions to the school board with an anticipatory attitude of fait accompli. Life, for superintendents, is no longer that simple, if it ever was.

## The Balancing Act

Regardless of a superintendent's orientation toward winning and losing, the situations he confronts in his daily work seem to require that he perform a continual balancing act. It is a delicate condition, its delicateness (to continue the metaphor) probably being related to (1) how high the tightrope wire is off the ground and (2) whether or not there is a safety net in place should he lose his balance. The height of the wire refers to how important the situation is to the superintendent personally or to the school system, and the safety net to the amount of support he has with the school board, the teachers, or the community, depending on the case at hand. The superintendents in this study made numerous comments about the balancing acts they engaged in. For example,

> Well, for instance, you know the union is going to be up in arms if I want to cut back staff. They're going to come out strong against it, "We need smaller class size, we need this, we need that." Okay, I understand that. Another group says we have to have more guidance people. Another wants more speech therapists. Another wants to cut the budget in half, and another says that we can't have any increase. So you have to do a balancing act. Sometimes you're in the middle, and it's kind of fun to be there because you have to keep things on an even keel.

* * * * *

> Yeah. For example, you have building principals who literally detest certain teachers. I have one who detests the president of my teachers' association. You name the adjectives. This guy [the principal] will use them. Now I've got to live with this guy. It's a political reality, and I'd like to have him in at least a decent frame of mind. So I have to do a balancing act. I lean on him at times, but then I buy him off by giving him something he wants. It's not totally honest, but it keeps things somewhat peaceful.

* * * * *

> Yes, it's a continuous balancing act, particularly when you're new and until you've built up your credibility. After a time, though, I've been able to build up my own power base. I become freer and can tilt things in my direction easier.

* * * * *

> It's always a balancing act because there are so many pressure groups. More so than ever before and the funny thing is that we have made it happen that way. We have really pushed the idea that everyone should be involved in the schools. So now I have so many different constituencies out there with so many different interests that my problem is to try and keep them appeased.

These are almost classical responses of people who understand that their success and survival in their positions depend on their political acumen—their ability to sense the character of the competing interests in a situation and to behave in ways that keep these interests and themselves in balance. It is important to realize, though, that merely keeping things in balance is not what it's all about. Tightrope walkers don't want to maintain their balance so that they can stand still—nor do most superintendents. For them, keeping things in balance—and performing their own act, as well—is necessary for movement, though there are times when the achievement of balance is of positive value in itself, particularly when a system has been racked with controversy. One superintendent reflected this idea when he said, "My problem is to keep them appeased." The district in question is a sprawling suburban one that includes a number of disparate socioeconomic and interest groups and in which the teachers' union is strong and militant. Balance here is indeed a desired goal in and of itself. There are undoubtedly times when such a goal is appropriate for all school districts.

We note, however, that some other cues in the remarks just quoted cast a different light on the need to seek balance and to balance oneself. For one superintendent, the politics of the balancing act are fun, particularly when he finds himself in the middle. One senses that this superintendent rather looks forward to those times when he must perform his own balancing act so that he can "keep things on an even keel." These are times, and for most superintendents they apparently occur frequently, that present a challenge to his political skills, thus creating a situation that for him is "kind of fun." This comment suggests a somewhat different concept of the superintendency as a win-or-lose game. To "win" in the arena of human affairs usually means to make one's views prevail in the conflict situation, and to "lose" is the opposite. There are certainly times, however, when one "wins" by being able to manipulate conflicting interests so skillfully as to keep the system in balance without major disruptions. Winning and the fun of winning, in these cases, has less to do with trying to ensure that one dominates a decision than it has with trying to ensure that the system remains in balance, or with keeping things peaceful, so to speak. Though he didn't suggest that it was fun, one of the superintendents just quoted specifically noted that a particular balancing act he had performed was designed to keep the peace—perhaps an armed truce—between a principal and the president of the teachers' association. That it wasn't fun can be inferred from the remark, "It's not totally honest, but,..." with reference to his "buying off" the principal. Totally honest or not, keeping things in balance seems to require a sense of priorities, and there are probably times when one's ethical values take second place to the higher goal of keeping the system in balance and peaceful. It is probably true, then, as Boyd asserted, that on many occasions the need for a superintendent to be politically shrewd leaves little room for an open display of honesty. Burlingame, as we noted earlier, is most forthright and courageous in discussing that point.

# NOTES

[1.] Is an abridged version of Chapter 4 of *The School Superintendent: Living with Conflict* (New York: Teachers College Press, 1985)

# REFERENCES

Boyd, W. The school superintendent: educational statesman or political strategist? *Administrator's Notebook*, August 1974, 22, 9.

Burlingame, M. Superintendent power retention. In S.B. Bacharach (ed.), *Organizational Behavior in Schools and School Districts*. New York: Praeger, 1981.

Hess, F. The political dimenstion of local school superintendency. *Council Journal*, New York State Council of School District Administrators. May 1977, 1, 125-37.

Katz, D., and R. Kahn. *The Social Psychology of Organizations*, 2nd ed. New York: Wiley, 1978.

Nolte, C.M. How fast is the power of the superintendent slipping? *American School Board Journal*. September 1974, 161, 9.

Chapter 3
# An Hispanic Female Superintendent's Leadership and School District Culture

*by Flora Ida Ortiz, University of California, Riverside*

School reform has focused on several aspects of schooling. One aspect currently receiving increasing attention is the relation of the superintendent to school district reform. This chapter addresses this issue indicating how a superintendent worked to produce common goals and a purposeful, constructive school learning culture with stability in a school district that was close to anarchy.

This chapter describes a superintendent's approach to altering a school district's culture, addressing the needs, sequentially, of the various layers in the district—the school board, the cabinet, principals and the building faculties.

Secondly, this report shows how institutions' cultures can integrate ethnically diverse groups in a complex organization.

This report is based on interviews and data from the files of an Hispanic female superintendent who assumed her post three years ago. Observational data are limited to large group public meetings. Documents analyzed include office memoranda, newspaper releases, school district materials such as board meeting agendas, curricular and activity announcements and correspondence of various sorts.

Willower (1987) wrote, "A special organizational culture tied to educational goals is not likely to be found in normal circumstances. It has to be a deliberate creation" (p. 93). Dr. Felicia Singer's leadership most clearly demonstrates how a superintendent deliberately worked to alter a destructive school district culture and create a more purposeful and positive one.

## The Setting

Superintendent Singer's appointment to the Willow Creek Unified School District was unanimously supported by the school board. It had been in a state of desperate instability since 1974, e.g., a dozen different superintendents had served in the last seven years. Cabinet turnover was equally high. When Dr. Singer assumed her post a three-year tenure indicated seniority in the organization. Instability was also reflected in the financial condition of the district. The major board and community issues were spending, bookkeeping, overcrowding, and aging school buildings.

Willow Creek Unified School District is one of the largest school districts in the state and consists of 29 elementary schools, four middle schools, three comprehensive high schools and one continuation high school. The district operates an adult education center, a regional vocational training center, 22 magnet school programs, alternative middle and high school programs, five summer schools and special education schools for infants, children and adults.

The enrollment in kindergarten through 12th grade is projected to be almost 32,000 in the 1989-90 school year. Since 1980 the enrollment has been rising at a rate of 1000 to 1500 students a year. The district employs 2,777 full-time teachers, administrators and classified workers as well as more than 300 part-time employees, substitutes and playground supervisors. More than 35 percent of the 1,377 teachers have advanced degrees. The total budget for the 1988-89 school year was $129 million. The district's preliminary budget for 1989-90 calls for expenditures of $130 million. This includes local, state and federal moneys.

The student population served by Willow Creek Unified School District is among the most diverse in the United States. In addition to a large Anglo, Black and Hispanic population, Stardust City is home to a large number of new citizens from Korea, Cambodia, Taiwan, Vietnam, India, Japan, Laos, the Philippines, and Central and South America. The major groups represented among the students are Hispanics, 33.9%; Asians and Pacific Islanders, 27.6%; Non-Hispanic whites 23.7%; and Native Americans, 1.2%.

## The Game Plan

The superintendent's initial encounter with the organization is an important consideration in establishing how a leader sets out to change the culture of a particular organization. As part of accepting the Chief Executive Officer's post of a school district, she identified the critical components to which she should respond: the school board, the community and her own sense of professional responsibility. She assessed the organization's state and she intentionally set out to change it.

For Dr. Singer, the school board's mandates were to change this school district to a stable one, instructionally and financially, and to integrate the diverse groups of students and school personnel.

The *community's information* about the school district was that it was bankrupt, had an unreasonable school personnel turnover and the students' performance was unsatisfactory. The description most often expressed was that schooling in the community was a political game with diverse groups combative to the detriment of the educational process. The overall image of the school district was that it was not a very good one.

She assessed the school district organization as one in disarray and turmoil. She described it as "This organization was like looking underneath the ocean. The waves were causing all of the top to turn over and be in a lot of turmoil, but the bottom was quite placid." She saw the high turnover and low morale among the central office personnel and some principals, and the consequences revealed at the school level amongst the teachers and students. She said,

"Students and teachers felt the commotion but did not fully understand what was happening. I could detect the incredibly low production and work ethic which was due in part to the absence of consistent and long-term supervision and the maintenance of standards."

The assessment of the organization's state, the understanding of the board's mandate and the community's expectations were summed up as, "Everyone wants improvements. The district needs instructional, financial and cultural improvements." She realized she had to propose actions in response: "That means to me that I must set some priorities and go to work."

## The School Board and Community

Superintendents' first responses are to the mandates of their board and responding to the community's expectations. This task is not usually conceptualized by the superintendent as changing a district's culture. They begin by "picking up" what the board and community relay. As they "pick up" they uncover actions which must be taken, decisions which must be made and persons who hinder or assist in the task.

In Dr. Singer's case, she early determined that all board members were not supporting her efforts. She felt that two board members' interests were lodged on themselves rather than on the school district. For example, the superintendent wanted to balance the budget by changing personnel and resources allocations. In doing so, one of the district's units would be greatly reduced. The school board members who opposed it were obligated to some of the unit's personnel politically and nepotistically.

It is not entirely clear what role the superintendent played in alerting the community to this difficulty and to the consequences. The data do indicate that community leaders emerged who systematically informed the community about the two school board members' challenges to the superintendent's proposed actions. The community leaders developed an argument that the superintendent offered an opportunity for the district's improvement and were successful in demonstrating how the two board members' actions reflected self-interest rather than institutional improvement.

When a board election was held, the two board members were replaced. The newly elected board members clearly expressed views which supported the superintendent's proposed actions. Dr. Singer described this incident by pointing out her view of her position and responsibility. She said,

Holding an executive position of an organization implies competence and confidence that that person can bring about organizational improvement. Not all board members appreciate the complexity and not all board members are personally motivated to act in the organization's interest. My proposed actions and decisions which were opposed by the defeated board members highlighted for the community the distinction between personal and organizational intentions. I am grateful the community rallied and elected officials who are genuinely supportive of school district improvement.

While the school board was realigning itself, Superintendent Singer set her priorities for the first two years. Her first major action was to balance the budget. The actions leading to a balanced budget were instrumental in the school board election. Each action was orchestrated through board meeting agenda presentations, board meeting interpretations and media announcements.

Three factors can be identified which are significant in changing a school district culture. First, the superintendent fulfilled the school board's mandate regarding the budget expeditiously and effectively. In balancing the budget, she educated the board, the community and the school personnel. She also fulfilled the community's expectation of school district improvement. In meeting both the board's and community's demands, Felicia Singer demonstrated competence and intention. Second, Felicia Singer carried out those actions because she holds a basic assumption that organizations are instruments and that "leadership is a willful act where one person attempts to construct the social world for others" (Greenfield, 1984, p. 142).

The superintendent was bent on improving the school district and she saw the critical importance of having a supportive school board whose interest was focused on school district improvement. Dr. Singer is unusual in the literature because she was able to strengthen her position by replacing two school board members, which occurred because the community's leaders aligned themselves with the superintendent and her proposed actions (Lutz & Wang, 1987).

## Personnel Changes

Balancing the budget and having a more supportive school board enabled the superintendent to proceed with personnel changes. Her early focus was on recruiting new teachers with specific skills and attitudes rather than increasing the central office staff, thus changing the context in which teachers could negotiate with the district. This strategy served to transmit a certain organizational norm and significantly reaffirmed that instruction and children were the focal elements in the school organization. Symbolically, the functions of schooling are highlighted; instruction, children and teachers do matter. Practically, new members in the teaching ranks infused new ideas, energy and work norms that contributed to changing the culture of the school district.

## Student Performance Improvement

Improving the performance of students was another major area of activity for the superintendent. The third, seventh and ninth grades were targeted for specific outcomes. The number of third grade youngsters who are on reading level is expected to increase. Seventh grade pupils are being prepared to pass the proficiency examinations to qualify for high school course programs. The ninth grade is targeted for reducing dropouts. Additional counseling and other resources for students are being directed to large classes beset with student problems. Contacts and relationships with parents and students were established to work towards the completion of ninth grade. The message is that the district is committed to increasing the high school graduation rate.

Associated with this targeted attention to students, Dr. Singer focused on the teachers who are failing children in the ninth grade. They are being helped to become better instructors. For example, in referring to what can be expected from teachers, Dr. Singer said,

> The state certifies that teachers can instruct by level, grade and subject area. Teaching credentials do not specify that teachers cannot be held accountable for student's performance based on their gender or ethnicity or race. Thus, better instruction to me means that teachers can teach all students well.

An associate superintendent for education services was hired who was especially qualified to provide assistance to teachers in instruction settings. In-service training, staff development and other teacher improvement strategies are being used to help teachers. The new teachers were hired to personify professional competence and a high work ethic and have been placed where they are expected to influence other teachers. The superintendent explains:

> I would like a culture of teachers that has a very strong work ethic. I would like to see everybody working twelve months because then you can plan things year-round such as staff development. Teachers who study and remain updated in their areas have adopted a lifelong learning attitude. Teachers who trust each other and respect each other create team building and self-esteem. Associated with this I would also like to see teachers here paid higher than anyone else. You can demand more when you pay well. We can, then, have procedures that are fair, ethical and well known and in this case reduce the bad feelings.

What can be deduced from her activities is that this superintendent has identified critical elements within the institution which must addressed. March (1984, p. 22) refers to this type of administration as one which "profits from ordinary competence and a recognition of the ways in which organizations change by modest modifications of routines rather than by massive mucking around. The modest modifications which took place were balancing the budget, replacing two school board members, hiring additional teachers, hiring an associate superintendent to help teachers become better instructors, and setting pupil outcome targets. She did not institute programs. She set outcome targets consistent with the institution's functions, for example, targeting third graders to read at grade level.

## The Superintendent's Personal Role Enactment

Dr. Singer made these changes but she also realized that the establishment of a work ethic, standards, improved morale, and production began with her. She had to personify what she expected of all school personnel and organizational members. She explained how when she first arrived, "No one was really concerned, except the board, if I had any commitment to stay or do anything. Most people felt that it was a stepping stone, that there was nothing to commit to. There was too much chaos."

Chester Bernard (1938) referred to the leader as an embodiment of the central purpose of the organization (in Greenfield, 1984, p. 164) and he "described the leader's task as being that which commits others to that purpose." Much of Dr. Singer's leadership was dependent on the image she projected. She stated,

> But I am very committed to the place, to the board. I do not want to go to another school district. I think that this is the place where I will make my contribution of my career. So I am extremely committed to making that contribution. If I can hang on to the superintendency and to my assistants this organization will be alright. That in itself will speak to a whole lot of things.

She established an image referred to in the media and community as unflappable. What it appears to mean is that this superintendent is loyal and committed, trustworthy and "up-front," industrious and stable, and that she has a "vision" of where the organization is headed. The image is consistent within the organization among the school board members and the community. The district and community are proud to claim her. Her personal attributes and achievements are widely acknowledged and the youth are ready to express wanting to be like her. The element she has released is hope. There is hope for the youth who are receiving its services and there is hope in the community that the district is moving towards positive comparability with others.

## School District Image

After establishing her image she concentrated on changing the image of the school district. She began by identifying a central office team which would project to the community that "talented people are in the district to serve in a place which is not such a bad place to work."

The team consisted of three: the associate superintendent for education services, Pat Yee; the assistant superintendent for business services, Jack Dash; and the assistant superintendent for personnel services, Nancy Johnson. A facilities planner is being sought to oversee the renovation and reconstruction of the district's aging buildings.

The team has contributed to the welfare of the district in several ways. First, the team is modeling team effort consisting of members from diverse groups. Second, the team is modeling competence and how they are interrelated. Third, the team is projecting a unified purpose which radiates across the school district to provide uniform and consistent educational services. The superintendent voiced it thusly:

> It is my sincere intent to insure that all schools in this district are comparable. I do not expect realtors to refer their clients to any one school because of quality differences. I do not expect to have teachers prefer to teach in some schools because they are better equipped or kept. The team I have working with me will monitor school sites in order to decrease differences among schools.

Projecting a positive image of the school district also involved integrating all of the groups within it. The cabinet was designed to project that intent. Dr. Singer refers to her cabinet as a rainbow cabinet. One of the members is a Chinese female, the businessman is a white male, the personnel woman is Black. The women are all mixed each representing more than one culture. The superintendent said,

> No one can claim any of these individuals. They claim what they can, but they can't get it all. That is what I call softening the racial tension. Let me explain. The Chinese woman has blue eyes. The Black woman's mother is American Indian. My mother is half Asian of some kind. We do not fit any stereotypical profile. We are, nevertheless, identifiable more with one group than with any other. The Hispanics do come to me. But by the same token, my husband is Jewish so they know I cannot possibly have total allegiance to the Hispanics. The Chinese woman's fiance is white. We are not exclusive to a group personally. So that, I believe, serves to permit people to act more neutrally. While we are claimed by any one group there is not a way to depend absolutely on our inclination to lean towards that group. For example, the white male feels that whites expect him to speak for them. He cannot do that too freely while he is being watched by the three of us!

The selection of the cabinet team carries symbolic significance because as March (1984, p. 32) states, "Whether we wish to sustain the system or change it, management is a way of making a symbolic statement."

Willow Creek Unified School District was a district in disarray, a district consisting of many diverse groups and a district which could not retain its administrative personnel. By hiring highly nationally recognized competent individuals and insuring the composition of the cabinet represented the community's diverse groups, a number of symbolic statements were transmitted. First, this district with a negative reputation drew competent individuals to improve it. Second, competence is present in all racial and ethnic groups and school organizations can staff their administrative cabinet with individuals from diverse backgrounds. Third, the care taken to select the cabinet implied an intention of permanence and stability.

Thus, the presence of this cabinet projected a quality of work life and organizational participation that differed from the previous ones. Dr. Singer, by her actions, is showing the community—in this case a highly diversified one — the extent of human potential. By having diverse groups represented across the district's organizational structure, each group can identify and/or attach itself to it. Students are also provided models and norms of behavior.

Image projection success is evident by the way the board has learned to perceive the cabinet. In comparison to the previous cabinets, the board thinks the present team it has hired is spectacular. The team members represent the district positively by being personable and professional. Their reputations for competence in their areas and experience serve to justify their rightness for their posts. Substitutes for all of them could be found but as a team they bring a constellation of experiences and personality that is being effective across the district.

Witnessing this highly diverse and competent team working towards a common goal has fascinated the school board. Their previous experience with administrators and themselves had been to respond to personal and/or group interests. With the present team, they are responding solely to the school district's organizational needs, that is, the improvement of instruction for children. An associated consideration is that the district can lay claim to the cabinet and its accomplishments. The superintendent found the members but they do not owe her an allegiance from years of past work with her. They are hers in the sense that they all share the same vision for the district and are willing to do what is required to fulfill that vision. This has allowed them to have a certain independence and display of self-confidence without the fear of being fired.

One characteristic of organizational cultures is the nature and quality of interdependence among the members. Willow Creek Unified School District had been portrayed as a district in which racial, ethnic and group interests continually fractured its structure. One of the necessary steps in Dr. Singer's intention to improve the school district was to develop interdependence among the members. The most visible and easily manageable group would be the cabinet. Thus, this cabinet, by virtue of its composition and its differentiated responsibilities could demonstrate across the district how interdependence works. Moreover, since this expression of interdependence can also be displayed at public board meetings, the community could witness this style of work. Interdependence among the cabinet members served to show how diverse groups' interests in schooling can be integrated in administrative actions to benefit the entire organization.

There were formal means by which the interdependence of the cabinet members was insured. They had very good "buy out" clauses in their contracts. It would be very expensive for the district to fire a member. The clause also serves to protect each member for a year or two until they can find another job. Informally, actions and decisions are coordinated and synchronized among the four persons. School board members cannot pit them against each other. School staff cannot bypass them. Procedures are agreed upon and adhered to across the district. March (1984) explains that "much of the job of an administrator involves making bureaucracy work ...and responding to the little irritants of organizational life" (p. 22). When the nature of the administrative task is understood and assumed, the results of organizational efforts may be spectacular. In light of the history of this school district, much of what the board perceived as spectacular cooperation and results was teamwork between the cabinet members.

## School Site Administration

Gaining control of the central office enabled the superintendent to turn her attention to the principals and the school sites. She realized there were several aspects which had to be addressed simultaneously. First, the principals would have to be in line with the superintendent's vision for the district. Second, the schools would have to portray the image that she held for the district. Third, the teachers would have to perform at levels consistent with her expectations. Finally, the students would have to improve dramatically in academic performance, school retention, and general citizenship. The purpose for all of these acts was to insure that each school site was engaged in fulfilling the major functions as she viewed them.

The socialization of principals took many forms. The superintendent engaged in various activities with the principals. She increased meetings with them. She met with them on a one-to-one basis. She called principals' meetings which varied by level or combination of levels. She formalized the relationship by creating a management team. This provided a forum for the superintendent and principals to clarify their intentions and for each party to display its competencies. It also provided the means for placing responsibility and obligation on each other. The consequence of this action is that the superintendent's intention to bring order and stability to the district and improve personnel and student performance is transmitted to the school site level. The responsibility and obligation for school site consistency with the district's intentions are delegated to the principals. The management team also provides a mechanism for systematic monitoring of principals' activities and decisions.

One aspect of school district management is the quality of the superintendent-principal relationship. How intensively and extensively should superintendents work with principals? Dr. Singer described this dilemma:

> School site management is imperative, but principals' efforts must be consistent with my vision of school district productivity. I do not want a favorite school. I do not want abandoned or slighted schools in this district. If uniformity across the district is going to take place, I am the person who has to insure that. Thus, I have to develop an intensive relationship with principals. A system of communication and interaction is necessary.

Dr. Singer engaged in "executing a large number of little things" (March, 1984, p. 22) with principals. The intent was to create a working group among the principals and to attach the principals to the central office. These "little things" included written communication, acknowledgements of a principal's efforts, central office reports and scheduled meetings of various sorts. Principals were encouraged to work together in the improvement of their schools.

They were encouraged to utilize the services of the central office and they were expected to run their schools consistent with Dr. Singer's vision. The central office staff, directed by the cabinet members, facilitated these working relationships. The consequence of this effort was that improvements among schools could be cited across the district. All district personnel and the total community could feel the impact of the superintendent's intentions. Particular neighborhoods could not charge district inaction.

The activities and consequences of these activities were tangible and widespread, while some were symbolic and/or contained within the principals' group. For example, how does a community claim its schools? One activity which demonstrates this consequence is the following. A picnic held in the park served as an occasion for a board member to acknowledge the school administrators to the crowd and provide an opportunity for mutual mingling.

How do principals and central office administrators get to know each other? One social activity in which principals participated was an eight-mile walk in the rain on a Sunday morning. This occasion enabled central office administrators and principals to get to know each other in a setting other than a meeting.

How do school people project an image of civic service? The administrative staff of the Willow Creek Unified School District participated in a local blood bank drive. Each of these activities appear trivial and irrelevant in the creation of a culture. But the combination and the execution of these activities serve to project certain values and expectations.

A school district culture is dependent on the quality of participation of the organization's members. Activities such as the Sunday walk signify—we are in this together.

Some activities were organized to deal with high priority issues. A voluntary management retreat was held to grapple with issues of student performance, behavior and retention. Those who attended enjoyed and benefitted from it, but they were a little resentful they had to pay and that it allowed some people not to go. A one-day inexpensive retreat was held in June and a two-day one in August. The issues dealt with were: gang activity, school policies and self-esteem. The retreats were conducted in a manner consistent with the envisioned culture. The first required personal expenditures so that it consisted of those most committed and interested. Since it was successful subsequent ones became possible. Now the board funds these activities and everyone must attend.

The retreats deal with issues which must be addressed in the quest for school improvement. Representatives from across the district are present. All schools are expected to address the issues publicly so that the total district contributes to the solution of problems and to improvement across the district. All principals and central office personnel know the status of their schools and they are engaged in efforts to improve the schools across the district.

The consequences of this socialization are varied: principal turnover decreased; instructional leadership roles were enacted; and the superintendent's expectations were implemented. The superintendent's personal and systematic style in working with the principals is being emulated by many principals as they work with their staff and faculty. The principals are projecting professional, industrious images providing role models for the teachers. Because all schools are projected to be equally excellent, principals don't have to compete for the allocation of resources. Resource allocation to each of them is designed to improve their schools. Status differentiation among them due to school assignment is virtually wiped out. Most principals are pleased. In addition to the reduction in turnover among the principals, there has also been a change in the work norm and positive attitude change. Stability among the group is being established. Similar expectations among the group are also present. Because the central office officials are in accord with the superintendent's intentions, the expectation that high performance is the norm is being fulfilled across the district. Veteran principals are astonished by the increase in good will among them.

Principals are also being integrated. The group of principals includes women and members of different ethnic and racial groups across the school sites.

## Teachers

Teachers are a major group which must be touched by the superintendent's intentions. Dr. Singer's appointment of a group of teachers in critical areas in schools has contributed role models and symbolic significance to the position. The in-service efforts have been directed to focus teachers on their tasks and expectations.

What do classrooms look like now? First, teachers are enthusiastic about teaching children from a variety of racial and ethnic groups. Second, teachers are being supported from the central office through in-service training and the provision of supplies. Classrooms, thus, consist of those materials which are necessary for teaching and the teachers are actively interacting with the students. There is a noticeable absence of work sheets, remedial programs, and children outside of the classroom for disciplinary reasons.

The intense attention given to principals by the superintendent has aided this process. Teachers are receiving more direct attention from the principals and the central office, particularly from Pat Yee, the associate superintendent for educational services. Student/teacher interaction is emphasized from the central office and the principal. The superintendent visits schools and classrooms, but in general, the visits are symbolic. For example, she attended a science fair for high school students in which the teachers and students were featured on a local television program. The exchange between the group was so impressive, the vignette was featured throughout the state to demonstrate how cooperation takes place between hierarchical levels, gender, and ethnic and racial groups. The task and the products were featured as process and outcome considerations in the conduct of schooling in America. Dr. Singer described it, "As corny as it may sound to many, a great number of the students in the school district do hold the American dream dear. Who am I to shatter it? I must do my best to enact it!"

Because Dr. Singer is only in her fourth year as superintendent, the data collected from school sites are incomplete and inconclusive. The first complete battery of tests are just now being administered. The base line data for determining student attendance, and other student profile information are just now ready to be used for growth comparison. Nevertheless, there are some tangible positive changes which are occurring which indicate Willow Creek Unified School District is a different and improved organization at the school site level than it was before Dr. Singer became superintendent.

What are the most visible indicators at the local site? First, the physical plant and the grounds are being improved. Even though resources are limited, the neighborhood has perceived the intent to better the schools, and community members have participated in helping to clean and refurbish the facilities and grounds. Many schools have volunteer gardeners and plant maintenance persons aid in the upgrading of the facilities and grounds.

The community is developing pride in its schools. Firms are asking teachers to bring their students to tour their plants. Agencies such as the police, fire marshal, and employment offices are volunteering their personnel to speak to students. Prior to Dr. Singer's appointment, the schools were places people avoided and criticized. Now the community is gradually claiming them. Dr. Singer explained, "The community must feel they own these schools and they are places to be proud of and to be loyal to."

## Equity and Excellence

Integrating minority administrators within the school district has required attention. Minority administrator attitudes regarding roles and lifelong learning have had to be fostered as they improve their administrative skills. The organization has instituted means to bring about equity. The racially mixed board, cabinet, principalships, and teacher ranks have changed the working climate. Interdependence, cooperation, and teamwork have resulted in procedures which facilitate action. At the district level, the proposed actions from the superintendent are accepted the first time they are presented. The board, as a body, is in accord with the superintendent's intentions and actions. Evaluation of and assistance with due process are being emphasized. An affirmative action plan, committee and officer have been approved. Progress is being monitored and reported to the community.

To affect the school site level, the district has begun a national recruiting effort including the various locations where individuals representing ethnic groups and specialties can be found. The focus is to provide at the school site level competent individuals who represent the racial groups in the Willow Creek Unified School District.

## Superintendent/School Board Relations

Insuring district-wide stability and order is dependent on the working relationship between the superintendent and the school board. The composition of the board changed during the first year of this superintendent's tenure. The new board's intentions were more compatible with her agenda. The superintendent cites the example of a recent incident. One board member was ill so various actions proposed were a vote short of passage. The split board took advantage of this situation. A board member opposing a proposed new hire said, "We have layers and layers of administrative crud. Hiring any more offends me." The superintendent objected to the remark and at the end of the meeting asked the board to meet in closed session. The audience expected the superintendent to resign.

The superintendent explained to the board members how a remark from one of them has an effect. She said,

> The thing that is going around here about this administrative crud is creating rumors or jokes like, where are you? Are you a top layer or bottom? Are you a thin layer or a fat one? Are you a hard layer or a soft layer? It is not funny around here. The board has no right to talk to us that way.

The local paper's report indicates to the community that the board and the administration are not getting along well. This is not so. They are getting along. It was just a careless remark made by one board member. The nature of the incident and the potential consequences demonstrate how fragile superintendent-board relationships are. Felicia Singer said,

> They do not always mean to be bad but they are. Sometimes we go faster than we should and do not communicate as well as we need to. We know we do not have a lot of time to make an impact. If we dare stop, something comes in to fill the vacuum and creates a wedge. It becomes real hard to get it back together again. The board is our boss and we appreciate that very much. They asked us to come. We are working very hard. People can see that some things are changing. They are hopeful. We believe that we are making an impact.

The superintendent instructs the board to realize the impact of its members' statements. The board can tell the administrators what they want but they have to allow them to figure out how to do it.

Aside from racial and ethnic characteristics, board members can bring other attributes which may contribute to incidents of conflict. This particular board consisted of a retired principal and three former teachers from the district. They have been residents in the town all along. Sometimes these members confuse things they have seen happen, have done, and have been successful in with the proposed actions from the superintendent. They get scared about new things and different methods.

What is evident is that the superintendent's intentions to establish order and stability require attention to every level of the organization. She summarized:

> It is just bit by bit, little tiny steps, but just like bad things get blown up, so do good things. We are just trying to give people good things to talk

about. It doesn't have to be important. It just has to be positive. Make somebody feel good so they will tell somebody.

# CONCLUSIONS

What can be learned from this case? This superintendent created a school district culture by attending to eleven basic actions. They were: l) balancing the budget, 2) replacing two school board members, 3) hiring additional teachers, 4) hiring a cabinet consisting of individuals representing diverse racial groups, 5) providing staff development to teachers, 6) establishing pupil outcome targets, 7) establishing a personal image, 8) establishing a school district image, 9) engaging in an affirmative action plan, 10) focusing attention on principals and school sites, and 11) establishing superintendent/ board relationships.

Some of these actions are highly interdependent. For example, hiring additional teachers and the associate superintendent for instruction and providing staff development to teachers were actions directly designed to improve pupil performance across the district. Establishing a personal image and a school district image required the institutionalization of an affirmative action plan. The composite of all of the actions resulted in the creation of a culture which is reflected at the school site level as well as district-wide.

The elements of the school culture emerge from these actions. The balanced budget reflected a healthier organization whose resources would be redirected for instructional purposes. A supportive school board and the personnel changes, such as the hiring of the cabinet and the additional teachers, highlighted the common purpose to which the organization is directed. The integration of diverse groups across the organization signified individual and group potential and provided opportunities for team work. Establishing intensive interpersonal relationships between the superintendent, the central office staff, and the principals bonded the hierarchical levels to each other. The concentration on hiring teachers served to support the process of rebuilding a productive work norm and to reinforce the value of instruction and children across the district.

Stability, a common purpose, and hope characterize the present Willow Creek Unified School District. The community, the school board and the superintendent are confident the organization is engaged in schooling. The central office staff, principals, teachers and students are engaged in the conduct of schooling.

Since schools are organizations created to fulfill educational goals, a culture designed for that purpose must be recreated or maintained. In this particular case, the community, school board, and school personnel were unable to sustain a school culture while the district was leaderless. Dr. Singer was hired to recreate a school culture emanating from the classroom and school site to span the district. Dr. Singer is fulfilling that mandate. This case illustrates how organizations are person dependent. Superintendents shape the culture of a school district by complying with the school board's mandate and the community's expectations. The superintendent's own capabilities and intentions are directly related to the nature of compliance. Superintendents who comply with board members' mandates create school district cultures which contain excellent, mediocre, and inferior schools within them. Superintendents in this case accept the differentiation. In the case of Dr. Singer, she sought that all schools within the district be equally excellent.

Superintendents develop cultures through routine, systematic, focused decisions and actions, rather than through heroic deeds. Dr. Singer did not import special programs nor did she dismantle the organization. Instead, she balanced the budget, hired a new cabinet, socialized the principals, hired and critically placed exceptionally competent teachers, and set targets for student performance. This point is important when considering equity and excellence. For Dr. Singer, the provision of excellent educational services for all was her priority. Her intentions were fulfilled by focusing on the general tasks of schooling rather than on responding to individual or group interests. Her regard for minorities was exemplified by surrounding herself with individuals representing all groups rather than by dwelling on board and community conflict.

## REFERENCES

Bernard, Chester. (1938). *The Functions of the Executive*, Cambridge, MA: Harvard University Press.

Carlson, R.O. (1972). *School Superintendents: Careers and Performance*, Columbus, Ohio: Charles E. Merrill.

Greenfield, Thomas B. (1984). Leaders and schools: Willfulness and nonnatural order in organizations. In *Leadership and Organizational Culture: New Perspectives on Administrative Theory and Practice*, Thomas J. Sergiovanni & John E. Corbally (eds.), pp. 142-169. Urbana and Chicago: University of Illinois Press.

Lutz, Frank W. & Wang, Lee-Yen. (1987). Predicting public dissatisfaction: A study of school board member defeat. *Educational Administration Quarterly, 23* (l), pp. 65-77.

March, James G. (1984). How we talk and how we act: Administrative theory and administrative life, in *Leadership and Organizational Culture: Perspectives on Administrative Theory and Practice*, Thomas J.Sergiovanni & John E. Corbally (eds), pp. 18-351. Urbana and Chicago: University of Illinois Press.

Willower, Donald J. & Smith, Jonathan. (1987). Organizational culture in schools: Myth and creation. *High School Journal, 70* (2), pp. 87-94.

# Diversity in Student Cultures

# Chapter 4
# Implausible Endings: Teenage Mothers and Fictions of School Success

*by Nancy Lesko, University of Indiana*

This paper examines the culture of an alternative high school for teenage mothers by closely examining one of its ritual practices, student panels. Panels of students regularly speak to different audiences about their experiences as pregnant teenagers, as school dropouts, as students at Bright Prospects School[1], and as young mothers. Public panel discussions provide the forum for girls to recount their former "wildnesses," declare their new selves, and provide evidence of their maturity and responsibility. The panelists' stories provide evidence of success at two levels: both the girls and the school are successes.

These panels provide a glimpse inward toward the dialogue of appropriate school practices and outward to the social dialogue regarding the problem of teenage pregnancy. This paper proceeds by investigating both the content and the form of the success stories told in the student panels. The success stories have plausible endings. In order for endings to be "plausible," they must be grounded in norms or maxims (Miller, 1981). Thus, to understand school success stories (whether real or imagined), one needs to probe the underlying norms, which include rationality, individual achievement, and child-centeredness. Another dimension of these success stories of teenage mothers is the autobiographical form, which rests upon and, in turn, reinforces certain conventions of female lives.

In addition to examining the norms underlying perceptions of student and school success, the analysis also seeks to illuminate what school-aged mothers might gain from the achievement of school success and what they might lose (Smith, 1987; Walkerdine, 1985). Since all stories are partial, only some of all possible interpretations are represented in a particular rendering (Smith, 1987; Whitson, 1988). This perspective allows a reading of multiple and conflicting layers of school success stories.

## Plausible Endings

This interpretation of one school's success stories begins with a now-classic film about high school groups, *The Breakfast Club*. The film tells the story of five students, who spend one Saturday high school detention together and through which they are changed. Each of the five represents a recognizable school clique: the three boys typify the jocks, freaks, and brains; the two girls portray the socialites and the outcasts. This film about relations among high school peer groups has several themes, one of which revolves around changes, transformations. For example, after the despised anti-school freak locks the assistant principal in a closet, the five are transformed from adversaries who look down upon each other to acquaintances who move a little toward understanding each other as human beings with strengths and weaknesses. The transformations, of dislike to acceptance, of conflict to understanding, help produce the happy and plausible ending of the film.

Schools participate in the cultural preoccupation with transformations and the belief that change is a plausible and happy ending to life stories. For example, schools gain prestige from "turning kids around" or staffs acquire recognition for "turning a school around" (Kirp, 1989). Schools for at-risk students are especially attuned to this mission (Wehlage, Rutter, Smith, Lesko, and Fernandez, 1989). An alternative school for teenage mothers likewise seeks to transform its students. The understanding of teenage pregnancy as a "problem" underlies the need to transform these girls (Rains, 1971; Lesko, forthcoming). In light of the problem of teenage pregnancy, the transformation of the outcast girl, Allyson, in *The Breakfast Club* is of special interest. At the beginning of the film, Allyson is pale, dressed all in black, with her hair hiding her face. She speaks only when pressed by her peers. Eventually she admits that she lies compulsively and only came to detention because she had nothing else to do. She appears to be a mess: emotionally and socially; this is analogous to the emotional "mess" attributed to girls who get pregnant (*Time*, 1985).

But when Allyson begins to open up and admit the truth of her life, she begins to accept and be accepted by the others. Near the end of the film, the socialite girl, Claire, takes Allyson up to the mezzanine of the library to re-make her appearance. Allyson emerges dressed in a soft, scoop-necked, white sleeveless dress. Barrettes hold back her hair from her face and she wears light shades of rouge and lipstick. At the film's plausible and happy ending, Allyson has changed her attittude and her appearance, accepting middle class norms for dress and social interactions and being taken under the wing of an upper middle class girl. This new look is also connected to her pairing up with the jock. Allyson discards her black frock, her angry silence, and unconventional behavior, to be attired in white, to act "normally," and to become sexually attractive to a male athlete. Allyson's "power" to be looked upon with approval (by Claire, the jock, and the audience), to be noticed, and listened to via her new self: new appearance and attitudes. She drops her anger, talks to people, feminizes her appearance, couples romantically and, thereby, is deemed worthy of attention by the peer audience and the film audience.

The harmony of the group transformation and, especially, the romantic coupling of jock and outcast stimulate a "happy feeling" in viewers, feelings based upon an acceptance of its plausibility and the norms underlying the changes. Near the end of the film, Claire admits that these Saturday friend-ships will be short-lived. When school reconvenes on Monday, she says, the higher status students (herself and the jock) will not speak to these other three, at least not if other higher status friends are present. Despite this restatement of social class realities, the romantic couplings prevail in establishing a plausible, happy ending. The happy ending to *The Breakfast Club* is normatively connected to students reducing conflict by talking about their feelings and the ways in which they are all put down by their parents. But this group unity gives way for the "real" happy ending, which is premised upon the norm of heterosexual coupling.

Several of these norms which undergird the plausible, happy ending of *The Breakfast Club* are present at Bright Prospects School. As will be shown, changes in attitudes are conceived as the basis for happy endings to students' stories. These attitude changes are normed by middle class values and experiences. Heterosexual coupling remains the implicit norm, since economic success is otherwise jeopardized. The happy ending of *The Breakfast Club* illuminates norms underlying plausible school success stories. Analysis of school stories with happy endings, in turn, provide insights into school culture as it intersects with culture beyond the school.

## Theoretical Background of the Study

This paper looks at how a panel of students speaking to outside audiences provides an occasion to analyze the meeting of inside school and outside school cultural themes which operate to produce "success stories." To avoid merely "grafting on context" (Walkerdine, 1988) to studies of schooling, this analysis seeks to understand school practices as necessarily drawing upon social concepts to give meaning (Geertz, 1973; Whitson, 1988; Henriques, Hollway, Urwin, Venn, and Walkerdine, 1984). This approach views all social utterances, whether vocal, behavioral, stylistic, ritualistic, as part of ongoing social dialogues. The meaning of utterances is understood by seeking to understand the specific and general dialogues in which utterances are situated (Bakhtin, 1981). This does not mean that the conscious realities of students are unimportant or ignored. Rather, this analytic approach seeks to examine the discourses within which students must operate in order to be social participants (Whitson, 1988; Bakhtin, 1981).

This analytical approach is based upon structuralist and poststructuralist perspectives on meaning-making and communication. Meaning, sense, and communication proceed through difference, or in Bakhtin's framing, through *dialogue* among different perspectives. One cannot participate in social communication unless one uses terms already part of the ongoing dialogue. It would be like trying to communicate in writing without knowing any of the conventions of writing, punctuation, spelling, grammar, or the words for expressing ideas, feelings, and thoughts.

Narratives, or stories, are fundamental ways by which human beings understand their lives (Gee, 1985; Levi-Strauss, 1963; Wexler, 1982). The stories that are told and retold about successful and unsuccessful students articulate elements of school culture, social perspectives, and the structures of meaning through which success and failure are understood, legitimated, and accepted (Lesko, 1988). Storytelling can also be analyzed as social rites, a conceptualization which places emphasis on both the form and content of the stories (Varenne, 1977; Turner, 1969; McLaren, 1986; Lesko, 1988). The student panels at Bright Prospects School were scrutinized for their place within the school's internal dialogue about what is successful and what are its roles and tasks. But the panels will also be scrutinized as utterances in the dialogue across schools and social groups about the "problem of teenage pregnancy" with its characters of "good" and "bad" girls. While the transformation from "bad" to "good" girls is counted as success on the level of the within school dialogue, looking at the girls as single mothers, they are not glowing success stories. By narrowly focusing upon certain symbolically weighted characteristics, the success stories are created. When we look at other dimensions of these girls' lives and prospective futures, Bright Prospects' achievements are dulled.

This analysis is also informed by feminist perspectives on society and schooling (Rich, 1979; Howe, 1984; Gordon, 1988, 1974; Sidel, 1986; Arnot and Weiner, 1987; Martin, 1985; Roman, Christian-Smith, and Ellsworth, 1988). Feminist perspectives vary substantially but, in general, attend to how schooling contributes to the marginalization and subordination of women in society. How do the apparently neutral knowledges and practices of schools contribute to inequities of power and knowledge of women, and especially of women of color?

This analysis raises several interwoven questions: What is school success and what norms do stories of school success rely upon? What is school success for young mothers and how is that related to their post-secondary school lives? How is school success for young mothers related to a transformation of aspects of their previous lives? And what relationship do the transformations of females have to the broader social discourse and gendered relations of power?

## School Setting and Research Methodology

The data from Bright Prospects School were gathered during four weeks of participant-observation spread across a school year. The analysis includes data gathered through observation of classes, interviews of staff and students, examination of curricular materials, and the viewing of a videotape of a student panel discussion.

At the time of the study, Bright Prospects School occupied a former middle school building situated at the intersection of a four-lane and a six-lane road in the area of town sprouting the newest and finest shopping malls, office buildings, and hotels. The school was a dusty yellow stucco, surrounded by several large, handsome cottonwoods which shaded the children's outside play areas. Temporary buildings flanked two sides of the school. The building clearly denoted what it was: an urban school. However, when a visitor entered the school and encountered its long main corridor brightly carpeted in red and its female students with infants and toddlers in tow, it became clear that this was an unusual urban school.

Bright Prospects is unusual in that it is a school for young mothers, not just a program for girls while they are pregnant. Girls typically choose to enroll in the school when they are four or five months pregnant and their changing body "starts to show." Pregnant girls' other options in this district are to continue in their regular school or to drop out of school until they give birth. The program is designed for a one-year stay, until the child is 4-6 months old, when girls are encouraged to return to their "home" schools. However, girls who have no child care provisions or who do especially well in the small, nurturant setting, remain until graduation. Girls must apply for continuation in the program and are chosen by staff on the basis of need and a positive response to the program in the past. Of Bright Prospects' students, 86% complete high school, while only 60% of teenage mothers nationally (by age 19) do so (Guttmacher Institute, 1981). This high graduation rate is part of what attracts visitors, reporters, and commendations from across the country.

The city's ethnic diversity is reflected in the school population of 54% Hispanic, 30% Anglo, 8% American Indian, and 7.5% Black. The Bright Prospects' staff describes its students as poor. Despite low incomes, they live in their own houses and are members of extended families. The girls are perceived to be from homes where women maintain traditional roles, and education for girls is not highly valued. One teacher estimated that 50% of the students live in families which are "in crisis," families in which alcoholism, physical, sexual, or psychological abuse, chronic unemployment, or drug abuse are present. Students range in age from 12 to 21 years of age. In the year of the study (1986-87), over 50% of the students were 16 or 17 years old; 16% were 15 years old and 13% were 18 years of age.

Central to Bright Prospects' program are its three child care centers in the building; 75 infants through toddlers receive care while their mothers attend classes. All students assist in a childcare center for a class period each day. The nurseries are also used as "labs" for the study of child development. Three staff nurses, supplemented by visiting health clinics from the state university medical school, provide regular health care for the babies and the mothers.

Its graduation rate, comprehensive program, 18-year history, and strong funding from the public school district (over 90% of its funds come from the school district) make it a model program. In addition, Bright Prospects' teachers continue to develop curricular materials (e.g. in math, in pregnancy and motherhood) that are used across the country. This brief overview must suffice as an introduction to the school. The next section looks more closely at the stories told during a student panel.

## A Student Panel: Success Stories of Responsible, Rational Mothers

The image of a young girl with swollen belly dominates the discourse on the problem of teenage pregnancy. The *Time* (December 9, 1985) cover presents her as the problem that "rends the social fabric." She stands sideways, to accentuate her fully pregnant, fully sexual body. Her ripe body is juxtaposed with her child's face, which communicates sadness, pessimism, and confusion. Her face forecasts uncertainty—the apparent consequences of irresponsible sexuality. This image signals "disorder" or "alarm": a child having a child, a young woman too soon sexual, a spectacle, a grotesqueness (Russo, 1986).

The images of success, of socially redeemed young mothers, are directly connected to these images of spectacle and disorder. The images of successful young mothers are less sensational, but nevertheless gripping. In one of many panel discussions for different audiences, six Bright Prospects' students sat behind a V-shaped table and looked at a group of about 20 adults, mostly women. Two of the six panelists were Anglos, three were Hispanic or American Indian, and one was Black. Five fashioned their shoulder length hair after Farah Fawcett in the 1970's television show, "Charlie's Angels." They all wore pants and simple blouses or tee shirts. Within the last 12 months each could have posed for the "Children Having Children" cover of *Time*.

The six were introduced as "representative" of most Bright Prospects students, who would discuss what it meant to be "combining the roles of parent and student." The girls ranged in age from 16 to 19; four were single mothers, two were married. For thirty minutes they told the audience of strangers (and a video camera) how they responded when they found they were pregnant, how they came to Bright Prospects, why they had previously dropped out of school, and how Bright Prospects helped them. Along the way, they also discussed the difficulties of being mothers, single mothers, and continuing their education.

The woman conducting the panel, a former Bright Prospects staff member, began by asking each panelist to tell a little about herself. The girls responded by telling their ages, how old their babies were, and how long they had been enrolled at Bright Prospects. The moderator asked, "Tell us how you came to be at Bright Prospects."

In responding to this directive, the panelists followed a formula in which they first recounted their reckless pasts, getting pregnant, dropping out of school, and feeling hopeless. Then they narrated how they have changed and how their futures have been shaping up. Across different settings, Bright Prospects' students were very willing to talk about themselves, to make sense of their lives through such stories (Lesko, 1988), and, thereby, to redeem themselves through the "new" selves they presented.

The panelists spoke of themselves as previously "wild" or reckless. Arlynn described herself when she got pregnant: "I was headed for dropping out; I was headed down. I hadn't been doing well in classes." Esther recounted a similar past, "Before [I got pregnant] I didn't go to school; I partied all the time... Now I respect myself more. I don't do things to embarrass myself." Dolores volunteered, "I was bad. I would go home, take a shower, pack a bag and leave for two weeks. My mom was getting really upset with me. We were fighting a lot." Each time a panelist spoke, other heads bobbed in recognition.

Then, with the realization that she was pregnant, each girl discussed how she came to recant her previous behavior. Each student said that having a baby made her more mature. Having responsibilities for another and having that other totally dependent were circumstances that forced her to be consistent, dependable, to consider the consequences. What the girls meant by becoming "mature" was to leave behind behaviors dubbed immature. Michelle said, "I miss being crazy, being wild. I was a really wild kid." Esther added, "You can't do that anymore [sit around drinking and smoking pot]. If you do that, they'll grow up to do it, too. You have to set an example for your kid." Charlene noted, "It seems when you get pregnant, you mature just like that. We're not old," she added quickly. "You just mature." Michelle said that Bright Prospects intended "to help you take care of your baby and to take responsibility."

This responsibility and maturity theme centered upon taking care of their babies. The oldest panelist, Carla, admonished the audience to remember, "Young teenagers can take care of their babies." Once again the other five panel members nodded in agreement. Carla acknowledged that she often wanted to get out of her situation with a "crying baby, a hungry husband, dishes, ironing." She wondered aloud: "Why did I do this?" Then she concluded, "You have to give someone else your life; you have to put your husband and your child first."

In addition to becoming mature and responsible mothers, the panelists emphasized their regular use of birth control. They laughed among themselves when Dolores said, "I have my son on my lap. There is *no way* I will forget to take my birth control pill with him there as a constant reminder." Most of the girls said they wanted more children but not until they were ready. "Maybe when I'm out of college and I don't have to depend on anyone, when I can take care of myself." Esther summarized, "I know not to do it again [get pregnant] until I'm ready."

Every panelist described herself as now wanting to attend college. Esther said, "I think of college now, before I didn't want to. I want my baby to have whatever he wants." Dolores saw college as a prerequisite for a good job. And a good job meant self-sufficiency. Esther expressed her strong dislike of living with her mother, "I want to support me and my child, not have to live at home. I don't like that idea. I feel like me and my baby are a burden to my mother."

The panel moderator asked what difficulties students encountered in being mothers and attending school. Arlynn, the other married young woman, spoke of her particular difficulty: a husband who didn't want her to finish school. "He didn't graduate and so he doesn't want me to finish," she said solemnly. She also valued that at Bright Prospects "you get some time to get to know yourself."

The panelists spoke in only glowing terms about Bright Prospects School. Cindy said, "I couldn't imagine there was a school where I could leave my baby while I go to classes." Carla said, "It's a really loving atmosphere here." Another panelist commented, "It's like a second family." "I can't believe that there's a place where I really fit," exulted Marilyn. Several girls thought that the regular high schools should look at how Bright Prospects did things. For example, "Other schools treat you like little kids; here they treat you like an adult," said Delores. "I would have been kicked out of any school, because when I was pregnant I was sick and I missed more than 11 days," added Charlene.

The moderator's last question was, "When it is so hard to get your baby ready and yourself ready and get to school, why do you do it?" The panelists responded with fervor: "This is an opportunity that I can't pass up." "Not everybody can go to this school. There's a waiting list. I'm going to take up my space and use it good," said Delores.

The final statement on the video was Charlene's. She summed up how she felt about the Bright Prospects Program: "Because of this school, I'm going to make it."

## First Reading of School Success Stories

On first exposure, the stories of these representative Bright Prospects' students appear to be unqualified successes. The girls will likely complete high school; they have learned a lot about taking care of children; they are given time away from their child while in school classes. Each panel member was energetic, determined, and confident of her future success in school and/or in the workplace.

It would seem that the stories presented are straightforwardly cases of transformations of young women, from "wildness" and irresponsibility to grounded responsibility, acceptance of their fates, and strong hope that they can salvage good, sound lives for themselves and their children. It would seem that, like Allyson in *The Breakfast Club*, they have been transformed from "outlaw" or freak status to "good girls." They are centrally concerned with their children's welfare and rationally planning for their future. They are no longer sexually irresponsible, in that they use birth control. They are sociable and willingly speak to strangers, and they smile when they speak about their lives. They are not emotionally disabled. These girls are not grotesque; they are not spectacles. They seek conventional paths: to be good mothers, to be successful students in high school and in college, to earn a decent income to support themselves and their children, and, for a few, to get to know themselves and what they want in their lives.

The story of Bright Prospects School also appears to be a simple success story. The school's comprehensive program has saved the girls from fates of dropout, low self-esteem, and emotional disabilities. They are instructed on how to be good mothers, and their continuation in the program beyond the initial year hinges, in part, on their behaving in ways that show staff members that they are benefiting from the program and applying the things they learn, especially in the realm of child care.

The stories of difficulty and redemption held the attention of their audience. Their willingness to confess their crimes, recount their deviance, and boldly and confidently declare, "Because of this school, I'm going to make it" were startling. Why would young women willingly volunteer for these public "confessions?"

These public panels function as rites of social redemption for the teenage mothers. These girls' statements calm the fears raised by the discourse on the problem of teenage pregnacy (Lesko, forthcoming). The confessions of these girls reveal that they are not "emotionally disabled," but young mothers with "regular" problems of children and schoolwork (*Time*, 1985). The ordinariness of the panelists is soothing. Thus, this panel proclaims that these teenage mothers are no longer women with unusual problems or people who will cause problems for others (Gusfield, 1986). In embracing good motherhood, responsibility, rational life-planning, and optimism for self-sufficient futures, these girls publicly complete their redemption. Their deviancy began in the public limelight; their sexual young bodies were necessarily publicly displayed. And their deviancy ended publicly with stories of maturity and hope. The audience represents "society" who finds plausible the stories' happy endings.

However, the panels also serve the school; an alternative school program is always in jeopardy of being eliminated as an "extra" or "frill" in a school district budget (Wehlage et al., 1989). The panels verify and personalize the real successes of Bright Prospects School and the importance of the program for the students it serves. Thus, these panels proclaim that both the girls and Bright Prospects are successes.

Is this not a simple story of students' success and school success? Are these not plausible happy endings?

## Second Reading of the Stories of Teenage Mothers: Narrative Power and Identity Politics

However, this smoothly successful, seamless narrative arouses suspicion on a number of levels, which challenge its credibility, its naturalness, its "happy ending." Post-structuralist analyses examine the power woven into representations, into narratives, into all knowledges, from history to medicine to architecture (Walkerdine, 1988; Foucault, 1977; 1978; Weedon, 1987; Whitson, 1988; Henriques et al., 1984). These analyses help to unpack the relations of power and the perspectives interwoven in all representations, which are present in both the form and content.

## Confessional mode

The form of the autobiographical tellings is significant. Foucault (1977) suggests that the telling of private stories, whether in religious settings, medical, or therapeutic, all partake of a new, modern form of social control through self-revelation. The power in the "confessional mode" is with the audience, the listeners. The speaker seeks to understand what will be listened to, be considered legitimate, and be responded to. In written autobiographies (Smith, 1987) and in oral recitations (Foucault, 1977), the audience has the power to accept, praise, condemn, reject the speakers who tell their life stories. Individuals are judged, can be listened to or rejected by these audiences. The categories and meaning-systems of the members of the audience are relevant to the speakers who must communicate within those meaning structures.

From this perspective, the panel of Bright Prospects students wanted to have a certain effect on their audience. They wanted to be listened to, empathized with, understood. They wanted to touch their audiences with their honesty and with the details of their stories. They wanted to be seen as sympathetic young women, worthy of school support and supportive of Bright Prospects' program. So, the dependence on a favorable audience response suggests that the life stories of the girls will be told according to certain conventions, which are likely to be heard, sympathized or empathized with. The works of Foucault and Smith point to the importance of life-tellings, as experiences through which individuals construct their lives and, at the same time, as events in which audiences actively interpret social behavior according to certain criteria. Life-tellings are moments of intensive social and individual identity construction; times when "society" is actively present as an audience, helping to shape individuals' representations of their lives.

## Autobiographical conventions

Smith's (1987) study of women's autobiographical writing finds four scripts used by female writers in this genre. They are the scripts or roles that allow women to appeal to their audiences and to be seen in a good light. Smith dubs these roles "power narratives," because they serve the writer by giving her the power of an audience. By writing within one of the four scripts, female autobiographers gained an audience for their works. Smith suggests that the autobiographers would likely have been shunned and unread if they did not adhere to one of these conventional scripts. The four predominant life scripts, or autobiographical identities, available are: the nun, the queen, the wife, and the witch.[2]

Within these autobiographies, certain womanly traits are admired and normative. For example, a nun receives social approbation for her chastity, and for her non-worldly, self-effacing, spiritual life. The wife receives acceptance and legitimacy from her audience with descriptions of "wifely" acts and attitudes, which include:

> the narrative of feminine goodness, a silent plot of modesty, naivete, virtue, dependency, innocence and self-concealment (Smith, 1987, p. 89).

The exemplar of the true feminine may inhabit an autobiography as the writer's mother: "an ideal of timeless beauty and devotion, an image of female perfection that is cloistered, quiescent, eternal" (Smith, 1987, p.92). But the model woman can also be portrayed through the weaker sides of her personality:

> the representation of herself as foolish, uncomfortable, ignorant, fearful, bashful, and speechless in public testifies to her superior virtue, the basis on which her true merit as a model woman rests (Smith, 1987, p.93).

And, of course, the life story of the ideal woman demands the repression of sexual desire.

The "silent plot" of modesty, naivete, virtue, dependency, innocence, self-concealment, foolishness, ignorance, fearfulness, bashfulness is both selectively upheld and violated by the autobiographers Smith studied. Smith's view is that the "poetics" of women's autobiography arise in the intricate fashioning of self-stories invoking some aspects of the "womanly" norms and violating others.

Teenage mothers clearly violate that "silent plot" of the ideal woman's life: teenage mothers are neither innocent nor self-concealing. Teenage mothers have been sexual outside the confines of marriage. They have "stepped into the limelight out of turn" thereby making spectacles of themselves (Russo, 1986, p. 213). However, women's crimes can be forgiven; women redeem themselves in autobiographies in several ways. Teenage mothers can admit ignorance, foolishness in their pasts and claim to be changed, transformed. They can demonstrate their adherence to new, positive characteristics: child-centeredness, rational control of sexuality, and striving for economic independence.

The transgressions of teenage mothers are enumerated in numerous publications about the problem of teenage pregnancy (e.g. Children's Defense Fund booklets, reports by the Alan Guttmacher Institute, and cover stories in *Time*). Reports of the problem of teenage pregnancy reiterate three main themes: teenage mothers are social problems because of sexual irresponsibility, likelihood of being bad mothers, and the likelihood of being economically dependent.

The Bright Prospects panelists tell stories which include a changed perspective on each of those formerly problematic area. First, they have been irresponsible: dropping out of school, running away from home, and being wild, usually involving drugs and sexual activeness. Second, the panelists portray themselves as child-centered mothers. Third, the panelists emphasize their desire to go to college and to be independent. From Smith's autobiographical perspective, they are following a female autobiographical convention of admitting stupidity. They acknowledge acting impulsively, foolishly, willfully. However, for female autobiographers to redeem themselves fully, they must do more than admit past follies. They must act positively, consciously, oriented toward their futures, as they move toward one of the conventional female life scripts. The most likely one is of wife [and mother]. Even though the student-autobiographers are not all wives, they are all mothers. It is this script which allows the panelists to win the approval and sympathy of their audience.

## The Curriculum of Rationality

The Bright Prospects curriculum appears to overlay "rational order" onto the lives of its students. The "representative" students on the panel unanimously provide evidence that they have become rational and orderly in viewing their lives, their responsibilities, and their futures. The Bright Prospects curriculum, as represented in the life-stories of student panelists, inculcates a male-identified conception of self. Smith argues that to write autobiography is to use conventions of self-representation that are consistent with male experiences, values, social relations, and psychological orientation.[3] Autobiographical lives emphasize rationality, individualized thought and action, orderliness, and a consciously constructed unfolding of purposeful action over time. Smith argues that autobiographies leave out the uncontrollable and unnamed side(s) of human existence: "that which is fluid, immediate, contingent, irrational" (Smith, 1987, p. 40). Autobiographies attempt to impose a view of orderly progression on life events, which might have been experienced as chaotic or ambiguous. To tell autobiographies is to rewrite lives from a phallocentric perspective. The norm of change, illustrated in the happy ending of *The Breakfast Club*, is clearly present in the success stories of Bright Prospects students. The girls admit mistakes and stupidity and give evidence of their transformation into responsible, child-centered young women who strive for economic independence. These stories are told within acceptable autobiographicl scripts available to young women. The panelists' life stories have been examined for their participation in the broader social dialogue about norms for young women. In the next sections, the focus shifts to how the panelists' stories also participate in the within-the-school dialogue about successful students in a program for teenage mothers.

## Curriculum of Individualization and Mothering

In the within-the-school dialogue, the meanings of the student panels are located in their messages regarding what it means to be a successful student. Successful students are ones who accept the rules of the game. One major rule is that each student succeeds or fails alone. The process of becoming schooled is a process of seeing oneself as an individual who is separate from others, whose interests are distinctive, whose person is unique (Bellah, Madsen, Sullivan, Swidler, and Tipton, 1985; Lesko, 1988; Martin, 1985; Bernstein, 1976). The panels are rituals which differentiate rather than unify students (Bernstein, 1976; Lesko, 1988). Again, the autobiographical format "valorize[s] individual integrity and separateness... and devalues personal and communal interdependency" (Smith, 1987, p. 39). Walkerdine (1985) argues that school is the phallic order; to succeed in school is to become incorporated into patriarchy, with its emphases on individualism, competition, and autonomy.

However, being a successful female student involves modification of the standard of success. Being a successful male student may mean expectations focus upon being inquiring, discovering, inventive and creative (Walkerdine, 1983, p. 83). Successful female students often fail to exhibit these "good" characteristics, and are viewed by educators as "only" hard-working: girls follow rules and do rote memory work. The girls at Bright Prospects show themselves to be successful students by plodding along in their courses and their credits, not by being brilliant or aggressive.[4]

The second part of the curriculum complements the emphasis on the successful, striving individual. Mothering provides the perfect vehicle to transform rule-breaking young women into rule-followers. This part of the curriculum, and parts of the autobiographies, provide the formerly wild young women a path to conventionality, toward a form of power (albeit defined and circumscribed by men). The curriculum teaches mothering in many overlapping ways: first, in the nurturing way adults treat students, bending the rules, always giving students another chance; second, in the required courses which focus directly on mothering; third, the child care centers help initiate the students into the importance of raising children and the knowledge which attends "good mothering." These different channels of mothering and nurturing seemed to foster, or support, a child-centeredness which developed among the girls. Although many had never considered going to college before they had a baby, as mothers they planned to go to college for their child's welfare.

The curriculum of mothering helps teenage mothers become school successes. This curriculum has positive dimensions, for example, that young mothers learn how to care for their children. In a broader perspective, certain conventions of the female self, rule-following, nurturing, passivity, are reproduced in a school curriculum and integrated with an individualistic, autonomous, rationalistic curriculum to produce young women who appear to be successes for the school staff and for the broader society. This hybrid— a middle class value system grafted onto working class single mothers— appears to be an unmitigated success. It accomplishes this by speaking on the two levels of discourse: the level of within-school student success and the level of correcting socially problematic people.

## Problems with the Curriculum of Individualization and Mothering

On closer inspection, these success stories appear untenable on both philo-sophical and practical grounds. Philosophically, it is an untenable hybrid because students are learning to value independence, autonomy, rational-planning when all the evidence suggests that women, and especially women of color, meet extraordinary difficulties in being single mothers and living above the poverty line (Sidel, 1986; Zinn, 1989; Collins, 1989). The success story is untenable because it suggests that if girls become good, follow the rules, develop positive (i.e. independent, rational, autonomous) attitudes, they will succeed. This view of what it takes to succeed discounts the continuing significance of both gender and race in U.S. economic realities. This myth further enhances the individualistic ethos in placing all the responsibility for success or failure on individuals. There is no education around the social realities of women, and minority women, and the labor market. "The advice to the poor seems to be that the sole requirement to lift oneself out of poverty is to think and behave like white, middle class men and women" (Collins, 1989, p. 882). This is the norm which underlies the transfor-mation of Allyson in *The Breakfast Club* and the plausibility of its happy ending. She changes her attitudes and all the other factors fall into place.

Even though Bright Prospects' own child care is the single most impor-tant feature of its program, the child care is the social support which allows girls to attend school. But its formal curriculum is blind to the importance of social supports, social context, for success. While it supports its students with free child care, it instructs that success is grounded in individual ambition, autonomy, and following the rules.

A second philosophical issue is the failure of Bright Prospects to develop any collective unity among its female students. The school resembles a social service delivery system more than a collection of individuals across time. Although each student panelist comments on the quality of the Bright Prospects program, a central ritual of the school focuses upon individualized, autonomous autobiographical stories. What begins as experiences in common of being a pregnant teenager, a "norm-breaker," being seen as a social problem is transformed into individualized, unique autobiographies. The common experiences of "outsider" status have the potential to unite and educate these girls about political and economic realities of women and of single mothers. But the school curriculum individualizes those experiences thereby undercutting a potential power base for recognition and push for change.

This section has examined how student panels are condensed statements in a dialogue within school about good students and in a broader social dialogue about non-problematic young women. As in all rituals, these student panels can be assumed to have an impact on participants' meanings and understandings of themselves and their lives, especially since they are reinforced by other messages in schools and in society. The form of the panels is autobiographical. This form carries numerous conventions. It emphasizes the autonomous, rational, consistent individual, for it is a phallocentric genre. The form also carries a value of independence. This form dovetails nicely with the radical individualism taught in schools; the autobiographical structure of the panels contributes to the dialogue on successful students, in helping to create students who view themselves as unique, autonomous individuals whose success or failure rests solely in the hands of each person.

The autobiographical form and content together present stories which are virtually assured of being positively received by audiences, in that they participate in two dialogues, one about successful students and one about caring, devoted mothers. The stories of these transformations are powerful, culturally weighted with conceptions of the "good," the "just," and the "right."

## Implausible Endings: Collective Identity and Social Resources

Let us imagine a different ending to the film whose plot and theme introduced this analysis, *The Breakfast Club*. Rather than Allyson being transformed into a non-problematic, "good" girl, smilingly attired in white, let us try to imagine a story unfolding differently: Allyson's anger, her negative view of the corruption of adults and social institutions, strikes a deep chord in the four other students. The other girl, Claire, is strongly influenced. In the latter part of the film Claire is transformed more into Allyson's image: she dyes her hair black, switches to mostly black clothing, and begins to show an anti-conforming attitude. The three boys also participate in this change of perspective and the five begin to brainstorm about how they think they are being neglected in basic social and personal dimensions. After considerable time, the five organize to make demands of the school for special programs for students like themselves who have been neglected and abused by the system. They demand that the community agree to give them jobs with living wages when they complete school.

This is an "implausible ending" and would surely land on the cutting room floor of any major film company, for its implausibility would affect its box office success. Such an ending to a film like *The Breakfast Club* would be generally unpalatable to audiences raised on individualism, independence, and success stories built upon individual hard work and positive attitudes. People working together to claim identities based upon different norms and to demand social resources are likely to be seen as a threat, a problem unto itself, rather than a solution to the problem of antagonistic social cliques in high schools.

A school program that helped school-age mothers understand how they are discriminated against, illuminated the sexist and racist nature of society, and provided opportunities to develop a sense of unity and linked futures is an equally implausible story of school success. Such a school program might lead to young women cooperatively starting a child care center, which would alleviate their most pressing need if they are to have even a chance at post-secondary education. Collective action might take the form of applying pressure to expand child care at all levels, pressing for equal pay, and examining forms of discrimination against women of color. The common sense of expecting that all young women will think and act like middle class white girls is hard to dislodge and critique. It appears grounded in expectations of middle class women and mothers. A nuclear family norm is also tacitly in place. Unmarried women, especially those who are actively sexual, seem to deserve whatever they get. The norms for individual and school success appear grounded in traditional views of women's correct place in a nuclear family and middle class views of how striving leads to success. The Bright Prospects School program did nothing to examine the applicability of that norm to its students' lives.

A program which raised questions about women's place in society would also also likely end on the cutting room floor for its failure to conform to cultural myths and values related to individual struggles and success. These cultural myths and values strongly constrain the nature of programmatic aims of any school program, but especially school programs for at-risk students, those students so obviously needing some modified programs.

## Conclusion

This analysis has sought to make several points about the culture of schools and schooling for teenage mothers (or any "problematic" group of students). The cultural theme of transformations—transformations from a "wild," problematic status to a "good," successful, autonomous, independent, non-problematic status—is woven into schools and all other social organizations. The success stories which result from school policies and programs are shaped, in part, by this cultural theme. To put it differently, schools and school programs participate in the dialogue about success and are affected by the culturally valued, male-dominated, individually oriented characteristics of success. We can speculate that all schools will have to participate in this dialogue and respond to how they have produced successful students, argue against those criteria, or lose their own credibility.

In the case of teenage mothers, the characteristics of success seem like a suit of clothes made for someone else. That is, given what is known about the economic plights of single mothers, and of women of color, the training to be independent, autonomous, rational, and unique seems like a cruel joke. Given the economic situations of most single mothers, no amount of those characteristics will allow them a decent living wage. Good affordable child care remains unattainable and discrimination against women and, especially, against women of color usually results in lower salaries. In the face of institutionalized sexism and racism, independent attitudes may carry a woman nowhere beyond a high school diploma.

When the possibility of continued success in post-secondary schooling or work diminishes, single mothers must fall back on the other dialogue in which they have gained "success" and "acclaim": being a mother. The problems in the first dialogue may eventually spoil the success of the dutiful, devoted mother unless mothers are able to transform the privatized, domestic domain of good mothers and develop another dialogue, a mother-generated and mother-centered dialogue on mothering, which redefines the good mother in collective and socially situated ways (Martin, 1985).

For educators, this analysis points to the central problem of radical individualism in schooling. For any "problematic" group of students, the success stories based upon radical individualism may be just as unsatisfactory as failure and maintenance of an anti-school identity. If we are to have different success stories, which allow for the success of groups, not just isolated individuals, both the form and content of autobiographical "happy endings" must change. Possibilities for collective identity and success must exist. Then the rituals and myths of school will nurture a greater variety of success stories and a greater number of students.

## NOTES

[1] All proper nouns are pseudonyms.

[2] Cultural anthropologists have similarly documented the limited roles of women, e.g. Rosaldo and Lamphere, 1974.

[3] This conclusion rests upon feminist scholarship, like Chodorow's (1978), which argues that since women are primarily the child-rearers, the initial connection of male and female children with the mother is different. This object-relations theory focuses upon identity created in relation with parents. Since women do most child-rearing, girls grow up with a sense of self based upon continuing connectedness with the mother, since they are also female. Male children, according to Chodorow, must separate from the mother in order to become non-female, or male. Thus, Chodorow argues

that foundational male identity, at very early ages, is formed by separation, distinctiveness, and autonomy from the mother.

[4] Evidence for this statement was in a conversation with the vice-principal of Bright Prospects in which she said that when she first began working at the school she believed all the girls needed a course in assertiveness training. However, with time she came to believe that the school did not have the right to "introduce conflicting ideas" into the lives of students. I understand this change of view as evidence of the program's curricular thrust on a staff member. I hypothesize that students would be similarly influenced.

## REFERENCES

Arnot, M. and Weiner, G. (Eds.). (1987). *Gender the the Politics of Schooling*. London: Open University Press.

Bakhtin, M. M. (1981). *The Dialogic Imagination* (C. Emerson and M. Holquist, Trans.). Austin: University of Texas Press.

Bellah, R., Madsen, R., Sullivan, W., Swidler, A., and Tipton, S. (1985). *Habits of the Heart*. Berkeley, CA: University of California Press.

Bernstein, B. (1975). *Class, Codes, and Control*, Volume 3. London: Routledge and Kegan Paul.

Chodorow, N. (1978). *The Reproduction of Mothering: Psychoanalysis and the Sociology of Gender*. Berkeley, CA: University of California Press.

Collins, P.H. (1989). A Comparison of Two Works on Black Family Life. *Signs, 14* (4), 875-884.

Foucault, M. (1977). *Discipline and Punish: The Birth of the Prison* (A. Sheridan, Trans.). New York: Random House.

Foucault, M. (1978). *The History of Sexuality, Volume I* (R. Hurley, Trans.). New York: Random House.

Gee, J.P. (1985). The Narrativization of Experience in the Oral Style. *Journal of Education, 167* (1), 9-35.

Geertz, C. (1973). *The Interpretation of Culture*. New York: Basic Books.

Gordon, L. (1974). *Woman's Body, Woman's Right*. Harmondsworth: Penguin Books.

Gordon, L. (1988). *Heroes of Their Own Lives*. New York: Viking Penguin.

Gusfield, J.R. (1986). *Symbolic Crusade*. Urbana, IL: University of Illinois Press.

Guttmacher Institute. (1981). *Teenage Pregnancy*. New York: Alan Guttmacher Institute.

Henriques, J., Hollway, W., Urwin, C., Venn, C., & Walkerdine, V. (1984). *Changing the Subject*. London: Methuen.

Howe, F. (1984). *Myths of Coeducation*. Bloomington, IN: Indiana University Press.

Kirp, D. (1989). Education: The Movie. *Mother Jones* (January).

Lesko, N. (1988). *Symbolizing Society*. London: Falmer Press.

Lesko, N. (in press). Curriculum Differentiation as Social Redemption. In R. Page and L. Valli (Eds.), *Curriculum Differentiation*. Albany, NY: State University of New York Press.

Levi-Strauss, C. (1963). *Structural Anthropology*. New York: Basic Books.

McLaren, P. (1986). *Schooling As a Ritual Performance*. London: Routledge and Kegan Paul.

Martin, J.R. (1985). *Reclaiming a Conversation*. New Haven: Yale University Press.

Miller, N.K. (1981). Emphasis Added: Plots and Plausibilities in Women's Fiction. *PMLA, 96* (1), 36-48.

Rains, P.M. (1971). *Becoming an Unwed Mother*. Chicago: Aldine.

Rich, A. (1979). *On Lies, Secrets, and Silence*. New York: Norton.

Roman, L., Christian-Smith, L., and Ellsworth, E. (1988). *Becoming Feminine*. London: Falmer Press.

Rosaldo, M.Z., and Lamphere, L. (Eds.). (1974). *Woman, Culture, and Society*. Stanford, CA: Stanford University Press.

Russo, M. (1986). Female Grotesques: Carnival and Theory. In T. deLauretis (Ed.), *Feminist Studies, Critical Studies*. Bloomington, IN: Indiana University Press.

Sidel, R. (1986). *Women and Children Last*. New York: Viking.

Smith, S. (1987). *A Poetics of Women's Autobiography: Marginality and the Fictions of Self-Representation*. Bloomington, IN: Indiana University Press.

Turner, V. (1969). *The Ritual Process*. Ithaca, NY: Cornell University Press.

*Time* Magazine. (1985). Children Having Children.

Varenne, H. (1977). *Americans Together*. New York: Teachers College Press.

Walkerdine, V. (1985). On the Regulation of Speaking and Silence. In C. Steedman, C. Urwin, and V. Walkerdine (Eds.), *Language, Gender, and Childhood*. London: Routledge and Kegan Paul.

Walkerdine, V. (1988). *The Mastery of Reason*. London: Routledge and Kegan Paul.

Weedon, C. (1987). *Feminist Practice and Poststructuralist Theory*. London: Basil Blackwell.

Wehlage, G., Rutter, R., Smith, G., Lesko, N., and Fernandez, R. (1989). *Reducing the Risk: Schools as Communities of Support*. London: Falmer Press.

Wexler, P. (1982). Structure, Text, and Subject: A Critical Sociology of School Knowledge. In M. Apple (Ed.), *Cultural and Economic Reproduction in Education*. London: Routledge and Kegan Paul.

Whitson, J.A. (1988). The Politics of "Non-Political" Curriculum: Heteroglossia and the Discourse of "Choice" and "Effectiveness." In W.F. Pinar (Ed.), *Contemporary Curriculum Discourses*. Scottsdale: Gorsuch Scarisbrick.

Zinn, M.B. (1989). Family, Race, and Poverty in the Eighties. *Signs, 14* (4), 856-874.

# Chapter 5
# Black Visibility in a Multi-Ethnic High School

*by James Stanlaw and Alan Peshkin,*
*University of Illinois, Urbana-Champagne*

The linguist George Lakoff and the philosopher Mark Johnson have argued that metaphors are not only instrumental in our everyday lives, they also structure our thinking in various direct and subtle ways.[1] Regardless of whether or not Lakoff and Johnson have overstated their case, the metaphor of "invisibility" characterizes the status of blacks in America. Though early black writers used the term[2], it was Ralph Ellison's novel *Invisible Man* that brought the notion of black invisibility into the popular parlance:

> I am an invisible man....I am invisible, understand, simply because people refuse to see me. Like the bodiless heads you see sometimes in circus sideshows, it is as though I have been surrounded by mirrors of hard distorting glass. When they approach me they see only my surroundings, themselves, or figments of their imagination—indeed everything and anything except me.[3]

What we choose not to see, we need not deal with: if blacks are invisible, we can ignore their plight. Black anthropologist John L. Gwaltney alludes to this on a broader scale when he speaks of how "Euro-American culture, for a plethora of conscious and unconscious considerations, has often chosen to deny the very existence" of black culture, black heritage, and black genius. It has been argued[5] that much of the unrest in the 1960s was an attempt by blacks to force whites not just to acknowledge social injustice, but to recognize their existence as legitimate and sentient beings.

Among educators, Rist has used the term invisibility, though in somewhat different fashion. He describes how a well-intended white school administration in Portland, Oregon, tried to achieve integration through racial assimilation. Ironically, by ignoring black cultural differences and personal individuality—by taking a "colorblind" approach to integration—the administration only perpetuated an insidious kind of invisibility:

> Day after day...Black students came off the bus to a setting where the goal was to render them invisible. And the more invisible they became, the greater the satisfaction of the school personnel that the integration program was succeeding![6]

Other images of invisibility have been used elsewhere in the literature to describe, for example, the problem of black families in America,[7] the plight of the elderly in a Jewish retirement home,[8] and the psychology of the pariah caste in Japan.[9] Rarely found, however, are instances of a favorable, visible minority or ethnic presence. In our study of Riverview High, a multiethnic integrated high school in northern California, we found not merely nonblack acceptance and tolerance of blacks, but a true black visible presence, as well.

At Riverview, integration has occurred without the assimilating invisibility (as Rist describes) that so often happens when different ethnic and racial groups are thrust into a mainstreaming school. In fact, we will argue that blacks are more than a visible presence at Riverview High School; they are a group to emulate. Concerning music, fashion, communicative style, and the general persona students carry, blacks seem to be the pacesetters. In what follows, we will describe this particular positive black visibility, how and where it occurs, and the different ways it is manifested. Though the "whys" of Riverview's black visibility—the causes of their unusual social presence—can not be definitively established, we will explore several possibilities. Since any of the reasons for black visibility are necessarily connected to the particular place of Riverview, we will begin by describing the town and the high school, their history and interrelationships, after first briefly describing the composition of the study.

# THE STUDY

This ongoing research is the fourth in a series of investigations of American communities and their high schools.[10] Riverview was chosen because of its size and ethnic mix. Specifically, the research hopes to answer questions about how a school with a diverse ethnic composition operates, e.g., How and why do students get along? Is ethnic identity an issue in deciding what to teach? How do teachers respond when they face a class of Asians, blacks, and Hispanics?

## The Unity of the High School and the Town

Riverview is an ethnically diverse working class town surrounded by predominantly White upper class communities and takes pride in, and identifies with, its high school. Approximately twenty percent of the faculty and staff were graduates of Riverview High. In sports, where intercommunity jealousies and hatreds can be symbolically battled out, the Riverview residents support their team with an enthusiasm and loyalty granted only to the most blessed major professional franchises. It seems that the high school, the town, and the team are all great unifying symbols: whatever differences individuals might have among themselves, be they personal or racial, are set aside when confronted by outside challenges.

## Black Visibility and Invisibility

As mentioned, the image of "Black invisibility" is common in the literature. However, to hold fast to this notion without qualification is somewhat simpleminded. Any black man would probably feel quite visible walking down the streets of Beverly Hills, as indeed he would be. It is likely that he would be noticed by the neighbors, stared at by children, followed by the police. Sometimes there are positive aspects to being invisible or not being out of the ordinary. If you are black and you have no special "place" in your town, you can operate normally and unself-consciously with no feelings of pressure. It is not a simple matter, then, to look only at visibility or invisibility; we must also look at their positive and negative consequences as well. As a heuristic device, the following schematic might be used:

|  | Negative | Positive |
|---|---|---|
| Invisibility |  |  |
| Visibility |  |  |

We have already mentioned the common theme invisibility as described by Rist, Ellison, and others. We will now look at its antithesis—positive visibility—which we claim is a predominant theme of Riverview High School.

## The Positive Visibility of Blacks

Blacks are outstanding at Riverview High, both literally and figuratively. They wear their FILA shirts, caps, and sweats.[11] They play basketball at lunch on four outdoor courts, and rap with friends in class. Black students exude confidence, class, and style. If any one group sets the styles for others to follow, it is the blacks. Among Riverview black teenagers, there are few invisible young men and women.

A rough indication of just how visible blacks are on the Riverview campus can be seen from our interview data. As Table 6 shows, blacks probably comprise about 25 to 30 percent of the student body. Among those questioned about what the percentage of black students at Riverview might be, no student ever underestimated the number of blacks: many even claimed the school was at least half black, with whites and other ethnic groups being noticeable fractions, but nonetheless definitely a numerical minority. Black students, too, gave similar answers, inflating the black population (though none ever guessed that the school was half black or more). When questioned in both the formal and informal interviews as to who generally set the pace on campus, students answered—if at all—that it was "the blacks."

Black visibility was not just a matter of blacks being the most outlandish or conspicuous in appearance; several other groups contended for these honors. Among these groups were mods, punks, or new wavers (who dressed, to varying degrees, in black or loud, antique, used clothing, with teased, dyed hair, and heavy make-up), thrashers (hardcore skateboarders, oblivious to pain or the idea that clothes need not necessarily have holes), or *cholos* (an Hispanic subgroup whose males are especially known for driving "low-rider" cars with modified suspensions).

Particular areas where blacks are especially visible include:

*MUSIC.* If Black culture truly dominates any one aspect of life at Riverview High School it is in musical taste. Top 40[12] black artists, like Whitney Houston or Lionel Richie, of course are popular. Also popular, however, are particularly black music idioms such as rap, beat, and soul. Such artists as Dougie Fresh or Run-DMC, who are usually not heard on top 40 radio and are not too popular in the surrounding areas, have a great following among both black and non-black Riverview students. Primarily black-influenced music is played at school dances, assemblies, and other school functions. All the school dances we attended were hosted by a black DJ,[13] playing mostly black-style music.

*FASHION.* There are perhaps a dozen or more labelled and readily identifiable groups of students at Riverview. These include "jocks" and "cheerleaders," "preps," "nerds," "brains," as well as largely ethnically based groups such as Hispanic *cholos*, Filipino "hoodies," or white "stoners." Though each particular group at Riverview has its own special clothing, the influence of blacks on the general fashion scene is substantial. Stirrup pants, mega shirts, FILA sweatshirts, and painter's caps were all popularized by black students; black students also promote the general acceptance of exercise wear as everyday apparel.

*SLANG EXPRESSIONS.* Sociolinguists have long recognized the major influences of the black spoken vernacular on white speech; some scholars even claim that upwards of eighty to ninety percent of the common idiomatic expressions in white speech have black origins.[14] Also, the emphasis on stylistics and performatives in the black speech community has been well documented.[15] Riverview substantiates these findings, and, if anything, extends them. Many white students use particular black vocabulary items such as "blood" (a black man, but generalized by white males to refer to any other male), "touch your toes" (a metaphor for sexual intercourse), "freak" (fuck), or "fly-girl" (a girl of questionable morals). Many of the grammatical rules of the black-English vernacular (as described by Labov) were incorporated into the speech pattern of non-black students. For example, the first day of school in a general freshman English class we heard a white teenage male say to his half-Hispanic/half-white friend "Dang, blood, what was you doin'? You be trippin' with her?" Depending on the intonation, in more typical white slang this might be rendered as "Hey, man, what was going on? Were you two really hanging out?"

*COMMUNICATIVE STYLE.* Kochman has shown that white and black speakers differ not just in dialect (the formal code) but also in the way their dialects are used (the communicative style). For example, Kochman claims that in a classroom setting, whites debate an issue as impersonally as possible, stressing objective ideas detached from whoever expressed them. Black students, however, engage in more personal arguments. They consider "debate to be as much a contest between individuals as a test of opposing ideas. Because it is a contest, winning the contest requires that one outperform one's opponents: outthink, outtalk, and outstyle them."[16] The latter form of argumentation was certainly most pervasive at Riverview.

The attitude of Riverview students, then, towards the black dialect and black rhetorical style is not just one of tolerance (i.e., "non-rejection") but one of acceptance and prominence. Non-black students do not criticize blacks for speaking "black," nor are blacks assertive about their right to talk black. White parents sometimes complain that "black talk comes home," but the students give it the label of normality and place the burden of understanding on mom and dad.

*STANCE: BEING COOL.* Associated with the above discussion on communicative style is the idea of "being cool." An attempt at a definition will not even be made, but as everyone knows, being cool is not a way of life for teenagers, it is life. Whether deserved or not, black students, especially males, exude the social confidence, the savvy, and the street-corner poise needed to be appropriately cool. Admittedly, this is one of the more subjective evaluations we made, but it is hard not to notice the distinctly black swagger in a Filipino or white boy's walk.

*LEADERSHIP AND ACTIVITIES.* Because of the effort of a number of key individuals, blacks were among the outstanding leaders at Riverview High School in the 1985-1986 academic year. Blacks had more than ample representation on the cheerleading squads, student council, and yearbook staff. The Black Student Union had about fifty members and took an active part in most school functions. One black student leader also read the daily announcements over the intercom in the mornings. Riverview's earlier yearbooks indicate that blacks have been a dynamic and felt presence for at least the past decade and a half.

*HOMECOMING KING AND QUEEN.* Two popular blacks students were elected homecoming king and queen at Riverview during our 1985-1986 fieldstay, no small achievement given that non-blacks predominate. No teacher or student indicated that it might be unusual to have both these positions filled by blacks, and when it happened it was thought to be a rather ordinary and natural occurrence, unworthy of comment. The significance of this event is further highlighted when we remember that a homecoming king or queen is not necessarily a school's best scholar, most talented athlete, or most active leader; these are positions of *pride.* Students select those whom they want to be a symbol of their class and their school.

*SPORTS.* Considering the interest in sports and the size of the populations, it is not surprising that Riverview High School blacks are well represented on all JV and varsity athletic teams (save the new soccer and tennis organizations).[17] The first-string varsity football team was more than half black, and the varsity basketball team had only one white member. The men's and women's track teams were predominantly black and fielded several champion black runners.

Though blacks were not the majority of the cheerleading squads, they were well represented. More important than that, however, was the fact that black dance styles, and sometimes even cheers in Swahili, were used and readily accepted by both fans and cheerleaders. As one black teacher commented in class after a big victory, "Our ladies know how to GET DOWN!"[18]

BLACKS AS A SYMBOL OF RIVERVIEW HIGH SCHOOL. There has been a fifty-year rivalry between Riverview and its immediate neighbor Jericho. Though Jericho shares a common history, similar economic backgrounds and family ties with Riverview, it does not have a significant black population. This difference makes the animosity between the towns passionate, perhaps irreconcilable.

Each fall this friction is symbolically vented in the annual Big-Little Football game ("little" in that it is not necessary for the conference championship, but "big" in that it is just as important). This event attracts thousands of spectators, and requires the presence of the police departments from both towns. Tempers are hot, not just among the students but among the parents as well. Old newspapers and alumni are full of accounts of past fights, vandalism, and vendettas.

The 1985 game was enacted with all the usual competitive festivities, but one incident stands out which is germane to the argument here. Midway through the third quarter some Jericho fans held up a banner making derogatory remarks about the Riverview team. It included a black football player riding in a Cadillac convertible holding a watermelon. In response, some white and Filipino Riverview residents walked up and down the sidelines with a sign depicting the black epithet "Yo' Momma!" (with the back saying, "And yo Daddy, too!").[19]

Outsiders view Riverview as little more than a crime-ridden black ghetto. Insiders view it as something different, of course, but they also know about the images folks "over the hill" have of them. The response (whether by white or black) to the discrimination and denigration afforded to all people from Riverview is a kind of "black pride." This underdog role often takes the form of coming on rough, macho, or "bad ass."[20]

## Favorable Black Invisibility

It would be wrong to assume that blacks are always outstanding, are always a visible presence, at Riverview. This overstates the case; furthermore, such a situation could never occur in a town that is truly integrated. At Riverview High, black students are usually thought of simply as "persons," as opposed to "black persons." The high school no longer teaches any black history or black culture courses; for the new special accelerated college-prep EXCEL program, race is particularly specified not to be a factor in the selection of candidates. Students told us that the fights which occur at school are due to personal disagreements rather than to racial differences. The fact that a white student would even think of starting a fight with a black student without being thought a racist clearly testifies to how far integration has come at

Riverview.

These attitudes, of course, are not simply confined to the school. One black teacher told us how strange it felt when he first came to Riverview. In contrast with his native Texas, blacks in Riverview had no special "place" in the community. A white woman could even talk to him on the street without fear of chastisement. Older white residents sometimes speak of the blacks they grew up with as being just "dark-skinned Italians": "Lamar Robinson didn't know he was black until he was ten years old, and then we had to tell him." Of course, whether these blacks felt the same way is not always clear; Lamar Robinson, however, is the current mayor of Riverview.

## Why Riverview?

The social situation just described may not be unique, but it certainly is far from typical in American schools, where physical integration is underway but true equality for blacks and other minorities remains to be achieved. In fact, some observers[21] fear that with rising minority populations, declining economic opportunities, and a new influx of immigrants, trouble-free integration may be even more ephemeral in the 1980s and 1990s than in the 1970s. The questions are, then, what happened in Riverview? What did Riverview do, if anything, that was right? Are there lessons to learn from Riverview and its high school? We propose three general explanations: (1) a "magic" population ratio, (2) the particular history and development of Riverview, and (3) similarities in communicative styles of the black and non-black communities.

## A "Magic" Population Ratio

This hypothesis argues that there are optimal numbers of a minority population in a town or school which maximize the possibilities for cooperation, friendship, and mutual trust and respect. If the minority is too few in number, they cannot help but feel threatened and alone. A fortress mentality of "them" vs. "us" sets in, and it is hard for the minority to feel comfortable interacting with the majority. Much time is spent "circling the wagons" and little, if any, real communication takes place. However, if the minority is too present, it is the ever-decreasing majority that feels threatened, often responding aggressively, harshly, and without thinking. What exactly this magic number might be is very difficult to guess, but St. John[22] suggests that between 15 and 40 percent minority enrollment is optimal in a school.

While this explanation has some merit, it certainly fails even to begin to depict the situation found at Riverview. First, there are other schools in America with similar demographics, but (at least as reported in the literature) their racial/social integration is not like that found at Riverview. Second, as described before, there are a variety of different ethnic groups in Riverview, all within the optimal "magic" range, but why is it that it is the blacks who have become the style-setters, the group to emulate, the notably *visible* people?

## The Particular Historical Development of the Riverview Community

The inadequacies of the first hypothesis suggest the second: there must be something unique in the Riverview experience that has created this distinctive social matrix. Once again, however, it is difficult to specify what this might be. Historical explanations for the contemporary black visibility are certainly possible. However, the real increase in the black populations, and, thus, the present of blacks as a potential influence, did not occur until after World War II. Also, in the late 1960s Riverview suffered from racial unrest, as did many towns and cities in America at that time. The phenomenon of black visibility, then, seems to be something that has happened in the past ten or fifteen years. But what has happened in these fifteen years?

*NON-FORCED INTEGRATION, AND A GENERATION OF PEACE.* The students we saw at this year's high school graduation ceremony are the first to have thirteen years of relatively trouble-free education. In the sixties and seventies Riverview experienced some unpopular attempts at busing, but this never profoundly affected things at the school or in the town. The natural plurality of the community has kept Riverview High from being a "rich school," a "black school," or any special kind of school at all. Accordingly, children have attended school for thirteen years with everyone in town. This is an ordinary, everyday event.

Thus, either through intent or accident, integration was never something that "occurred" at Riverview High. How the racial interactions that developed in this kind of setting differ from those which develop when integration is forced or artificial can only be guessed at. However, the literature strongly suggests that in most cases of forced integration, the resulting interracial social relationships are strained, cautious, or even hostile.[23] In Riverview, integration is a natural and stable fact of life. It occurs without substantial busing, magnet schools, or any of the other devices communities use to desegregate their school districts. Thirteen years of this kind of interaction culminates in a homecoming ceremony where the crowning of a black king or queen is a mundane, almost unnoticed, event.

*BLACK LEADERSHIP.* Riverview has been fortunate in having politically astute black leaders who possess the proper qualities to facilitate compromise and cooperation. For example, Lamar Robinson, the current mayor, is a black man trusted by both the black and white communities. Having been born and raised in the old Italian section of town, he has the virtue of being looked upon as a neighbor by whites. Though a peacemaker, blacks know Robinson has never bought the status quo: they expect him to earnestly represent and fight for black interests. It is hard to estimate the effect of such an individual on race relations in town. Certainly, the presence of men like Robinson can only be a beneficial influence, both in times of trouble and calm.

*MINORITY REPRESENTATION.* While the country was suffering from racial unrest in the late 1960s, Riverview blacks and others formed effective political organizations which successfully challenged the old guard and its nepotism. Thus, while no minority feels totally comfortable with the way things are, most believe that the local political structure offers a viable forum for their grievances.

*THE SCHOOL BOARD.* It is commonly assumed in Riverview that there is a certain kind of rationality and common sense on the school board; its members are thought to be well-intended and sensitive to the needs of the total community. Though not revolutionary, they are perceived as being sufficiently responsive to minority requirements. Again, the presence of certain key individuals may be significant. Oswald Davis, an articulate and educated black man, has been on the board since the troubled times in the early seventies; Tony Messina, the son of one of the older influential Italian families, has been on the board almost since his high school graduation fifteen years ago. Both men are accepted and trusted by the black and white communities, and can act as bridges when divisive issues arise.

*THE SCHOOL ADMINISTRATION.* The Riverview community seems to have similar kinds of feelings about the school administration as it does about its school board. Both the district superintendent and the high school principal are locals, products of the Riverview school system. They are generally thought to be available, responsive, and sympathetic to minority needs. Their own statements reflect this concern. Both have said that they invariably assess the effect of their decisions on minority students, and they consider how the minority community might interpret their actions.

*HOUSING.* It is well known that one of the biggest obstacles to school desegregation is residence patterns. Thus, if a district boundary does not contain sufficient numbers of a certain kind of people, artificial steps must be taken to alter the ethnic or racial mix. In the 1960s, Riverview was no better (though probably no worse) than any other town in America as having segregated housing. Urban renewal, with all its implications, was a fact of life in Riverview, too. Most important, however, Riverview had several ambitious developers who built more houses than there were white people available to buy them. This meant that if blacks had the financial means, they could disperse rather readily throughout the town, thereby moderating the ghetto effect often associated with black neighborhoods.

*COMMUNICATIVE STYLE.* Another possible explanation concerning black visibility in the Riverview community is communicative style. Kochman[24] claims that, generally, black rhetorical devices are diametrically opposed to white methods of communication. Thus, in many places, when blacks and whites interact frustration or intransigence occurs. For instance, one of Gwaltney's informants mentions that

> There are probably many white people who are as honest as we [blacks] are. Well, there certainly are some. I guess there can't be many or the

country would not be as rotten as it is. *Anyway, since I can't tell the good ones from the rest, I have as little to do with any of them as I can.*[25] [emphasis added]

It was argued previously that most students in Riverview High share a common mode of argument, one that is similar to the rhetorical devices found in black speech. If all students indeed share a common style of communication, it is possible, and even likely, that such conflicts and attitudes can be avoided.

## Black Visibility Outside of School

Before the war, some Italian families would not let their daughters talk to a black boy on the street, even though these people might have sat next to each other every day in high school, or danced at the homecoming ball. An analogous situation occurs today upon graduation. What happens, say, to the highly visible black football star after graduation when he goes to work in town? Does black high school visibility become real-world invisibility?

In political and social terms, the answer is no, though blacks and non-blacks clearly mix less, and blacks enjoy less prominence. In economic terms, the answer is yes, both inside and outside of Riverview. When jobs and economics become the issue, whites have the advantage. Black unemployment is double that of white unemployment in town, even though federal and state monies have been granted to provide temporary and permanent jobs for minorities. As one white teacher said about several of his black students who were tossing paper on the floor, "I tell them, I don't care if you throw that shit on the floor now, because you're just going to be coming back here a couple years from now and picking it up every day."

In light of these facts, we asked teachers and townspeople if they felt that Riverview gave black students a false sense of security. In other words, did they think that blacks got the wrong impression of the rest of the world? Did they generalize from how their life was in Riverview High School? Many thought this not to be the case. They said that blacks realized Riverview was different and would expect more indifference, prejudice, or discrimination elsewhere.

In spite of this, however, Riverview High presents a number of dilemmas for both white and black students. There is a certain "party line," an unwritten code of conduct, among students: "Don't trip off people's color." It is un-cool to be prejudiced, and it is discouraged in all kinds of subtle and obvious ways. Perhaps in a place as ethnically diverse as Riverside this is not only a sensible way to behave, it is necessary. But to say that it is un-cool to be prejudiced is not to say that it is cool to be ethnic, that it is cool to be black. In one sense, blacks need to be somewhat bicultural in order to leave the Riverview environment: "I know I got to behave different when I go to Jericho or over the hill," says one black football player. "I got to be a little less, you know, intense." But how can he learn what being "less intense" is if he attends a school where his intensity is encouraged, if not emulated, by those around him?

The problem, then, is this: Riverview High School students have created a world relatively free of overt prejudice, a world full of ethnic pride that celebrates ethnic diversity. But the cause that they celebrate is, in real-world terms, lost. Once outside of school, other norms apply for both black and white students. It is not clear how, or if ever, these contradictions can be reconciled.[26]

# NOTES

[1] George Lakoff and Mark Johnson, *Metaphors We Live By* (Chicago: University of Chicago Press, 1976).

[2] Frederick Douglass, *Autobiography of Frederick Douglass* (New York: Fawcett, 1845 [1963]). W.E.B. DuBois, *The Souls of Black Folk* (New York: Fawcett, 1962), pp. 343-345.

[3] Ralph Ellison, *Invisible Man* (New York: Vintage, 1947), p. 3.

[4] John Gwaltney, "Common Sense and Science: Urban Core Black Observations," in D. Messerschmidt, ed., *Anthropologists at Home in North America* (Cambridge: Cambridge University Press, 1981), pp. 46-61.

[5] H. Rap Brown, *Die Nigger Die* (New York: Dial, 1969). Richard Gregg et al., "The Rhetoric of Black Power," in A. Smith, ed., *Language, Communication and Rhetoric in Black America* (New York: Harper & Row, 1972).

[6] Ray Rist, *The Invisible Children: School Integration in American Society* (Cambridge: Harvard University Press, 1978), p. 244.

[7] Herbert Guttman, *The Invisible Fact: Afro-Americans and Their Families* (New York: Pantheon,1976).

[8] Barbara Myerhoff, *Number Our Days* (New York: Harper and Row, 1979).

[9] George DeVos and Hiroshi Wagatsuma, *Japan's Invisible Race: Caste in Culture and Personality* (Berkeley: University of California Press, 1966).

[10] Alan Peshkin, *Growing Up American* (Chicago: University of Chicago Press, 1978); *The Imperfect Union* (Chicago: University of Chicago Press, 1982); *God's Choice: The Total World of a Christian Fundamentalist School* (Chicago: University of Chicago Press, 1986).

[11] FILA is a popular brand of sports clothes.

[12] "Top 40 Radio" refers to the current forty most popular records that are being listened to at any given time.

[13] "DJ" refers to "disk jockey," or someone who plays records on the radio or for a live audience.

[14] William Labov, *Language in the Inner City* (Philadelphia: University of Pennsylvania Press, 1972); Thomas Kochman, ed., *Rappin' and Styling Out: Communication in Urban Black America* (Urbana: University of Illinois Press, 1972); J. Dillard, Black English (New York: Vintage, 1972).

[15] Roger Abrams, *Talking Black* (Rowley, Mass.: Newbury House, 1976); Kochman, ed. *Rappin' and Styling Out;* Claudia Mitchell-Kernan, "Signifying and Marking: Two Afro-American Speech Acts," in J Gumperz and D. Hymes, eds., *Directions in Sociolinguistics* (New York: Holt, Rinehart and Winston, 1972),p. 24.

[16] Thomas Kochman, *Black and White Styles in Conflict* (Chicago: University of Chicago Press, 1981),p.24.

[17] "JV" means "junior varsity," or the junior-level sports team. There seems to be some association between certain sports and ethnic groups: Hispanics and Asians with soccer, Filipinos with tennis, and blacks with basketball and football. However, these are not strict pairings, and all ethnic groups can play in any sport they desire.

[18] "Get down" is slang for dancing well, with much enthusiasm.

[19] "Yo' momma" is a slang expression which translates as "[Fuck] your mother" or "motherfucker."

[20] It might be argued that the reasons for the particular social configurations found in Riverview are due to whites, rather than blacks, being a minority. Other minority groups may join with blacks in a solid front against the mainstream "majority" (i.e. white) culture, which happens at this time to not be in a position of strength. We found little evidence to support this view. If anything, there may be more rivalry between the minorities (e.g., blacks vs. Hispanics, Filipinos vs. Hispanics, all vs. Southeast Asians) over school resources, social prestige, and so on.

[21] Marvin Harris, *American Now* (New York: Torchstone, 1981).

[22] N. H. St. John, *School Desegregation: Outcomes for Children* (New York: Wiley, 1975).

[23] Raymond Mack, ed., *Our Children's Burden: Studies of Desegregation in Nine American Communities* (Chicago: University of Chicago Press, 1968); John Egerton, *Education and Desegregation in Eight Schools* (Evanston: Center for Equal Education, 1977); Rist, *The Invisible Children.*

[24] Kochman, *Black and White Styles of Communication.*

[25] Gwaltney, "Common Sense and Science," p. 53.

[26] In a similar vein, Lois Weis (personal communication) asks, What is the role of the high school in such a situation? Is the school being racist if it insists on conformity to mainstream culture? Or is the school being negligent if it succumbs to the easy (though ultimately detrimental) temptation to indulge minority non-mainstream behavior? These questions, obviously, are no less difficult to answer than those posed in the text.

# Cultures of
# Teaching in a Time
# of Change

# Chapter 6
# The Culture of Teaching: Stability and Change

*by David H. Ost, California State University*

> Muhammadans are Muhammadans because they are born and reared among that sect, not because they have thought it out and can furnish sound reasons for being Muhammadans; we know why Catholics are Catholics; why Presbyterians are Presbyterians; why Baptists are Baptists; why Mormons are Mormons; why thieves are thieves; why monarchists are monarchists; why Republicans are Republicans and Democrats, Democrats. We know that it is a matter of association and sympathy, not reasoning and examination; that hardly a man in the world has an opinion on morals, politics, or religion that he got otherwise than through his associations and sympathies.[1]

Twain thus eloquently illustrates the intuitively obvious—people do not objectively choose their positions on religion, politics, education, and morals. The label of Baptist, Monarchist, or Democrat not only describes how a person behaves but also carries a connotation of what the person believes—in short, the culture (or subculture) to which the individual belongs. To understand why Republicans are Republicans or why teachers are teachers, we must develop an understanding of how they came to be a part of that specific group, as well as how and from whom they acquired the beliefs that characterize the group's culture.

Culture, an ongoing focus of study in anthropology, is generally described in terms of observable, socially transmitted *patterns of behavior*. In this sense, culture can be characterized as, "Patterns of behavior, thought and feeling which are acquired or influenced through learning and that are characteristic of groups of people rather than of individuals."[2] It is recognized that behavioral patterns are manifestations of basic elements responsible for culture (beliefs, values, expectations, etc.). In this sense culture must be thought of as ideas or rules that direct the behavior of its members. To put it another way, culture is, "Whatever it is one has to know or believe in order to operate in a manner acceptable to its members.... It is the form of things that people have in their mind, their models for perceiving, relating and otherwise interpreting them."[3]

It is difficult to believe that the large sophisticated teaching repertoire and expected behaviors included in the teaching culture are acquired only through especially designed conditioning processes collectively known as "teacher education." In fact, some recent studies have shown that what makes good teachers is not their knowledge about teaching, but the beliefs they hold about themselves, their goals and purposes, and about students.[4] To understand the transmission and evolution of teacher culture, it is useful to review the mechanisms and processes of cultural evolution as understood by anthropologists and sociobiologists. This article is intended to establish an operational concept of the culture of teaching. The argument will be made that research in education overrates the importance of specific behaviors by ignoring the patterns and origins of the rules that govern the culture. A model will be presented to account in part for the evolution of the teaching culture. Expanding this conceptual approach provides a perspective for understanding: the mechanisms that stabilize the teaching profession, the need for changes in teacher education, and the kinds of strategies required for lasting school reform.

## Culture and Social Learning

The argument in support of the fact that culture is a semiautonomous, self-replicating entity that changes in response to natural selection is well documented in the literature.[5] The concept of culture in studying change in educational settings has been used by, among others, Sarason[6] and Goodlad.[7] The notion of culture implies a sense of identity with purpose. Purpose is tied to the notion that there are goals and objectives that are shared within the organization supported by the community. To this end, teachers and other members of the school community must believe themselves contributing and participating members of the culture.

A good example of "identity with purpose" is frequently associated with Magnet Schools. Magnet school teachers tend to have a clearly defined subculture characterized by a sense of cohesiveness, professionalism, and personal identity.[8] The clearly defined purpose of the magnet program results in the recruitment of teachers with specific kinds of personal commitment and motivation. These characteristics serve as a common denominator around which culture can form within the school and the constituency it serves. Of course, the power of the magnet school is that its unique culture is subsequently transmitted to the students. The major value of these schools lies in their ability to enculturate as well as educate.

Social learning experiments show that people learn by observation even where they cannot perform the expected behavior. The observer is able to collect and organize information as well as learn behaviors in the absence of immediate reinforcement. Bandura, for instance, summarizes the effect: "After the capacity for observational learning has fully developed, one cannot keep people from learning what they have seen."[9] Observational learning is a highly effective means of teaching behaviors and transmitting culture. Social learning research has also shown that individuals abstract rules from modeled behaviors. Children, as well as prospective teachers, are systematically exposed to social conditioning, as they seldom escape being rewarded or punished. Thus, an individual's learning from modeled behavior, by parents, friends, or teachers, results in a set of undefined abstract rules that govern action. These experiences are not lost to the members of the group.

Seventeen or more years of social conditioning establishes many of the behaviors of individuals who will become teachers. In this sense, social learning is a form of classical conditioning. Behaviors designed to be incorporated into the cultural repertoire of the prospective teacher (e.g., as provided through teacher education programs) must fit the rules the individual has previously synthesized through years of observational learning in classrooms. This is emphasized in a recent review of the literature on teacher education.

> Prospective teachers' expectations are acquired indirectly from early encounters with their own elementary and secondary teachers, social norms communicated by the general public, and the existing ethos on the higher education campus. The expectations formed from these sources typically carry a negative valence and reflect an awareness that teacher education is easy to enter, intellectually weak, and possibly unnecessary.[10]

Thus, potential teachers enter the teaching profession with well-developed sets of rules that will govern their teaching behaviors. According to Rosenthal and Zimmerman, "these cognitions in turn guide the observer...."[11] If the new teaching behaviors are to be carefully attended to in teacher education programs and retained, the behaviors must be congruent with the individual's set of rules.

There is considerable evidence that rules, not behaviors, are what are generalized to new situations. Markus believes that the individual builds on past experience and self-knowledge to extrapolate future behavior and goals.[12] Circumstances activate certain subsets or combinations of rules that direct behavior. A given cultural rule may lead to unexpected (teaching) behaviors in different environments (rural versus urban, large versus small systems, etc.). Localized variations may not be long-lasting changes in ideas but only modified expression of the rules through short-lived behavior.

## Change and Stability in the Teaching Culture

The elements of culture are in large part subliminal, rarely articulated and too self-evident to be the focus of study.[13] It is the quiet nature of culture that gives it much of its power; the competition among internal cultural elements occurs without recognition by its membership.[14] It is only when behaviors are identified as significantly different from a past norm that change in the culture is apparent.

Changes in teacher behavior do not necessarily mean that the culture of teaching has changed. For example, intense teacher in-service training may bring about changes in teacher behavior for a period of time, but reversion to the traditional culture can be expected. Similarly, when a strong school administrator establishes and enforces regulations which require changes in teaching, teachers will behave accordingly, but their action does not imply that they have changed their ideas, values, or beliefs. Although a change in the culture will generally result in changes of behavior, one must be wary of concluding that changes of behaviors are evidence of cultural change. That is to say, an individual can and will modify his or her behavior in response to stress conditions. This survival behavior is sometimes used to suggest that the individual has adapted to environmental conditions. A better description is acclimatized or adjusted. That is, the behavior is adjusted, but must fit within the parameters of the person's individual cultural heritage while the cultural elements remain unchanged.

In the strict sense, the concept of adaptation can only be applied to populations over time. Although an individual behavior can be "selected for or against," adaptation of the culture to changes in the environment takes place only if a corresponding quantitative change occurs in the cultural elements of the population. As the cultural elements (beliefs, values, rules, etc.) of the population change, it directs the evolution of the population. The environment interacts with the cultural elements through various forms of natural selection.[15]

The most commonly known form of natural selection is directional selection. A population will change in one direction in response to the systematic, continuous selection against (or for) specific characteristics. As adaptation of the population occurs either as selection against lesser valued characteristics or for a quality, the favored characteristic increases in frequency over a period of time (see Figure 1). In this way the organizational culture tracks environmental changes.

Selection does not always lead to progressive change, however. Under some conditions, selection operates against both extremes of a distribution or set of attributes. Removing the extreme ends of a distribution curve has the obvious effect of reducing the variance. Over time the cultural elements will stabilize but with lesser variation in the population (see Figure 2). Stabilizing selection results in a narrowly adapted or self-sustaining population.

The third type of natural selection, disruptive selection, occurs when a large diverse population is subjected to different selective pressures under different environmental conditions (Figure 3). The primary effect of disruptive selection is to divide a single common group into two or more new groups clearly identified as subpopulations or subcultures (see Figure 3).

One or more forms of natural selection will operate on any population that is not in total harmony with its environment. In terms of organizational theory, selection operates to fit the members of the organization to the organizational culture by selecting for or against the behaviors—values, and/or beliefs. In a similar manner teachers are subjected to intense selection prior to, and during, employment. Natural selection has a constant and usually undetected effect on the culture of the organization.

It has long been recognized that populations left to natural forces will track the environment through natural selection and adaptation. If, however, criteria are carefully employed in the process of selection the population or group can be designed. Artificial selection has long been used in agriculture to develop hybrid plants, to increase meat or milk production or to produce unique breeds of dogs. Designed populations of organisms can be maintained with any kind of variation as long as the artificial selection is maintained. If, however, the artificial selection pressure is reduced (e.g., allowing dogs to breed at random), natural selection will come into full operation and direct the population to respond to environmental forces. In the same manner organizational culture can be directed and maintained by using special criteria in hiring, promotion, and/or designing the organization's structure.

## The Life Cycle of a Teacher

By most criteria, teachers are a special group. They are not selected at random. Behaviors reflect specific values that make up the school culture.[16] The specific characteristics of the teaching culture are the result of ongoing selection. To understand best the relationship of selection and the culture, it is important to trace what might be termed the life cycle of teachers.

1) Establishing the population of prospective teachers. The first major selection point in the life cycle of a teacher occurs as youngsters drop out of school at the junior high school level (see Figure 4). Selection is against individuals who would not fit the teaching culture in the most gross sense. Dropouts who become parents transmit their values and beliefs to their children, future members of a pool of prospective teachers.

The students who continue with their education—a smaller pool of individuals—have learned what teachers do and how teachers behave. They have learned the "compliant" behavior necessary for success in school.[17] As the students enter high school, their basic values are solidifying and their identity is being formulated from experience. Recognizing that upwards of 50 percent of students never complete high school, it is clear that natural selection operates intensely on this population. Furthermore, the youngsters have begun to develop a perspective of the purpose and process of education, a view based on experience in schools as they currently exist. Since schools are the primary point of the interface of the culture and the individual at this young age, it is not surprising that dropout studies point to the influential role of the school and teachers in the decisions of students at this time. It can be inferred that students who can accommodate—schooling, teachers, and the teaching culture—will continue with their education. Those individuals who do not fit the "niche" of student (and of being a teacher) will elect other choices. Thus, the pool of prospective teachers is further refined and delimited.

To this point in the refinement of the prospective teacher pool, selection has been for students who fit the social constraints of school and who seemingly identify with the teaching culture to which they have been vicariously subjected. However, within the college student pool, there are those students who, because of various reasons, are not in the least interested in teaching (as they perceive the career), while there is the population of individuals who see teaching as a potential career. The latter group has developed an identity, value system, and perspective of education, which is the result of years of exposure to teaching and schooling. The two primary college student populations can be described as oriented towards careers in teaching and in non-teaching. (It must be noted that there is generally a third population of "undecideds.")

By the time a student applies for admission to a teacher education program, the selection process has produced a narrowly defined pool of candidates. It is only at this point that artificial directional selection is invoked in the form of admissions criteria to the teacher education program. Although professional education in institutions of higher education has evolved a powerful infrastructure and is itself the result of intense selection, it is ironic that there seems to be no generally accepted definition of "quality teacher" or of quality teacher education programs.[18] Applegate suggests that "when clarity of outcomes is lacking, there is little hope that successful selection criteria can be developed."[19] There is essentially no uniform application of even basic criteria to admit prospective teachers to teacher education programs.[20]

Thus, there is no formalized process of positive selection (neither artificial nor natural) for teachers with specific teaching strengths or attributes. It is recognized that there is natural selection specifically against those individuals with ideals and values consistent with educational reform. An excellent case can be made that this negative selection can be countered through carefully planned artificial selection at the point of admission into a teacher education program.[21] Yet, the application of criteria through artificial selection, no matter how meritorious, will be directed at an already highly refined pool of potential teachers.

The influence of various categories of people changes as the individual ages.[22] Peers, professional colleagues, and other adults influence the prospective teacher entering and establish the probability of the teacher remaining in the teacher subculture. Negative selection will continue throughout the teacher education program.

2) The honing of teacher behaviors. Prospective teachers begin their professional preparation programs already having served a lengthy "apprenticeship of observation."[23] Values, identity, career objectives, and perception of education have been refined by years of intense natural selection. Natural selection, specifically stabilizing selection, has operated to produce a teaching population that is narrowly fitted to its environment as perceived and communicated by continuing teachers and other professional educators. The minor influence of artificial selection in the final stage of admitting prospective teachers to the teacher education program can do little to change the basic qualities of the cultural pool. The years of experience in schools have resulted in idiosyncratically derived rules for teaching behavior. Under these conditions new knowledge, advocated through teacher education programs, will be carefully screened. Only those teaching behaviors that fit the individual's rules will be accommodated into teaching repertoires.

If the "knowledge base" of teacher education consists of maxims of practical knowledge and cultural knowledge some have advocated,[24] then the teacher has considerable option and subjective choice in accepting new knowledge. Many candidates begin their teacher preparation believing they have little to learn about teaching. This perception establishes a context (both at the individual and collective peer level) in which the offerings of teacher education programs are experienced.[25] The invention and trial of new ideas or strategies will be discriminated against by preexisting ones.[26] As individuals are predisposed to adopt the newer ones, then these favored strategies or behaviors will increase in frequency (and correspondingly the others will decrease).

Thus, even though the population accepted to a teacher education program is subjected to minor admission criteria, the existing teaching culture swamps artificial selection for new attributes. Natural selection has predetermined the pool of potential teachers and has determined what individuals will accept from the teacher education program. Accordingly the individual will choose strategies of instruction and forms of behavior that insure his or her survival in the teaching culture.[27] The acquisition of knowledge and skills by a prospective teacher must fit the individual's perception of teaching and the teaching culture.

3) The continuing teacher population. Natural selection does not stop with the establishment of a pool of new teachers. As the individual begins his or her career, the influences of the organizational culture of the school and the culture of teaching tend to merge. Stabilizing selection results in what appears to be contradictory beliefs and values. According to a study done by the National Center for Education Information, "Teachers are generally satisfied in their jobs and personal lives, more so than college graduates or people in general."[28] The fact that a significant proportion of the continuing teachers are content with their position is further substantiated by the 1984 and 1986 Metropolitan Life surveys that concluded that 40 percent and 33 percent, respectively, were "very satisfied." Yet, the same poll found that 27 percent of teachers will leave the teaching profession for a new occupation;[29] evidence that there is intense selection against specific teachers. As young professionals leave the teaching culture through attrition, variation is reduced and the continuing teaching culture is stabilized.

The norms of teacher behaviors have been correlated with values and beliefs and are reasonably well summarized.[30] Considerable knowledge exists of teacher beliefs and perceptions concerning items such as classroom structure, teaching in groups, the principal's role, conflicts between teaching as a job and teaching as a profession, about stereotypes, and teacher socialization. These norms shape the teachers' approach to work, to furthering their professional education, and to all other aspects of the teaching environment. Unfortunately, the information is not synthesized into a holistic view of the teaching culture.

## Implications of a Cultural Approach to School Reform

The teaching culture is a mechanism that serves two major purposes: 1) providing identity, and 2) helping individuals avoid anxiety and uncertainty. Any attempt to change culture must include strategies that assist the population cognitively to redefine its identity (purpose) while maintaining security. However, the basic assumption of therapeutic and self-insight models is that the culture as represented by individuals is motivated to change. Quite to the contrary, stabilizing selection has resulted in a culture that carries minimal variability. There is no evidence that the teaching culture is desirous of change. To unfreeze the cultural perceptions, new ideas must be introduced through people who have not been fully subjected to the natural selection process. Small closed systems may accomplish this under local conditions with expert external help.

If long-term school reform is to be attempted it is clear that strategies and mechanisms must be developed that focus on changing the culture of teaching. These strategies should be designed to counteract the power of selection to delimit and define the teaching culture. The strategies should stimulate diversity rather than allow the culture to stabilize and be self-perpetuating. The following examples of strategies designed to change the teaching culture are drawn from a synthesis of mechanisms that have been used successfully over the past two decades in directing the evolution of organizational cultures.[31]

a) *Hybrid introduction*. This is a process of selectively filling positions with persons who are familiar with the culture but whose personal assumptions are somewhat different from the mainstream culture. For this strategy to function, values and mechanisms must exist external to the school, which will support change. There must be individuals in positions of leadership (school administrators at the state or local level, school board members, etc.) who have identified missing elements in the teaching culture and who have the authority or ability to introduce the missing substance. Although administrative positions must be targeted, teaching positions, too, can be filled with "hybrids." These must be provided with support systems that will facilitate change in the organization.

Hybrid introduction in education is not without precedent. Efforts to increase the numbers of women and minorities are based on the premise that it is important to introduce a specific quality into the culture. It must be recognized that there will be an undefined cost usually in the form of trade-off. For example, in some technical fields of education, the most qualified teachers will be those with current business or industrial "experience." To get these individuals into a school setting requires modification of regulations concerning teacher licensing. Furthermore, to get the potential industry-based teacher released from his or her current employment will require close cooperation with the private sector. Those partnerships will have many positive spin-offs and can be powerful tools for fostering a change in the teaching culture and eventual education reform.

b) *Technologic seduction*. This is an effort that is, in effect, the instituting of a new form of artificial selection within the continuing teacher population. It can range from the wholesale introductions of technologic innovations and other new technologies to the deliberate, managed introductions of specific educational technologies that require alternative behaviors. In both cases the technology causes individuals to undergo self-selection and/or be subjected to a new form of selection. The power of this approach lies in its dual effect, on the individual as well as on the organization. The impact on the teacher is due to the fact that the effort "is linked to real transformation in people's lives, jobs, hopes and dreams."[32]

Orchestrated introduction of technology into a culture will cause the members to review values, beliefs and assumptions as old patterns of behavior are disrupted. It must be noted that "technology is a rubric that includes management systems and other behavior modification techniques for working with students and colleagues as well as hardware (computers, teaching devices, etc.)." Education technologies have not been well received by teachers, but technologic seduction could be a powerful force to improve school efficiency and the culture of teaching.

c) *Alternative credentialing efforts.* These provide individuals with alternative paths to teaching careers. Initially conceived as a response to teacher shortages, the model not only offers alternative pathways to teaching but can be a strategy to diversify the teaching culture. The mechanisms are in place to infuse the culture with different values by implementing "hybrid introduction" or by fostering "technologic seduction."

Individuals entering the teaching profession via such routes will be subjected to intense selection by the established teaching culture. The products of alternative credentialing efforts will not have gone through the same processes as those of the members of the "continuing teacher" population, and thus may not be readily accepted. Appropriate support systems will be needed.

d) *Early recruitment.* This can be a technique that not only broadens the pool of potential teachers but can also be used to modify the culture. The current natural selection of prospective teachers must be addressed early in the education of youth. The Magnet School concept, originally used to recruit and provide students with specialized education in the sciences; mathematics; vocational, technical, or fine and performing arts, is now being tried as a means of addressing the problem of recruiting specially targeted young people into teaching.[33] As this effort matures, the admission criteria currently used at the teacher education level could be refined for use at the 9th- and 10th-grade levels or lower. This would be an effective strategy to counter natural selection in the K-12 years by building a sense of identity and purpose early in a prospective teacher's career.

Although scholarships, active recruitment programs, and marketing strategies may function to bring in new teacher candidates, these processes do not address the culture of teaching. There is no reason to believe that individuals brought into teaching via such routes will remain in the profession. The cost will likely outweigh the benefits.

e) *Counteracting the influence of the existing teaching culture.* This must be strategically planned to challenge directly the culture of teaching perpetuated by the continuing teacher population. In addition to the four processes described above, counteractive strategies are needed that will help first- and second-year teachers (whether products of traditional or alternative programs) ward off the conservative self-perpetuating cannot be simple "support groups" to comfort the new teacher. qualities of existing teaching culture.

Efforts cannot be simple "support groups" to comfort the new teacher. Counteractive strategies must defend the new teacher and her or his values while modifying the teaching culture. Administrators must allow and even encourage new teachers to exhibit behavior that could be judged as nonprofessional by current beaching cultural standards. The support system must be sophisticated enough to confront the oppressive qualities of the beaching culture while at the same time reflecting what is known of good beaching.

f) *Exposing myths and misrepresentations to the public*. This is a powerful cultural change mechanism. It is not uncommon in education for "espoused theories" to be in conflict with accepted theories-in-use.[35] learners may not be the same as how the school treats students. Or, what For examples what the public is told about how children are treated as a superintendent hears from a principal may be very different from what actually occurs in a school. In many cases such problems are the result of a closed decision-making process.

Carefully engineered leaks of information to the right place at the right time can be powerful inducements to cultural change. Such leaks are often termed "whistle blowing," in the sense of exposing inconsistencies internal to organization and precipitating serious consequences. Since whistle blowing has the potential for forcing examination of the cultural assumptions, one can see why entrenched members of the culture are reluctant to take action and why the organization wishes efforts to expose myths and misrepresentations.

g) *Managed change through structural changes*. This can be used to challenge embedded assumptions and establish a new pattern of operation. As old procedures, beliefs, and values are weakened, new organizational leadership can revitalize the organization. A current example of this strategy is the university-school partnerships being established in various areas of the country. They are designed to affect school culture by joining schools and other educational agencies into a cohesive unit.[37] The partnerships bring together diverse professionals by systematically addressing educational policy curriculum and instruction, educational technology, and training needs. Given time, these partnerships will have a direct effect on the teaching culture.

These seven strategies can be used in different ways in different environments. While any one of them could be used in a narrow manner (such as simply providing better instruction in technical fields), their full potential in affecting schools will not be reached unless they are simultaneously used to foster change in the teaching culture.

Although the notion of "school culture" is gaining credibility in the literature, the concept of the teaching culture is not well defined. Research focuses on behaviors, teacher evaluation instruments teacher education competencies, predictive measures all emphasizing behaviors—the exclusion of the underlying rules that establish the culture. Behaviors are fleeting manifestations of the established culture and frequently actions induced under stress. Behaviors are not a solid conceptual structure upon which to build a rationale for change or educational reform. As Combs summarizes: "The behavior we observe at any moment is only the external expression of what is going on inside."[38]

What teachers believe and how they behave is a result of their culture; the culture is a product of natural selection that operates unaddressed by teacher educators and school reformers. Behaviors can be temporarily modified but, if long-term reform is to be a real goal, attention must be given to the teaching culture. It is argued in this article that the culture of teaching is being transmitted to the next generation of prospective teachers on a continuing basis of 15-20 years. The population of individuals who will assume the role of teacher is subjected to rigorous natural selection. By the time artificial selection is invoked in teacher education programs the pool of prospective teachers is already highly solidified and defined; the behaviors, underlying values, and rules of operations are thoroughly established in the individuals of this population. Furthermore, the variation in cultural elements that remains in the population of newly certificated teachers will be subjected to intense stabilizing selection during the first several years of teaching; individuals who do not fit the norms of the profession will exit to alternative careers.

Some years ago Sykes argued that the teaching profession was seriously imperiled and that the efforts under way to improve matters were insufficient, misguided, or both.[39] Although the attack on the problems has been strengthened and become more orchestrated, it must still be classified as *piecemeal*. It is argued here that the quality of teaching in America will only improve when attention is directed at the single most powerful barrier to change — the culture of teaching.

## NOTES

[1] Mark Twain, "Corn-pone Opinion," in *On the Damned Human Race* (New York: Hill & Wang, 1923, 1964), p. 24.

[2] Marvin Harris, *Culture, Man and Nature* (New York: Crowell, 1971), p. 136. Also see, Marvin Harris, *Cultural Materialism: The Struggle for a Science of Culture* (New York: Random House, 1979).

[3] Ward H. Goodenough, "Cultural Anthropology and Linguistics," in *Report of the Seventh Annual Round Table Meeting on Linguistics & Language Study*, eds. Paul L. Garvin and Leon Dostert (Washington, D.C.: Georgetown University Press, 1957), p. 167.

[4] The work of Arthur W. Combs and his associates is particularly revealing. See, e.g., Arthur W. Combs, "New Assumptions for Educational Reform," *Educational Leadership* (February 1988): 38-41; Arthur W. Combs, *A Personal Approach to Teaching* (Boston: Allyn and Bacon, 1982); Arthur W. Combs, Anne C. Richards, and Frank Richards, *Perceptual Psychology: A Humanistic Approach to the Study of Persons* (New York: Harper and Row, 1976).

[5] For a review of the evolution of culture, see, Luigi Luca Cavalli-Sforza and

Marcus W. Feldman, "Cultural Versus Genetic Adaptation," *Proceedings of the National Academy of Science* 80 (1983): 4993-4996; Cavalli-Sforza and Feldman, *Cultural Transmission and Evolution: A Quantitative Approach* (Princeton, N.J.: Princeton University Press, 1981); Charles Lumsden and Edward O. Wilson, *Genes, Mind, and Culture* (Cambridge, Massachusetts: Harvard University Press, 1981).

6. Seymour B. Sarason, *The Culture of the School and the Problem of Change*, 2nd ed. (Boston: Allyn and Bacon, 1982).

7. John I. Goodlad, *The Dynamics of Educational Change: Toward Responsive Schools* (New York: McGraw-Hill, 1975).

8. Linda M. McNeil, "Exit, Voice and Community: Magnet Teachers' Responses to Standardization," *Educational Policy* 1 (March 1987): 93-113.

9. Albert Bandura, *Social Learning Theory* (Englewood Cliffs, N.J.: Prentice-Hall, 1977). Also see, Albert Bandura and Robert Walters, *Social Learning and Personality Development* (New York: Holt, Rinehart & Winston, 1963).

10. Judith E. Lanier and Judith W. Little, "Research on Teacher Education," in *Handbook of Research on Teaching*, 3rd ed., ed. Merlin C. Wittrock (New York: Macmillan, 1986), pp. 527-569, p. 542.

11. Ted L. Rosenthal and Barry J. Zimmerman, *Social Learning and Cognition* (New York: Academic Press, 1978), p. 79.

12. Hazel Markus, "Possible Selves," *ISR Newsletter* (Spring/Summer 1987): 1-2. [Ann Arbor, Michigan: Institute for Social Research, University of Michigan]

13. George D. Spindler and Louise Spindler, "Anthropologists View American Culture," *Annual Review of Anthropology* 12 (1983): 49-78; also, George D. Spindler, "Education in a Transforming American Culture," *Harvard Educational Review* 25 (Spring 1955): 145-156.

14. Mary Haywood Metz, "Teachers Pride in Craft, School Subcultures, and Societal Pressures," *Educational Policy* 1 (March 1987): 115-134.

15. This discussion of selection is drawn from David H. Ost, *Evolution*, 2nd ed. (Chicago: Development Systems Corporation, 1977).

16. Paul Heckman, "Understanding School Culture," in *The Ecology of School Renewal*, ed. John l. Goodlad [Eighty-sixth Yearbook of the National Society for the Study of Education] (Chicago: University of Chicago Press, 1987).

17. A good discussion of the power of compliant behavior in school culture is provided by Elliot W. Eisner, *The Educational Imagination: On the Design and*

*Evaluation of School Program*, 2nd ed. (New York: Macmillan, 1985), pp. 87-92, and the references cited therein.

18. Robert L. Fisher and Marilyn E. Feldmann, "Trends in Standards for Admission to Teacher Education," *Action in Teacher Education* 6 (Winter 1984-85): 59-63.

19. Jane Applegate, "Teacher Candidate Selection: An Overview," *Journal of Teacher Education* 38 (March-April 1987): 2-6.

20. Archie E. Laman and Dorothy E. Reeves, "Admission to Teacher Education Programs: The Status and Trends," *Journal of Teacher Education* 34 (January-February 1983): 2-4.

21. Thomas E. Barone, "Educational Platforms, Teacher Selection, and School Reform: Issues Emanating from a Biographical Case Study," *Journal of Teacher Education* 38 (March-April 1987): 12-17.

22. Alan P. Bell, "Role Modeling of Fathers in Adolescence and Young Adulthood," *Journal of Counseling Psychology* 16 (January 1969): 30-35.

23. Dan Lortie, *Schoolteacher* (Chicago: University of Chicago Press, 1975), develops a reasonable position that prospective teachers are highly influenced by prior classroom experiences and have served an "apprenticeship of observation." See, also, Perry E. Lanier and Joseph E. Henderson, "The Content and Process of Teacher Education: A Critique and Challenge," *New Directions for Education* 1 (1973): 1-102; Lanier and Little, "Research on Teacher Education," pp. 527-569.

24. Lee S. Shulman, "Knowledge and Teaching: Foundations of the New Reform," *Harvard Educational Review* 57 (February 1987): 1-22.

25. Cassandra Book, Joe Byers, and Donald Freeman, "Student Expectations and Teacher Education Traditions with which We Can and Cannot Live," *Journal of Teacher Education* 34 (January-February 1983): 9-13.

26. Donald T. Campbell, "Blind Variation and Selective Retention in Creative Thought as in Other Knowledge Processes," *Psychological Review* 67 (No. 132, 1960): 380-400. Also see, Donald T. Campbell, "Variation and Selective Retention in Sociocultural Evolution," in *Social Changes in Developing Areas: A Recent Expectation of Evolutionary Theory*, ed. H. R. Barringer (Cambridge, Massachusetts: Schenkman, 1965), pp. 19-49.

27. Robert Boyd and Peter J. Richerson, *Culture and the Evolutionary Process* (Chicago: University of Chicago Press, 1985).

28. C. Emily Feistritzer, *Profile of Teachers in the U.S.* (Washington, D.C.: National Center for Educational Information, 1986), p. i.

29. Louis Harris and Associates, *The Metropolitan Life Survey of the American Teacher, 1986* (New York: Metropolitan Life Insurance Company, 1986).

30. Sharon Feiman-Nemser and Robert L. Floden, "The Cultures of Teaching," in *Handbook of Research on Teaching*, ed. Merlin S. Wittrock (New York: Macmillan, 1986), pp. 505-526.

31. Edgar H. Schein, *Organizational Culture and Leadership* (San Francisco: Jossey-Bass, 1985), provides an overview of techniques and strategies used to manage the cultural change in business organizations. See, particularly, Chapter 12, "Organizational Growth Stages and Cultural Change Mechanisms," pp. 270-296 and the references therein.

32. Michael W. Apple, "Teaching and Technology: The Hidden Effects of Computers on Teachers and Students," *Educational Policy* 1 (March 1987): 135-157. Quoted from p. 153.

33. Blake Rodman, "In Houston Magnet, District 'Grows' Its Own Teachers," *Education Week* 7 (May 11, 1988): I, 18-19.

34. The need for support systems and induction programs for new teachers is documented. See, particularly, Arthur E. Wise, Linda Darling-Hammond, and Barnett Berry, *Effective Teacher Selection: From Recruitment to Retention* (Santa Monica, California: The RAND Corporation, 1987), and the references therein.

35. Chris Argyris and Donald Allen Schon, *Organization Learning: A Theory of Action Perspective* (Reading, Massachusetts: Addison-Wesley, 1978).

36. Research at the Sloan School of Management has provided considerable insight into organizational culture and change. See, William G. Dyer, Jr., "The Cycle of Cultural Evolution in Organizations" (Cambridge, Massachusetts: Sloan School of Management, Massachusetts Institution of Technology, 1984; unpublished paper).

37. Paul E. Heckman, *Exploring the Concept of School Renewal: Cultural Differences and Similarities between More and Less Renewing Schools* [A Study of Schooling, Technical Report No. 33] (Los Angeles: Laboratory in School and Community Education, University of California, 1982). Similarly, John I. Goodlad and his associates are constructing a network for educational renewal. A brief overview of the effort is provided by Lynn Olson, "Schools, Universities in 10 States have joined Goodlad's Network for Educational Renewal," *Education Week* 5 (April 30, 1986), 1, 16.

38. Arthur W. Combs, "New Assumptions for Educational Reform," *Educational Leadership* 45 (February 1988): 38-41. Quoted from p. 39.

39. Gary Sykes, "Contradictions, Ironies, and Promises Unfulfilled: A Contemporary Account of the Status of Teaching," *Phi Delta Kappan* 64 (October 1983): 87-93.

# Chapter 7
# Unlocking Cultures of Teaching: Working with Diversity

*by Nancy B. Wyner, University of Lowell*

If you want to know how theater works, you talk with actors and directors, attend stage performances and go backstage to observe the interactions of people who make theater happen. School "happens" when teachers and students interact within the culture of the school. The dynamic interactions of values, beliefs and goals among teachers and students make schools succeed or fail. Shared values are a distinguishing characteristic of effective schools.

In each school, teachers have their own workplace beliefs, values, traditions, and relationships that constitute the culture of teaching. Teachers' beliefs about what goes on—"the script" on social interactions or subject matter—are a significant source of collegiality or conflict in teaching cultures. This paper describes what happens "backstage" within the teaching culture when teachers do not agree on the script—the common purpose, values, goals and outcomes of education for linguistic minority students, and, more particularly, what is happening to bilingual and ESL teachers in the natural setting of the workplace.

Our interest is in understanding what conditions might enable teachers to integrate cultural diversity in schools, and so prepare students for effective participation and leadership in a more diverse society (Wyner, 1989).

Bilingual education presents new cultural knowledge, practices and beliefs to the teaching faculty of a school that may be "accepted, learned, and remembered, rejected, ignored or forgotten, depending on where one sits in the social order" (Erickson, 1987, p. 13-14). How some faculty deal with bilingual education is the subject of this essay. But these issues may not be peculiar to the ESL or bilingual educator. Special educators and Chapter 1 teachers also require reconceptualization of the mission and goals of education by mainstream teachers so as to positively integrate them into the culture of teaching with their school.

In this study, daily workplace events are reported as evidence of the bilingual and ESL teachers' growing awareness of their low status as "outsiders," and their isolation from the dominant mainstream faculty. The "deep histories" revealed in their stories are interpreted from one perspective as the influence of an institutionalized myth on belief patterns and relationships. Reflection on these stories and their mythic underpinnings help to further conceptualize cultures of teaching.

If collegiality is a hallmark of productive schools, isolation and staff segregation are impediments to school improvement and educational equity. Alternatively, school staff with a broader vision of who and what has value, work to dismantle cultural barriers, to create inclusive, satisfying workplaces that enable teachers to form friendships, value each other's professional knowledge, work collaboratively to increase quality education.

This essay concludes with proposals to engage all members of the teaching culture in rethinking educational goals and the mission of teaching in their school district and school; assessing the "people" strengths and barriers to positive working relationships; enabling teachers to broaden their cultural knowledge and understandings through dialogue and reflection on their own beliefs and alternative research-based practices in linguistic minority education; increased involvement of bilingual and ESL teachers in school-wide planning and decision-making with their colleagues. Staff will want to support new arrangements if these changes have a positive affect on them, on how things work when there is increased collegiality and appreciation of diversity in a positive workplace environment.

## Emerging research

In *The Preparation of Teachers*, Sarason, Davidson & Blatt (1962, 1986) were concerned with the disjointedness between the realities of schools and the substance of teacher training programs. They noted with distress that "we simply lack the kind of detailed description of 'live' teaching so we can gain a better understanding of what the different protagonists in the controversy actually mean and the degree to which their descriptions are consistent with stated aims" (p. 119). Sarason and his colleagues argued for the importance of moving beyond the surfeit of course descriptions and vague generalizations to probe, and question what teachers are experiencing and learning in teacher education and in the workplace.

In *The Culture of the School and the Problem of Change*, Sarason (1972, 1982) challenged researchers and educators to study the perceptions of "live" teachers and their social interactions in the workplace. As the concept of "the culture of the school" gained acceptance in education, research began to uncover the conceptual complexity of school culture phenomena.

Feiman-Nemser & Floden (1986) reviewed the cultures of teaching and correlated norms of teaching behaviors with values and beliefs about leadership and teaching as a profession. In general, these studies focused on the beginning teacher, the role of teacher education, and the influence of experienced teachers on the novice teacher. However, teachers' behaviors, values and beliefs about bilingual education and ESL had not been given attention in the literature.

One of Erickson's (1987b) conceptions of school culture, defined as meanings generated in political struggle, provided a starting point for the notions about the culture of teaching developed in this essay. "Cultural difference is seen as tracing lines of status, power, and political interest within and across institutional boundaries found in the total social unit..." (p. 13). Through social conflict, different interest groups become culturally separate and different, though they may engage in similar routines and regularities within the workplace of the school.

Ost (1989, 1991) suggested there are two cultural mechanisms that stabilize the teaching profession: providing identity and purpose, and helping individuals to avoid anxiety and uncertainty. The notion of a sense of identity is tied to the shared conceptions, goals and objectives regarding schooling, with members of the school community agreeing on the common script. Bilingual and ESL and the cultural differences they value and represent challenge narrowly defined norms of the profession. Through exclusion and isolation they are teachers at risk.

## Social changes and schooling

During the last fifteen years, significant changes have influenced the demography of our nation. These changes are evident in the scale of the newest migrations, and the distinct immigrant groups (refugees, undocumented and legal immigrants) arriving from Nicaragua, Guatemala, and El Salvador, from Puerto Rico and Mexico, and Southeast Asia. Kellog (1988) believes these demographic changes "are shaping a future that is perhaps not fully understood by most Americans and that is certainly not often reflected by our national policies. By the year 2050 the U.S. population will reach 300 million, and it will look as it never has before" (p. 201).

There are now between 2.1 and 2.7 million school-age immigrant students in the public schools. When these newcomers arrive they are placed with bilingual or ESL teachers until they are able to function in mainstream classes. The gradual infusion of racial and ethnic minorities and newcomer linguistic minority teachers into the teaching culture will significantly change the racial and ethnic composition of the workforce. The complexities of these demographic changes represent an important new dimension that is transforming schools, with dramatic effects on the culture within which teachers work.

## Centers of "differences"

Since the 1840s, underclass European immigrants have populated the cities of Lowell, Lawrence, Haverhill and other towns in the Middlesex Valley in Massachusetts. They worked long hours for low wages. The tradition continues. The legacy of poverty and hardship is evident today among Hispanic and Southeast Asian immigrant families who continue to arrive in the region, the setting for this report. Today, these families struggle against poverty, hoping they can protect their children from the drug culture, believing that education and employment will help them and their children to claim a part of the American Dream.

The largest Hispanic population in Massachusetts resides in the City of Lawrence. Of the city's total population of 68,000, it is estimated that 30,000 residents are Hispanic. The per capita income of the city's residents ranks second lowest in the state. Unemployment in Lawrence for February 1989 was 8.3% compared to the state average of 3.5%, well above most other cities in the state. Recent data indicate there are 11,334 people ages 15-24 living in Lawrence, and an annual school dropout rate of 14.5%.

Since 1984, Lowell's school-age population has grown from 24% to 41% minority students. The city witnessed the largest influx of Cambodian immigrants in the nation. Vietnamese and Laotian refugees also immigrated to the region. The need to provide specialized language services to these students grew accordingly. The public schools were unable to find adequate numbers of trained teachers for linguistic minority education. Minimal funding for teacher training and certification was provided by the state.

## Sources for this study

Data for this study were drawn from teachers enrolled in a bilingual education and English as a Second Language (ESL) certification program at the College of Education, University of Lowell. They attended a graduate course I taught on *The Culture of the School*. Students in one section of the course were primarily bilingual education teachers, mostly recent immigrants from Southeast Asia, Central and Latin America, or migrants from Puerto Rico. The second group of thirty students was made up of American-born native speakers of English. These two groups, with different racial and ethnic composition, areas of specialization and professional experience, faced disturbingly similar negative interactions with mainstream, regular education teachers.

## An Example of the Conditions within a School Setting:

On a visit to a school where several of my students were teaching, I asked a school administrator about the bilingual and ESL programs in his school. He responded:

> About 73% of our bilingual teachers weren't certified last year. We've got a lot of hairdressers and physical therapists and so forth who are teaching kids and they have never had a reading course in their life. So that's a problem... My bilingual teachers in this building have lunch together in a room separate from my teachers' room [notice the distinction made]. That's a concern for me. I just happened to be walking in the corridor and I saw all these people [the bilingual teachers and teacher aides] in a room all eating their lunch together. I am wondering if they tried and got driven out or if they just... I don't know.

No explanation was offered. No concern—just the observation. Were the bilingual teachers unwelcome in the teachers' room? Was this intentional exclusion? Perhaps socializing during a "break" should be discounted, unless we decide that these informal and formal interactions actually represent the school culture. Are these observable social groupings meaningful barometers of attitudes and values among the staff? The comment served as an introduction to an aspect of teacher interactions often hidden from view. The administrator did not clarify the situation, and yet he brought the matter to our attention. A puzzling episode, that illustrated the bilingual teachers' own experiences and comments during class.

If bilingual teachers are isolated from mainstream teachers, and administrators notice but do not open the issue for discussion and dialogue, the culture is stifled by isolation and segregation.

## Metaphors of alienation: Teaching in a coal bin, on stage in the auditorium, or at lunch "at the fourth table."

The plight of the itinerant, marginal teacher is illustrated by space and resource allocations. Schools are often overcrowded, especially urban schools. Space is a bargaining chip. When space is allocated the decisions are likely to reflect implicit, unvoiced priorities that don't include teachers outside the power lines. The problem is a familiar one to bilingual and ESL teachers:

> At my school class size is manageable. My ESL groups average 6-8 students. I conduct my classes on what used to be a small stage. A blackboard divides the room in half, separating two ESL classes that occupy the stage at the same time. The noise level can be intolerable. Students, teachers and entire classes walk up and down the hallway in clear view of the stage. Concentration can be difficult for students and teachers alike. Somehow teaching and learning do take place on the stage. I have a blackboard to write on, a bulletin board to hang my students' work on, and shelves for my books and supplies. The stage remains a mystery to the students from the regular classrooms. They are always asking me what I do, and if they can come up and watch. (Elementary ESL teacher)

*   *   *   *   *

> No room, books or materials during the first 3 months in the building. Eventually, the school's coal bin was petitioned. As an ESL teacher, I occupied one side; a special ed. teacher was on the other side. I saw groups of 15-18 students at a time, and she saw 6-8 students per period. I was often visited by administrators. My students were too vocal. I tried to explain that I use the oral-aural method, but the supervisor was not moved. She felt as though SPED kids took precedence over ESL needs. Should we have to choose? Eventually, I gave up the coal bin and established closer working relationships with my cooperating bilingual teachers. (Elementary ESL teacher)

*   *   *   *   *

> There are three long tables and one smaller round table [in the teachers' cafeteria]. Nothing has ever been said, but the same people always head for the same table when on a break. Aides always sit at the smaller table. Some of them make crafts and display them so everyone can look and order anything they like. The long table by the windows is considered the choice table. It is where most of the regular classroom teachers sit. In the morning before school begins, that table is so crowded the chairs are almost two deep all around. In contrast to the other tables, they never talk about school or their students. The third table is where you sit if you are late for your break. There is always a lot of complaining with that group. The fourth table is the bilingual table. The teachers moved it at

a right angle to the rest of the cafeteria and only Spanish is spoken.

These bilingual teachers felt as if they were outsiders; working with children as teachers, but not considered by the regular education teachers as legitimate. This sense splinters the faculty as an entity.

Behaviors of the dominant social group are experienced by "outsiders" as elusive, differential, arbitrary. Value patterns and norms are implied but contradict social norms of welcoming supportive communities, and reasonable social behavior. When values are not shared, institutional purpose is uncoupled, fragmented, and decisions relate back to the personal and subjective. The following anecdotes highlight the problem:

> Some of the regular teachers are against the bilingual program. They don't understand the value of bilingual education. They ask, "Why not English Only?" "Why do they need to learn the Vietnamese language or the Laotian language if they are going to stay in America?" They don't realize that bilingual education helps to make subject matter more comprehensible. *And* language is an important cultural resource for all Americans in this global society. (Southeast Asian bilingual teacher)

* * * * *

> Attitudes toward the Spanish bilingual student at my school have been changing over the last twelve years, gradually and slowly. My perception is that many of the Anglo staff have the idea that the bilinguals are somewhat an "untouchable" class. Now there is more acceptance. This changing attitude, coupled with the realization that 25% of the student population are Hispanic, has made people realize that the presence of the bilingual student group is not going to change in the foreseeable future. (Hispanic bilingual teacher)

## Time as a bulwark for integration...

Time has a powerful role in school cultures. Time is expressed by schedules, exam periods, beginnings, rituals, seasons, vacations, endings (when there is no more time). Time is what most teachers need to be able to plan, think, collaborate, experience and express collegiality, innovate, change. Leaders know the importance of time and reflect on ways to manage time effectively. Time can be used as a bulwark or facilitator of integration in schools.

> Integration into the main content areas is a major struggle because there is no central schedule for all classes. The bilingual student may lose his or her native language instruction to receive English, reading or math instruction. Two standard teachers would not consider altering their schedules for the sake of integration in any form. Schedules were dispersed last fall attempting to integrate all classes for lunch, music, P.E. and art. These teachers approached the principal with the lament, "We don't have enough uninterrupted reading time." They got their way.

* * * * *

> In our school there is no opportunity for integration of students during the school day. All of the art, music or gym classes are taught in self-contained classrooms. Actually, there is supposed to be integration. No one questions the principal about this practice, we seem to fear any kind of questioning of her authority. The only time the whole school gets together occurs when there is a movie. There has never been a movie shown in Spanish. At our "Student of the Month" assemblies all the children are seated in the auditorium for both praise and a lecture. Even though half of the school has bilingual classes, the Spanish language is never spoken. Too bad for the child who does not understand what is being said, whether it is in praise or whether a new rule has been announced. (Elementary bilingual teacher)

In these fragments of data there are puzzlements and provisional explanations of social behaviors and relationships among groups of teachers. Exclusionary behaviors seem to function as part of the daily routine of the life of the bilingual teachers in school. Attitudes displayed toward bilingual teachers were not very different from stories in the daily newspaper. The culturally learned attitudes of many school staff in these anecdotes reflect the social divisions and cultural experiences of teachers in their own communities.

In the view of bilingual teachers, they are apt to be tolerated rather than appreciated. Montero-Sieburth & Perez (1987) ascribed this to the fact that bilingual teachers are assigned to transitional classes "akin to a waiting room, where students are to stay until they are admitted to the mainstream" (p. 187). The authors concluded that the bilingual teacher comes to feel an inevitable sense of isolation "enajenacion," or a malaise that is also the fate of their students. In the settings where bilingual teachers work, there are few patterns and regularities that link the teacher to the standard teacher group. Consequently, the bilingual is afloat, marginalized, extraneous. A middle school teacher reflected on this experience.

> Our working conditions are fair and there is an equitable distribution of duties (recess, bus and sometimes lunch duty). We all have access to the different audio-visual materials available. We also have the opportunity to improve our teaching skills through participation in several workshops during the school year. Those workshops are intended to help teachers that belong to the regular program. I have not participated in two years in a workshop in which the topic is related to bilingual instruction in my school. (middle school bilingual teacher)

Montero-Sieburth & Perez argued that bilingual education will remain thwarted unless an effort is made "to understand the realities of minority experience, its diversity, and the challenges facing the teachers." (p. 187)

## Failures in communication deliver a message.

Teachers in this study often commented on the failures of the communication process. There were incidents when a school event was in progress, a video was being shown in one of the other grades and they were not invited to attend with their children. Or, the memo was sent to teachers but bilingual teachers were not included in the information loop. In these instances, the politics of legitimacy and exclusion reached out to affect student interests as well as the teachers' attitudes about their role in the school culture.

## An explanatory perspective: Mythmaking and mythkeeping

Myth is a language, a type of speech. In the Myth of Sameness the mythmaker or mythkeeper walks the Main Streets of Puritan New England or Jefferson's rural communities where everything is almost as it was: the library, the Town Hall that served as anchor, the Congregational Church, the clapboard schoolhouse. A place where townspeople held close the notion of racial and religious uniformity. Charles Ives captured the spirit of the symbolic New England town in his song, "The Things Our Fathers Loved," filled with tuneful references to Main Street and the village band.

Generations of Americans have internalized these images as the iconography of their cultural heritage. Through historical omissions, token representations, the myth of sameness postulates a kind of memory and past filled with a situation, a certain knowledge of reality, shapeless associations and expansive ambiguity. Myth prefers to work with incomplete images. It is a story at once true and unreal. Barthes (1957, 1972) observes that the principle of myth is that it transforms history into nature. As "depoliticized speech" myth does not deny things. On the contrary, it makes them innocent and natural. "In passing from history to nature, myth acts economically; it abolishes the complexity of human acts, it gives them simplicity of essences, it does away with all dialectics, with any going back beyond what is immediately visible, it organizes a world which is without contradictions because it is without depth, a world wide open and wallowing in the evident, it establishes a blissful clarity; things appear to mean something by themselves" (p. 143).

One image turned myth was that problems of poor immigrants were of their own making, the consequence of not working hard enough, being undisciplined. The problem, it was decided, was *cultural*, not political or economic. They were *different*. Educators were relieved of responsibility for their low-income minority students as the Myth of Sameness filled their imagination, developed a sense of its own importance.

Bilingual teachers are another group, enveloped in an image of incompetence and strangeness, who are viewed as different: their goals askew. They are miseducators, hence excluded.

This obsession with sameness as the safety net is explored by Donald Schon (1971) in *Beyond the Stable State*. Schon tells us about our collective need to believe in a "stable state," reached after a time of troubles. Such a vision, Schon realized, is only an image, "an afterlife within one's own life." He proposes a shift from belief in universal stability toward different views of reality that accept "zones of uncertainty" and "nonrational processes" as preconditions on which rational inquiry is based. Such zones of uncertainty characterize most if not all of the daily dynamics of the school.

In the anecdotal material reported, an emphasis on differences is prevalent, although there were mainstream teachers who reached out and promoted integrated classroom activities and collegiality with specialists and language education teachers. But integrated classes and activities were a rarity. And when cultural diversity is not welcomed or validated through positive recognition, the consequences are damaging for bilingual teachers and their students.

Despite the new realities of demography, the nature of pluralism is denied in teaching cultures bonded by sameness. The myth of sameness, created out of our need for a national sense of identity, preserved by a nation longing for an idealized past, hoping to restore an imagined wholeness, persists even as we forge ahead into an uncertain future. Continued reliance on the myth stalls our growth as a pluralistic nation in an era plunging toward a globalized world community.

In this essay, stories are told by bilingual and ESL teachers that reflect their experiences in their teaching cultures, their efforts as individuals, or with colleagues, to overcome the chilling myths of the past, to reach the possibilities of integration and cultural identity for themselves and their students, and to make meaning of the promise of educational equity and excellence.

Although the Myth of Sameness may be natural to some, it is unacceptable to many Americans who value ethnic and racial diversity. In this myth, we do not glimpse a role for ethnics, linguistic minorities, people of color, their living vital histories, traditions and cultures. This notion of an idealized past has tilted our cultural lens away from issues of changing demography, globalization and the realities that have transformed American society since the formative moments of our nation's infancy. Through mythweaving, radical cultural distortions spin off and settle in the culture of the school. Entrenched myths in the minds of educators wall off potential and possibilities for teaching and learning.

## Challenges to Cultures of Teaching

Reflection on the experiences portrayed here point to a hard reality in teaching cultures: the gap between idealized and actual belief values and social interactions. The challenge is to develop inclusive teaching cultures through ongoing strategies that support reflection, dialogue, positive working relationships, and sustained staff development, enabling all teachers to participate in educational change and effective teaching. School building leadership must be supportive and willing to facilitate and manage professional development opportunities. The following multilevel initiatives are suggested:

*Rethinking educational goals and the mission of teaching.* Rethinking district-wide and school-based educational goals, and the mission of teaching is a productive place for the staff to begin to question and reflect on assumptions, beliefs and norms about teaching. This perspective *begins with teachers, their own sense of purpose, their vision about teaching in multicultural schools.* When bilingual and mainstream teachers talk together about the needs of students and their mission of teaching, they are reflecting on the common ground and values they share as educators. Self-reflection and shared reflection could move participants to think about practice relevant to changes in student demographics and new demands on teachers and schooling. Creation of a new collective purpose, a new vision for an inclusive teaching culture in support of multicultural and bilingual education could be a powerful goal for these activities. Where there is great diversity of beliefs, values, and norms among teachers, it is more difficult to develop a common sense of purpose or vision. More difficult and more important to achieving effective education for all students.

*Assessing teachers' worklives.* A teacher-developed profile of the teaching culture—the natural networks, interactions, and concerns of teachers in the workplace—would make available "live" information for reflection and planning. What's happening and why? What is the level of teachers' motivation to participate in strengthening collegial relationships in their teaching culture. (This is crucial, since teachers are key to this process. Unless teachers are motivated or can be motivated to engage in improving the teaching culture, change is unlikely.) Does peer isolation exist? If so, what efforts have been made or can be made to deal with this chronic problem? What information is available within the school or district about successful collaboration or co-planning between mainstream teachers and ESL or bilingual teachers. What forms of resource or instructional sharing exists among mainstream and bilingual/ESL teachers? What are the "people" strengths, the typical problems, needs, barriers to productive and satisfying professional relationships in the teaching culture? Is there open communication? Does school leadership support teachers' professional growth? What does faculty think about teachers' social interactions and professionalism in the teaching culture? In thinking about changes in the teaching culture, what positive changes do they suggest?

*Setting priorities for building inclusive cultures of teaching.* Once staff reviews the information collected in the assessment process, planning begins. The following themes could be useful:

a) **Improving communication** is an essential factor in promoting collegial working relationships (see Fullan, Chapter 12 and Lieberman, Chapter 11) and appreciation of cultural diversity in the workplace. Ongoing access to information about school events is important if staff is to function as a part of the team. Stakeholders in the teaching culture should formulate alternate ways to spread news about school activities, teacher meetings, school visitors, problems, issues, concerns.

b) **Arranging equitable space and resource distribution.** Classroom assignments and resource allocations are inevitable stress points in school life.

When they are perceived to be made unfairly, resentments arise, sometimes anger is expressed toward the more vulnerable newcomer teacher. Changing conditions require rethinking use of classroom space. At the Washington Elementary School in Lowell, Massachusetts bilingual teachers were concerned that children and their teachers were mainstreamed for part of each day. They agreed to rearrange the location of classrooms to facilitate integration of bilingual and mainstream students during social studies, science, and informal activities. With this arrangement, mainstream and bilingual classes were neighbors. Teachers had greater opportunity to talk with each other about students, to plan activities together and to initiate friendships. Sharing was a more natural part of life in school.

c) **Increasing cultural knowledge** is an important ongoing dimension of professional growth. While it is likely that teachers teach from within their own cultural traditions, it is also possible to develop "a double perspective which requires an understanding of the limitations of their own cultural perspectives" and an appreciation "of separate ways of understanding and shaping the world" (Nichols, 1989). In building inclusive teaching cultures we propose that teachers and administrators as a collaborative group engage in dialogue related to their own beliefs and understandings about learning styles, linguistic needs and alternative research-based practice to stretch group awareness and understanding. Dialogue or "discussion of alternative conceptions and activities that in combination with some of the teacher's own conceptions form a view of warranted practice" (Richardson, 1990).

The multicultural environment of today's schools, must recognize the connections that link teachers, school curriculum and student success. Several teachers in this study reported they were not invited to attend cooperative learning workshops to learn this technique, yet it has been found to be highly effective with minority students. (See Sharan and Sharan, Chapter 10.) If mainstream and bilingual teachers were to attend cooperative learning workshops together, they could share their views on the appropriateness of this strategy, and share the outcomes of the learning activities as well. "Instead of each one of us doing our thing, we could share ideas!" remarked one third grade mainstream teacher. "Everyone gains, including the students!"

d) **Working together to increase quality parent involvement** can provide a significant focus for communicating, with opportunity for strengthening student academic performance, and community support for the school. Bilingual and ESL faculty have cultural knowledge, skills and community networks that can support outreach and development of parent programs. Sharing this expertise could benefit everyone.

e) **Facilitating critical reflection** has the potential of enhancing teacher relationships. Staff development strategies that couple teaching experiences with reflection must be treated as an ongoing, integrated strategy to promote new social connections and professional involvement. The staff arranges to have a facilitator to enable them to examine beliefs, practices and norms of teaching; and to question what they take for granted, spotlighting the inherent conflicts among personal values and professional purpose in the school culture. As teachers look at issues and problems from many perspectives—i.e. the sense of isolation experienced by the bilingual teachers—they come to see how relevant each member of the staff is to effective teaching. (See Mezirow and Associates, 1990.)

f) **Restructuring to enable positive working relationships** will help promote job satisfaction, effective professional development and school improvement. To foster collegial relationships, initiatives should focus on encouraging awareness of the options of isolation, exclusion and collaboration. Their impact should be debated and discussed by teachers and administrators *as it affects all staff—regular, bilingual, ESL, and special education specialists—teacher productivity, and the work environment*. Planning strategies aimed at grouping for project development, mentoring, coaching, peer supervision, and working collaboratively are techniques to strengthen and stimulate working relationships and improve the quality of instruction for all students. When teachers are sufficiently motivated to change, and choose to develop new ways of working together, there are endless possibilities for improving the professional worklives of all teachers.

## Conclusion

The discredited perspectives of bilingual and ESL teachers point to ways in which they are silenced, their voices ignored in their teaching cultures. Difference as a positive strategy focuses on changing mainstream practices and ideas through attentiveness to *relationships*. In stressing relationships, teachers must be encouraged to begin listening to a "different voice," to use Carol Gilligan's imagery. There is little more important today than the creation within education of cultures of collaboration and change, where schooling is an opportunity for listening and learning from each other, where *relationships* are nurtured—not only relationships among adults, but between adults and children.

Geertz (1988), reflecting on the role of ethnographic texts in the future, suggested that it will involve "enabling conversations across societal lines—of ethnicity, religion, class, gender, language, race..." He concluded, the next necessary thing is "to enlarge the possibility of intelligible discourse between people quite different from one another in interest, outlook, wealth, and power, and yet contained in a world where, tumbled as they are into endless connection, it is increasingly difficult to get out of each other's way." (p. 147)

## REFERENCES

Barthes, Roland (1957, 1972). *Mythologies*. NY: Hill & Wang.

Erickson, F. (1987a). Transformation and school success. In *Anthropology and Education Quarterly, 18*, 335-356.

Erickson, F. (1987b). Conceptions of school culture. In *Educational Administration Quarterly. 23*, 4, 11-24.

Feiman-Nemser, Sharon and Floden, Robert E. (1986). The cultures of teaching. In Merlin S. Wittrock (ed.) *Handbook of Research on Teaching*, 505-526. NY: Macmillan.

First, Joan M., (1988) *New Voices: Immigrant Students in the U.S. Public Schools.* Boston, MA: National Coalition of Advocates for Students.

Fullan, Michael (1982). *The Meaning of Educational Change.* NY: Teachers College Press.

Haney, Walter (1987). An estimation of immigration and immigrant student population. A paper prepared for the Immigrant Student Population Center. Boston, MA: Boston College.

Kellog, John B. (1988). Forces of change. In *Phi Delta Kappan.* (November): 199-204.

Lippitt, Gordon L., (1983). Can conflict resolution be win-win? *School Administrator, 40*, 3: 20-22.

Mezirow, Jack, and Associates. (1990). *Fostering critical reflection in adulthood.* San Francisco: Jossey-Bass.

Montero-Sieburth, M., & Perez, Marla (1987). Echar pa'lante, moving onward: The dilemmas and strategies of a bilingual teacher. In *Anthropology & Education Quarterly, 18*, 180-189.

Nichols, Patricia C. (1989). Storytelling in Carolina: Continuities and contrasts. In *Anthropology and Education Quarterly 20*, 3, 232.

Oakes, Jeannie. Classroom social relationships: Exploring the Bowles and Gintes hypothesis. In *Sociology of Education, 55* (October): 197-212.

Ost, David H. (1989). The culture of teaching: Stability and change. In *The Educational Forum, 53*, 2 Winter 163-181.

Richardson, Virginia. (1990). Significant and worthwhile change in teaching practice. In *Educational Researcher, V. 19*, No. 7, October.

Sarason, Seymour B., Davidson, K.S. and Blatt, Burton. (1962, reissued 1986). *The Preparation of Teachers: An Unstudied Problem in Education.* Cambridge, MA.: Brookline Books.

Sarason, Seymour B.(1972, 1982). *The Culture of the School.* Boston, MA: Addison Wesley.

Schon, Donald (1971). *Beyond the Stable State.* NY: Random.

Wyner, Nancy B. (1989). Educating linguistic minorities: Public education and the search for unity. In *Educational Horizons, 67*, No. 4, 172-176.

# Chapter 8
# Changing Faculty Beliefs About the Underprepared Student

*by Jacqueline Fidler Maloney, University of Lowell*

## INTRODUCTION

"You think we like seeing these failure rates, that's not why I came to teaching. I want to see my students do well, but I just don't know how to reach them anymore." *Senior faculty member at a meeting to study student failure rates in math and science.*

The culture of teaching in higher education has been confronted by drastic and continuous changes during the past two decades. A culture previously protected by elitist traditions is now faced with students who are characteristically underprepared and more diverse than generations previous (Boyer, 1987; Gamson, 1984). The complexity of today's world as a result of rapid changes in the economy, technology, and the growing interdependence of the world's nations all point to the need for an education that best equips students to learn on their own. Faculty are aware that existing curriculum and pedagogical practices no longer meet the needs of their students, yet they have been given little support to change them.

In this chapter I offer one participant's perspective of how an innovation was used to support changes in faculty beliefs about their students by enabling them to meet the changing needs of their students more effectively. The study focuses on the Freshman Year Program at the University of Lowell in Massachusetts. The purpose of this program was to enhance student performance through improved placement testing, orientation, advising and remediation, etc.

However, like other institutions, the University of Lowell found that its focus on student weaknesses was insufficient to meet the challenge. The University discovered there were several aspects of its culture that ran contrary to efforts to retain a broader base of students. In particular, the University discovered that the culture of teaching, characterized by the teaching practices and attitudes, had to change for "new" students to thrive. Without such change, efforts to retain students were doomed to failure.

I begin with an overview of the University of Lowell's history, goals; institutional leadership, faculty culture and students. The demographics and characteristics of an increasingly diverse student population are discussed as they impact the traditions of the institution. Finally, the change processes used to build the Freshman Year Program are described at length.

It will be argued that societal and demographic changes have adversely impacted the teaching culture and caused faculty to despair over their effectiveness as teachers. The University of Lowell's Freshman Year Program is proposed as a model that demonstrates how new programs can support faculty's efforts to become more effective in working with "new" student populations.

Innovative programs have to demonstrate a sensitivity to the faculty's dilemma and the critical importance of their role in improving student performance. Such programs should *support* the faculty's efforts to teach effectively and to cope with an increasingly diverse student body. In developing this program we learned that faculty can recover the intrinsic rewards of teaching if they are supported, acknowledged and valued for their efforts.

# BACKGROUND

## The University

The University of Lowell was founded in 1976 when Lowell Technological Institute and Lowell State College were merged as part of the reorganization of the Massachusetts public higher education system. Currently, there are approximately 9,000 undergraduates and 3,000 graduate students. It offers degrees in seven professional areas, but prides itself for its engineering program which has gained national prominence.

In the early phases of planning, the University followed Alexander Astin's reputational/resources model for developing universities (Astin, 1985). This model is built on the premise that higher education is driven by a hierarchical system related to institutional selectivity, a pedigree of degrees, amounts of resources, etc. Astin argues that institutions of higher learning compete with each other to build their reputations by building their resources. The more facilities, fields, labs or better SAT scores, the better the reputation of the school. The better the reputation of the school, the more resources you are granted. Institutions that wish to be respected in the academic community are forced to compete in this hierarchical and elitist system.

> Like most status hierarchies, our system comprises a few well-known elite institutions. This arrangement reveals a classic pyramid: Only a few institutions occupy the top levels, and the numbers increase as one moves downward. (Astin, p.5)

The University built its academic reputation by maintaining high admissions standards and enforcing a rigorous academic program that "screened out" unqualified freshmen. In fact, they had adopted the well-known engineering orientation lecture of "look to your right, look to your left, only one of you will be here in January." As a result, the University is currently a fairly competitive institution, claiming the highest average SAT scores of entering students in the state system.

Astin argues that the reputational model undermines efforts to promote equal opportunity by excluding certain students from the system. The

University of Lowell experienced this dilemma first hand. As a new University, it was imperative that the institution achieve a reputation of academic excellence. To accomplish this, extremely high academic standards have been invoked at the University to ensure accreditation in all of its professional programs and to build its graduate program. Yet, as a public institution, the University maintained a deep commitment to the community that surrounded it and adopted as its primary mission the "spearheading of the region's economic, social and cultural vitality" (University of Lowell, Strategic Plan, 1988). To accomplish this mission, the University had to overcome the long-standing paradox between equity and excellence in education.

*THE UNIVERSITY'S STUDENTS.* National demographics for the nineties point to a decline in the number of 18-24 year olds, the age group traditionally targeted for enrollment by higher education. This phenomenon, combined with compelling demands for a skilled workforce, has forced institutions to reconsider the reputational model and has led to an expansion in the "pipeline" to higher education as a result (Vetter, 1988). A privilege reserved for elite white male students until twenty years ago has become an aspiration to a vastly diverse population of nontraditional students including minority students, women in nontraditional fields, learning disabled students, and adult learners (Farber, 1987; Lee and Nishio, 1986).

From all accounts, these students are highly motivated to gain a college education. The percentage of students applying to some form of higher education has risen dramatically since the seventies. According to John Goodlad, higher education has replaced high school as the expected "universal level" of education for students, surpassing historical expectations for elementary and then secondary schooling (Goodlad, p.269).

Yet there is an alarming concern about the underpreparedness of entering college freshmen. Ernest Boyer (1987) recently concluded that "American undergraduate education cannot be strengthened unless and until the academic deficiencies of entering students are candidly confronted" (p. 77). Boyer and others point to this growing gap between the level of preparedness of incoming freshmen and the skills required to succeed in college as one of the most critical problems faced by institutions of higher learning.

The trends described reflect changes in the student population at the University of Lowell. Lowell Technological Institute served a virtually all-white male population and Lowell State College served primarily white females until fifteen years ago. In general, the University's students are hard-working and highly motivated; many pay their own tuition and/or support themselves. They are primarily first generation college students from working class backgrounds. They are very committed to their goals to earn professional degrees that will enhance their marketability as professionals. In two recent surveys, the majority of students reported they chose the University because of its academic reputation (as opposed to its reputation in athletics, student life, etc) and its reputation in the private sector. In this way, they could be characterized as serious students interested in achieving academically.

While they claim the highest average SAT's for entering freshman in Massachusetts' public system, they also suffer from the growing gap between high school preparation and expectations at the college level. "The students are less and less prepared each year," said one math instructor who reported a 30% failure rate of all students taking calculus. Though these "new" students bring richness in diversity, they also bring more complex needs for support services that will help them to achieve academically (Farber, 1987; Vandement, 1986).

The following conversation captures this challenge brought about by the changes described above. Lee Shulman was recalling a conversation with a colleague about a professor's student evaluations:

> They were bimodal—about half of the class always thought that he was extraordinarily good, and a good half of the class thought that he was absolutely horrible—"goes too fast, doesn't explain what he's saying, isn't well organized," etc.

> One of my colleagues on the committee, who was from the natural sciences and mathematics side said, "Now that's what I call a good teaching record." And I said, "What do you mean? He's leaving half these kids in the dust." He said , "Yeah, but those are probably the kinds of kids who shouldn't be studying physics anyway. Wrong kind of students. They shouldn't be here." (Shulman, 1989, p.8)

In short, should we choose and retain only the best students (reputational model) or should we foster the development of all students? More important, if we choose the latter, how do we enable faculty to reach these students?

*THE FACULTY CULTURE.* The faculty at the University are, for the most part, a highly credentialed, hard-working and academically conservative group of educators; like many faculty in higher education, they have grown discouraged by a general decline in the faculty condition (Schuster, 1986). "Working conditions for faculty members in the U.S. are deteriorating steadily; ...reductions in secretarial support, declining budgets for libraries and research instrumentation, poorly prepared students, ... overcrowded offices... and a host of well-intentioned (but sometime insensitively conducted) programs" have all contributed to a general decline in faculty morale (Schuster, 1986, p.22). Feiman-Nemser and R. Floden developed a conceptual framework for studying teaching cultures that will provide a backdrop in describing the teaching culture at the University (Feiman-Nemser and Floden, 1986). The elements of their framework include norms of interaction; concepts of rewards of a teaching career; and teacher's knowledge. This writer humbly submits the following description to the faculty culture at the University of Lowell realizing that is full of generalizations that do not reflect the beliefs of all of the University faculty.

## Norms for Interaction:

Many of the faculty were employed by the University prior to the merger. As such, they enjoyed the benefits of a small college atmosphere where colleagues worked closely together in professional and instructional activities, and where students were a central focus of their work. However, the fast-paced growth of the University, combined with the general decline of the conditions as described above, has diminished the opportunities faculty have to share their work with each other or to form bonds with their students. Forums that support interaction among the faculty or with their students are glaringly absent from this campus. In a report by the Faculty Council to Study Reorganization, the faculty expressed deep dissatisfaction regarding the level of activities and structures that supported faculty/faculty interaction, faculty/student interaction and student/student interaction (Faculty Council to Study Reorganization, 1988). In their final report they called for actions that would facilitate a sense of community:

> "...fragmentation draws lines between groups, it prevents the development of that sense of community necessary to ensure a spirit of lively academic inquiry for its faculty, students, and wider community. Such a sense of community is an essential ingredient to a vital, healthy, and competitive university" (Council to Study Reorganization, pp. 10-11).

## Concepts of rewards of a teaching career

Feiman-Nemser and Floden classify the occupational rewards for a teaching career in two categories: *extrinsic rewards* are those defined by salary, short working hours, elevated status, and significant power; *intrinsic rewards* are those related to satisfaction and pride in working with students.

The teaching faculty at Lowell have average salaries that are competitive and they enjoy abbreviated teaching schedules in order to accommodate demands for publications. They maintain higher prestige both internally and externally. The students generally admire the faculty as indicated by their responses on the surveys mentioned above. These factors would seem to indicate that the extrinsic rewards are present at the University.

Yet, like faculty across the country, the faculty complain that these extrinsic rewards are increasingly tied to demands for research and publication resulting in a lack of extrinsic incentives for instructional activities (Boyer, 1987; Student Life Committee Report, 1988). They describe their frustrations over these conflicting demands for their time. "If you want faculty to be more involved in teaching, then you have to prove to us that it is valued by the administration," said one senior faculty member (Student Life Committee Report, 1988).

How does one define *valued*? McKeachie asserts that an overemphasis on extrinsic rewards has had an undesirable effect on the motivation of higher education faculty (McKeachie, 1982). He maintains that faculty who entered teaching "to enjoy stimulation from colleagues and students and the satisfactions of being appreciated and respected by others" are denied such rewards in lieu of extrinsic incentives. This insight proved to be very true of the faculty at Lowell. The paucity of faculty interactions and their inability to serve their students effectively made the intrinsic rewards of teaching more difficult to realize. As McKeachie suggests, they pointed to the lack of extrinsic rewards as the cause of their diminished motivation to reach out to their students, when intrinsic rewards were just as sorely needed.

## Teacher Knowledge

The final dimension of teaching cultures proposed by Feiman-Nemser and Floden is the professional knowledge and expertise held by teachers. The faculty at Lowell are highly credentialed and therefore well respected for their knowledge in their disciplines. They publish papers and attend conferences frequently and are acknowledged for their expertise. They are proud of the rigorous academic standards held by the institution and consider it their responsibility to uphold the reputation of the degrees conferred by the school.

However, their interaction with the equity/excellence paradox has undermined their sense of efficacy as teachers, increasing discontent over their inability to motivate and teach the changing student population. Their sense of inadequacy changed to attitudes of bitterness against the students. According to Zelda Gamson, "even the most idealistic college teachers find themselves denigrating students" (Gamson, p.5). The faculty often lamented the underpreparedness and "laziness" of today's students. Many had been accustomed to teaching only "the better students" and were appalled by any notion to retain unworthy students. In some cases, their attitudes toward students were rationalized by comments like, "these students don't care about education, they don't put any time into their studies, and they won't go for extra help if you offer it."

One can easily see how scholars faced with underprepared students, increased demands for research, overcrowded classrooms and a lack of extrinsic or intrinsic rewards for teaching might feel resentful of programs to help students. The faculty openly resisted the Freshman Program during the first year. They viewed it as a waste of valuable resources that could have been put to better use by alleviating the poor teaching conditions. They wanted proof their investment in such a program would make a difference. Comments such as, "why should we mollycoddle these students," or "we have extra help offered in our faculty offices, they never come, why should we waste money on them, if they are not willing to get the help they need on their own."

The faculty believed it was their responsibility to weed out "the wrong" students from the right ones; they were committed to holding high standards and were fearful of any movements that might undermine them. They believed that the students flunking out deserved to flunk out because they either did not work hard enough or because they would not access extra help as needed. Until they had such proof, they were reluctant to invest their time or the institution's limited resources in these students. They were also overwhelmed by conflicting demands for their time and resented added responsibilities. especially in areas that would not be rewarded with tenure and promotion.

The next section describes how these obstacles were overcome by effecting changes in the teaching culture regarding the norms of interactions, faculty attitudes toward students, faculty rewards, and faculty expertise.

# CHANGING FACULTY ATTITUDES

> To the degree that we can help faculty members develop additional skills in teaching so that they have a repertoire of techniques and methods to draw upon, we are likely to increase the faculty members' satisfaction in teaching.

## A time of change

The President established a faculty commission to study the freshman year experience in 1987 in response to the growing concern about the institution's ability to respond to the needs of underprepared students. The Commission recommended that a comprehensive freshman program be established that provided academic support services. The President accepted the Committee's recommendations and created a Freshman Program which included limited computer and tutoring services. I was hired as Director for the Program because I had already established a reputation within the University as a program development specialist in working with disadvantaged high school students. I had also taught at the college level. Three existing staff positions were assigned to the program with a computer lab. Beyond this, there was little guidance as to the expectations for the program.

The literature was rich with ideas on how best to serve freshmen students and increase retention rates, but funding was so limited and the problems so overwhelming that the program had to find a way to help the most students with the least amount of money. Additional support would be forthcoming only if the program was proven successful to the faculty. Many faculty were antagonistic to the program. Unfortunately, many student service programs choose to ignore the antagonism that faculty feel toward them and reap adversarial relationships as a result.

> Defensiveness and/or exaggerated emphasis on the importance of one's own turf is counterproductive and frequently leads to reciprocal hostility... Sometimes, also, student affairs service providers may not be sensitive to the unique demands placed on faculty as they work within their departments and as they respond to the needs of their particular disciplines (O'Brien, 1989, p.285).

While it may seem expeditious in the short run to avoid faculty antagonism, these feelings often make such programs ineffective.

Faculty concerns were consistently acknowledged in developing the program, which was offered as an extension and support to their teaching.

Meetings were held in departmental and faculty offices to provide the basis for designing the Freshman Program. These meetings proved very painful to the staff because of the faculty's expressed antipathy.

## Freshman Centers

After several months of meeting with the faculty, defining and redefining the needs of students and faculty, the following mission statement was developed:

> The mission of the Freshman Year Program (FYP) is to enhance the freshman experience by facilitating a successful transition from high school to college. The center provides a climate of collegiality and a sense of community which fosters creative and independent thinking. Innovative educational strategies and technologies are incorporated to complement these efforts. By promoting communication and collaboration among students, faculty and staff, the FYP strives to inspire educational excellence and to insure the success of freshmen at U-Lowell.

As can be seen, this statement goes beyond the scope of a prototypical remedial learning center. The intent of the mission statement was to create a program that would change the learning environment at the University of Lowell by improving *both* faculty and student performance. To meet these goals, a comprehensive Freshman Year Program was designed that included: Freshman Centers which featured academic support services such as tutoring, computer labs, advising and study skills workshops; a freshman seminar course; and a Project Restart for students who fail their first semester. This discussion focuses on how faculty support was built for the Freshman Centers.

The Freshman Centers were designed to serve as the hub of the activity related to the program. Students and faculty could drop by the Centers and have easy access to services. Each Center featured an Educational Computing Program, a Tutoring Program and Advising Services. The first agenda was to get students and faculty utilizing the services. If the students did not come, the faculty would point to their lack of attendance as proof of their laziness. To overcome this obstacle, an aggressive outreach campaign was used to draw in faculty and students.

From the outset, the Centers focused on the development of publications for both faculty and students that featured timely information about University events and new programs. The Faculty Newsletter featured faculty innovations, progress reports on student usage and ideas for how the Centers could be used to improve student performance. Faculty who worked in collaboration with the Center were continuously and publicly acknowledged through the newsletter seeking to restore intrinsic rewards of teaching. The faculty were proud when their ideas were featured in the Newsletter and other faculty were motivated to try their ideas or to suggest new ones.

## Educational Computing

The goal of the Educational Computing Program was to provide computer expertise supportive of student and faculty efforts by providing training in state of the art technology. The faculty were particularly resistant to this area as many were not familiar with the potential utilization of computers in classroom instruction. For example, in a brief meeting with the English Department, faculty made many disparaging remarks about the utilization of word processing. While the science faculty had far more exposure to computer applications in the research, they had not considered its potential applications for instructional purposes. Many had never used computers at all.

To win their support, workshops were conducted for faculty on word processing, tutorial software, etc., and in ongoing training and technical assistance to faculty interested in utilizing computers. These workshops were successful because they enabled the faculty to overcome their fears about their future competence by upgrading their skills (Kantor, p. 194). It also provided the kind of technical support that Fullan says is so important in implementing change (Fullan, p.66-67).

The Center staff began to work in concert with the faculty to provide software support for a wide gamut of courses. Usages of computers at the Centers rose dramatically. Center hours had to be increased to evenings and weekends due to student demand. When the faculty witnessed the student response to these extended hours, their attitudes about students began to change. Students could be seen working in the Center throughout the day, evening and weekends, working on course projects. Faculty who required work done on computers began to boast about the improved quality of student reports. The faculty no longer pointed to student laziness as the problem. They began to realize that if support was offered in a meaningful way, the students would utilize it and show benefits. With faculty support, student usage has risen from approximately 7,000 the first year to nearly 23,000 usages presently. It is estimated that the Freshman Year Program teaches at least 3/4 of the freshman class to use personal computers each year.

## The Tutoring Program

The Freshman Center's Tutoring Program began by offering limited support only in high risk freshman courses such as physics, chemistry, calculus and college writing. Due to funding limitations, freshmen who needed tutoring services were forced to work in large groups of fifteen to thirty students on a drop-in basis without any diagnostic educational plan or consideration of their individual needs. The lack of initial funding for this program was symbolic of the institutional resistance. Most other institutions offer numerous forms of tutoring services on a variety of levels. Yet the University provided only a handful of tutors. Many freshmen were not served at all, due to the limited number of courses supported by the Freshman Center. The impact of these limitations was articulated by the students who utilized the

Center. In an evaluation of the Center's services, students expressed their frustrations with these limitations and asked for smaller study groups, more supported subjects and additional tutors.

The faculty were most resistant to this service because it is closest to their instructional activity. The faculty feel that instruction is their territory and tutoring activities necessarily invade that territory. I believe that some faculty were threatened by the possibility that others in positions of power would find out what was going in their classrooms and feared the related accountability. One faculty member said at a meeting about the use of tutors, "what if the tutoring sessions are better than the professors' classes, the students will stop coming to class and going to the student tutors instead, how do you answer that?" This professor happened to be a very committed teacher, his question helped him to get at his real underlying fear, was he still a good teacher? He knew that the solution was not in blocking a tutoring program, but in finding ways to help his students to learn more effectively. Fortunately, this same faculty member became one of the strongest advocates of the program.

To gain faculty support, we gave almost total control of the hiring and training of tutors to the faculty and offered the program as a service to them. The Coordinator of Tutoring met regularly with the faculty. Each time a faculty member would come forward with an idea, suggestion or complaint, the Program responded by altering the design to make it more responsive to faculty as well as student needs. For example, one faculty member argued that a major problem for students was their reading ability and general study skills. He suggested a "physics read aloud" session. A tutor would read a chapter aloud with students and discuss and answer questions. The program staff felt strongly that this would be unpopular with students. The first session attracted over 20 students and grew in popularity quickly. Due to popular demand, tutors in other subjects also conducted read aloud sessions within one month.

The faculty have been instrumental in building this program in a number of ways. They became involved in referring students, generating tutoring techniques, assisting in training tutors, and developing appropriate instructional materials. It was the faculty who demanded expanded services from the president, which gave the president permission to fully fund the tutoring services. These have been quadrupled in the past year. This kind of support from the faculty is virtually unheard of in higher education.

## SUMMARY

Within three years' time, the Program has grown into a comprehensive academic support program to all undergraduates and has gained national attention for its innovative design and successful work. The Massachusetts Board of Regents, the governing board of public universities and colleges in the state, chose the University to host an annual conference on Freshman Programs as part of the state's efforts to respond to the needs of its freshmen.

The Program's success is attributed to the strength of its relationship to the faculty. Our success provides support for Fullan's five assumptions for meaningful change to occur: change takes time and is not a linear process; initial stages always involve anxiety; staff need ongoing technical assistance and psychological support; change involves learning new skills; and fundamental change occurs when cognitive understanding is reached. The following summary relates how adherence to these assumptions enabled this innovation to facilitate change in the teaching culture of the University of Lowell.

First, Fullan suggests that most people vastly underestimate the amount of time needed to implement a change (Fullan, p.68). This faulty assumption leads many innovations to failure. The Freshman Year Program took at least three years to gain the acceptance and support of the faculty at the University. While this support has grown, it is still tentative and many faculty remain skeptical. The faculty needed time to adjust their attitudes toward their students and the Program needed time to examine its strengths and weaknesses in order to improve itself. This structure provides a model for self-renewal that was not a part of this institution's teaching culture previously.

Many service programs ignore Fullan's second assumption regarding anxiety or fear of change (Fullan, p.69). This anxiety is best captured by Kantor's description of emotional reactions to change such as loss of face, excessive uncertainty, fear of more work, and fear of future competence. As a result, many programs are sabotaged by those affected by the change (Kantor, 1983). The early outreach to the faculty and the manner in which this outreach was presented served to diminish faculty fears about this change. By listening to faculty concerns, we were able to shape the program as a service to them as well as their students. In this way, the program served the need of the teaching culture to enhance their knowledge base with new teaching strategies for reaching their students.

The program provides extensive technical support to the faculty and rewards those faculty who extend themselves on behalf of their students. This support has enabled the faculty to develop the new skills that respond to the changing characteristics of their students. Faculty referrals to the program have risen nearly 60% since the first year of the program. While this has been an important first step in making Lowell a more student-centered institution, the program has not succeeded in enabling faculty to examine or improve instructional activities inside the classroom. However, we continue to raise concerns about instructional strategies through the extensive feedback we are able to generate from students. New norms for interaction were also established as the Centers became a forum where faculty could meet and discuss ideas, strategies and innovations informally and formally. It is not uncommon to see faculty sitting beside a student in a computer workshop on graphics or spreadsheets, an anomaly just two years ago.

Finally, Fullan suggests that meaningful change occurs when cognitive understanding is reached. This third year of the program has brought evidence that faculty understand the problems faced by their students on a much deeper level and are now prepared to address them. Faculty frequently call upon the program staff for assistance in implementing new ideas they believe will improve student performance. For example, a math professor suggested we put all of the program's tutoring schedules, workshop announcements, etc. on overheads to enable the faculty who lecture to post this information before class. This system has saved faculty time and effort in making referrals. Other faculty are beginning to develop tutorial software for their courses that enable students to learn the course material more effectively. These faculty have indeed reached a new level of understanding about the needs of their students. Their belief in themselves as teachers is being restored.

An extensive system of feedback/evaluation aided in the development of the Program. (see Fullan, 1982, p.69). Each program component has its own evaluation tool which facilitates student feedback about the quality of services provided by the program. This feedback is shared with the University community openly so that changes and improvements can be considered by the entire community. In this way, the program provides a model for maintaining continuous growth.

Finally, this writer has learned a great deal from this experience. As an experienced change agent, I felt confident of my abilities to impact on the culture of this institution. However, I have been reminded that being a change agent, like being a parent, is a humbling experience. Sarason suggests:

> I confess that I find it somewhat amusing to observe how much thought is given to developing vehicles for changing target groups and how little thought is given to vehicles that protect the agent of change from not changing in his understanding of and approach to that particular instance of change. (Sarason, 1971, p. 217)

I am hopeful that Sarason would be pleased to know that his reflections have caused this change agent to take a much deeper look at her interaction with the change process and to be far more sensitized to the complexities and difficulties that are a part of any meaningful educational change.

The Freshman Year Program has undergone many changes and continues to evolve as an integral component of learning at the University. The Program's growth and success have become symbolic of a change in the teaching culture of the University of Lowell that is increasingly supportive of student development at all levels and that has the capacity for self-renewal and growth. The Freshman Year Program recently expanded its mission to provide academic support services to all undergraduates and is now called the Centers for Learning and Academic Support Services. This expansion is reflective of the kind of support the Program has received from the faculty and the administration, and is symbolic of a change in the ethos of the institution which, previous to this innovation, had not invested any of its resources in such services.

# REFERENCES

Astin, A.W. (1975). *Four critical years*. Jossey-Bass, Inc.

Baldridge, J. V., & Deal, T. (1983). *Dynamics of organizational change in education.* McCutchan.

Boyer, E. (1987). *College: The undergraduate experience in America.* NY: Harper and Row.

Cohen, M., & March, J. (1986). *Leadership and ambiguity.* MA: Harvard Business School.

Cuban, L. (1987). Cultures of teaching: A puzzle. *Educational Administration Quarterly, 23* (4), 25-35.

Faculty Council's Study for Reorganization. Final Report, University of Lowell, 1988

Farber, S.L. (1987). The diversity of student needs in higher education. Presented at the Annual Meeting of the California Assoc. for Counseling and Development, ED 283 067.

Feiman-Nemser, S., & Floden, R. (1986). The cultures of teaching. In M. Wittrock (Ed.), *The handbook of research on teaching* (pp. 505-526). NY: Macmillan Publishing Company.

Forrest, A. (1985). Creating conditions for student and institutional success. In N. & S. Levitz (Eds.), *Increasing student retention.* CA: Jossey-Bass.

Fullan, M. (1982). *The meaning of educational change.* NY: Teachers College Press.

Gamson, Z. (1984). *Liberating education.* CA: Jossey-Bass.

Goodlad, J. (1985). The great American schooling experiment. *Phi Delta Kappan, 67* (1-10), 266-271.

Hodgkinson, H. (1986). Reform? Higher education? Don't be absurd! *Phi Delta Kappan 68* (4), 271-275.

Hodgkinson, H. (1975). Courage to change: Facing our demographic destiny. *Currents*, July, 9-12.

Joyce, B., & Showers, B. (1988). *Student achievement through staff development.* NY: Longman.

Kantor, R. (1983). *Managing the human side of change.* Cambridge, MA: Goodmeasures Inc.

Lee, R.A., & Nishio, A. T. (1986). The implications of changing demographics on serving a changing student population (Summary). *Academic Affairs Resource Center.*

McKeachie, W. J. (1982). The rewards of teaching. In J. L. Bess (Ed.), *Motivating professors to teach effectively* (pp. 7-14). Washington, DC: Jossey-Bass, Inc.

O'Brien, C. (1989). Student affairs and academic affairs: Partners in higher education. *NASPA Journal, 26* (4), 284-287.

Ost, D. (1989). The culture of teaching: Stability and change. *The Educational Forum, 53*, (2) 163-178.

Rosenholtz, S. J. (1987). Education reform strategies: Will they increase teacher commitment? *American Journal of Education*, 95 (4) 534-536.

Saphier, J., & King, M. (1985). Good seeds grow in strong cultures. *Educational Leadership*, March, 67-73.

Sarason, S. (1982). *The culture of school and the problem of change* (2nd ed.). Boston, MA: Allyn and Bacon.

Schuster, Jack (1985). Faculty vitality: Observations from the field. In R. Baldwin (Ed.) *Incentives for Faculty Vitality* (21-33). CA: Jossey Bass.

Selznick, P. (1957). *Leadership in administration*. Los Angeles, CA: University of California Press.

Shulman, Lee (1989). *Toward a pedagogy of substance*. American Association for Gigher Education, *41* (10). (8-13)

Vandement, W. (1986). The ten-year study to improve college student retention (Summary). *Academic Affairs Resource Center*.

Vetter, B. (1988). Demographics of the engineering student pipeline. *Engineering Education*, April, 735-740.

Weick, K. (1978) Educational organizations as loosely coupled systems. *Administrative Science Quarterly, 23*, 541-552.

# Chapter 9
# School Culture in Multicultural Settings

*by Leonard C. Beckum, Duke University*
*with Arlene Zimney, City College, New York*

## INTRODUCTION

A brief review of studies examining the academic performance of cultural and linguistic minorities in urban public schools and an analysis of current educational activities responsive to the academic needs of these students points to a disastrous state of affairs in American education. Every indicator of educational success: achievement scores, dropout rates, attendance patterns, and post-secondary education completions confirms that large numbers of children, and particularly minority children, are not being served appropriately by our schools.

Providing educational programs to meet the needs of students whose cultural orientation is different from the mainstream, who may speak a native language other than English, who have a family income classified at the poverty level, who are frequently from single parent homes and who may be homeless, has proven to be an overwhelming challenge for the educational system. It is a challenge that cannot be met if our schools continue to do business as usual. Schools need to create a "new deal" for these students which realistically addresses the schooling process from both academic and social-cultural perspectives.

Conflict between the adherents of traditional and nontraditional educational philosophies is not new to education. Competing views of the schooling process, its purposes and its priorities, become more important as the number of poor, multiethnic and multilingual students increases in our schools.

Much research has focused on trying to isolate the factors contributing to the low academic achievement of large numbers of minority and working class students. Some researchers have suggested there is an inherent biological, intellectual and moral inferiority that influences the academic performance of these students. This hypothesis has been widely challenged. Alternatively, different, and sometimes, poor socialization, environmental and cultural experiences have been suggested by other researchers to explain these students' lack of achievement. A third point of view, of primary interest to us, relates classroom failure to the inability to develop a classroom culture which successfully integrates the individual cultures of students and teachers.

The primary purpose of this chapter is to review some current thinking on cultural issues and to discuss ways in which these theories could influence the reconceptualization of teaching and learning. Two major needs emerge central to us:

1. to recognize the impact of diverse ethnic and linguistic cultures on the design and implementation of a more effective schooling process; and

2. to refocus teacher training programs to incorporate the understandings and culturally appropriate classroom strategies for students in their classrooms.

## School and Classroom Culture:
## Responses to Multicultural Student Bodies

In recent years, many researchers and writers have added substantially to our understanding of the roles played by language, cultural values, and contextual experiences in students' adjustment to the culture of the school and the classroom (Truebe, 1988; Cole and Scribner, 1974; Ginsburg, 1986; Cummins, 1984; Erickson, 1986, 1987; Ogbu, 1982, 1985). The work of these researchers has provided a breakthrough in our understanding of how these characteristics influence the learning process and has led to a more objective assessment of the extent to which students' culture or language can be used to enhance the teaching and learning process. Their studies have also offered plausible explanations for why student failure has increased in contexts where effective integration of school, teacher and student cultures does not take place. These latter concerns have become particularly significant as schools with large numbers of failing or at-risk students search for solutions to improve the academic performance and achievement of these student groups.

Culture is most frequently defined as a composite of valued traditions, standards of judgment, knowledge and perceptions evident in behaviors and artifacts, transmitted and learned over generations. Cultures are not static. They evolve historically, and are continuously modified and augmented to give meaning to life and to help their members cope with problems encountered in their changing environments. Individuals are influenced by national and family cultures and individual experiences. Like the Russian babushka dolls, where each doll may be opened to reveal ever smaller units, characteristics of individual cultural experiences fit, one into the other. Most persons tend to believe that their personal experiences and value systems constitute the norm. When teachers enter the classroom, they do so with cultural orientations and expectations which reflect their own or adopted, usually, mainstream culture, and do not recognize or understand the cultural values and expectations held by their minority students. While faith in one's own value system is equally true for teachers and students, the teacher's value system will dominate the content of the curriculum and the organization of the students' learning experiences. School and classroom culture is a domain of competing interests through which dominant and dominated groups make sense of their life circumstances and conditions.

Vygotsky (1962,1978) and others (Scribner and Cole, 1981; Wertsch, 1985; Moll & Diaz, 1987; and Truebe, 1988) have explained cognition or cognitive development as culturally or socially based, challenging the notion that intelligence is static, and that the ability to learn is inborn, quantifiable and determined by a narrow set of factors which are measured by traditional IQ tests. The hypothesis of these researchers is that the activities and learning processes experienced and internalized by students in school, home and community contribute to the intellectual development of the evolving individual. These determine how the individual learns to think and master reflective operations. Understanding these processes is crucial to developing teaching and learning activities which support maximum individual growth. Approaches that attempt to incorporate an understanding and appreciation of these students' cultures and learning styles should be based on familiar cultural references. The ability of the teacher to use alternative methods for organizing and relating curriculum to the child's learning patterns is of primary importance.

Among the basic tenets of effective instructional decision-making is that teachers develop pedagogy based on their students' cultural and linguistic backgrounds and experiences. But suggesting that cultural differences should lead to different ways of perceiving and organizing learning experiences does not mean that expectations, standards and achievement outcomes should vary based upon cultural differences, nor should these cultural differences be used to support any notion of cultural inferiority.

## Classroom Culture

Since classrooms and schools serve heterogeneous populations, reflecting social class, racial, and linguistic differences, it is necessary to understand how these characteristics come together to form a "classroom culture," if we are to understand the full impact of the school. The schooling process, however, cannot be viewed in isolation from the community or society of which it is a part. According to some researchers, the norms, ideals, values or even prejudices of the community or society influence and, in some cases, dictate school and classroom practices and activities (Bernstein, 1961, 1972; Apple, 1979; Rist, 1970). Furthermore, these researchers also suggest that because the school is influenced by the greater society, poor, ethnic, racial, and language minority groups often undergo educational experiences which serve to maintain the dominant culture, and result in their further marginalization, socially and economically. In other words, the manner in which the school's messages are organized and transmitted through teaching methods and teacher-pupil relationships constitutes a cultural code. The values transmitted through this code act as a mechanism designed to maintain the dominant culture's influence and to make it difficult, if not impossible, for diverse cultures to assert their influence.

Since culture influences standards of perceiving, believing and evaluating, it plays an important role as teachers select and structure experiences in their classrooms. Interactions between the teacher and students are dictated by the cultural orientations each brings with them into the classroom. Terminologies such as "classroom social climate" or "classroom ethos" have long been used to describe the normative conditions, such as role relationships and expectations which characterize "classroom culture" (Sprinthall and Sprinthall 1977). In fact, Labelle (1972) considered all teaching and learning both inside and outside the classroom to be related to one or more cultural traditions, suggesting that the activities were handed down based on the teacher's internal and external experiences and orientations. Thus, the ways in which classrooms or schools are organized and structured, the patterns of discourse, the subtle distinction between gender categories, classroom control mechanisms, the systems of reward and punishment, and the topics chosen for classroom study are examples of culturally loaded activities.

The teacher plays an important role as an "intercultural broker" (Erickson, 1986). In this role teachers are in a position to bridge or fail to bridge the cultural gaps which may exist in the classroom. This is not an easy role for teachers who come into the classroom having grown up in or adopted the values of the dominant society. These teachers most likely have completed their formal academic training in an educational institution that transmits knowledge in keeping with the dominant cultural perspective. When they arrive at the schoolhouse, they find similar or corresponding cultural conditions in place. The teacher proceeds to prepare for instruction expecting and behaving as if all of the students entering the classroom share the same cultural orientation as is held by the teacher and the school. When problems arise and it becomes apparent that the expectations of the school and the teacher are clashing with those of the students, the teacher is at a loss to explain why and immediately casts the blame on the students' lack of academic potential.

One such example occurred when the student body in a New York City high school, which had been predominantly white, upper middle class, rapidly became a multicultural student body of varying socioeconomic backgrounds. The faculty, many of whom had been there for 10 years or more, perceived themselves as successful classroom teachers. One social studies teacher, who prided herself on her ability to link content with real life experience, came into the principal's office quite upset about her students' apparent lack of understanding. When questioned about her visible distress, she explained that she had attempted to teach an economics lesson about consumerism using advertisements from the New York Times. She used two department stores, Alexander's and Saks Fifth Avenue, to illustrate her point, examples that had worked well in previous years. Now, none of her students understood what Saks Fifth Avenue was or how it represented consumerism. They had never or seldom frequented these stores. How was she to teach such a group? It did not occur to the teacher to reexamine her approaches to teaching or to consider her students as a resource upon whom she had to draw if learning were to take place.

The students' life experiences which shape their cultural orientation are often ignored or discredited and the perspectives of the teacher, representing the dominant culture, are imposed. Given this scenario, some students may drop out of school, others fail a course, and still others continue with their education, but often with a damaged sense of personal worth and self determination.

A classroom culture can be viewed as having two main dimensions: an external dimension that refers to the classroom practices that directly reflect the demands of the dominant culture (community, school as an institution, family), and an internal dimension (student, teacher) that emerges from the dynamic interaction of student and teacher when they come together in the classroom. The school is called upon to integrate these differing realities. Teachers must develop a frame of reference that utilizes the differences to enhance the academic success of all students. By becoming aware of student culture and concentrating on interactive educational experiences that unify the classroom, teachers can significantly improve the opportunity for positive student development, thereby enhancing the entire schooling process. The local classroom is a cultural amalgam composed of diverse cultural elements and thus can be very different from the mainstream society.

The primary paradigm used to study classroom interactions has been process-product. This outcome-oriented methodology, which relies upon standardized tests, does not sufficiently account for the outcomes since it does not incorporate extenuating conditions such as social and economic factors, language or cultural influences.

More recently, a holistic position has been used which reflects the integration of the constructivist and developmental perspectives (Sivan, 1986). These assume that classroom tasks, which are the enactment of the curriculum, involve an inseparable relationship among the cultural, social and cognitive dimensions. As Vygotsky (1978) points out, thinking is not simply an internal action, but is the "transaction between the individual and his environment: people, objects, learned values, signal systems and communication systems." The schooling environment and the instructional processes are culturally fashioned activities reflecting the cultural orientation of the school and the teacher. If the classroom instructional activities are to reflect more than the view of the dominant culture, it is important for the teacher to incorporate the thinking about and the influence of the students' own cultural experiences. These experiences are significant because they operate in a dialectical manner to provide the context which helps to shape the classroom culture, and promotes or impedes students' intellectual and social development.

The teacher has the responsibility of designing the task environment and encouraging student engagement in the classroom setting. The task of creating meaningful instructional experiences is to use all available resources, including social, environmental and cultural, as well as verbal, emotional and sensorimotor capacities, to help children construct coherent systems of meaning about the activity or subject matter (Green, 1987). If educators are to create classroom environments which focus on nurturing children's capacity to learn how to learn, they must understand and be committed to integrating students' various experiences, skills, cognitive approaches and motivational orientations into the daily routines of the classroom.

## How Successful Teachers of These Children View Their Success

Beckum, Otheguy, Garcia, Zimny, Perry, & Rollett (1988) sought information on the personal, professional, and intellectual characteristics of successful teachers of minority children. Although much has been written on the subject of teaching effectiveness in general, few studies have concentrated on the characteristics of good teachers whose students come mostly from racial or linguistic minority groups. Knowing what makes an experienced teacher of minority children successful may point to the directions teacher training programs should go to serve populations where such children predominate.

While the focus is on environments for minority students, the project was carried out in three different countries, drawing material from minority educational settings in Austria and England as well as in the United States. In this manner, findings regarding traits of successful teachers of Black and Latino children in New York can be supplemented by investigations into the characteristics of successful teachers of Afro-Caribbean, Asian, Pakistani, Turkish and Yugoslavian children in London and Vienna. It was our hope that by learning something about effective teachers of children who are in a racial or linguistic minority, but who come from different backgrounds and live in different societies, we would be able to arrive at a broader set of conclusions.

Some of these expectations appear to have been met. One of the interesting results is the considerable similarity in the findings that turned up in the different research sites. While there are important differences of emphasis, it is apparent there are striking parallels between the kinds of traits that are considered relevant for success by teachers of minority children in all three cities.

The institutions that took part in this project were the Universitat Wien in Austria, the London South Bank Polytechnic in England, and the City College of New York in the United States.

THE SCHOOLS. In all three cities, we looked for schools deemed to be doing a good job of educating minority children, seeking the roots of success. This goal is best met by looking for competent teachers who are part of a broader pattern of effectiveness rather than exceptions to a generally negative rule. The areas were located by the investigators familiar with the demographic characteristics of each city. Within the chosen areas of each city, participating schools were selected. In London, schools were picked by inspectors employed by the Education Authorities (an education authority in England is roughly equivalent to a school district in the United States; an inspector is an educational advisor working at the Authority level). In New York and Vienna the schools, like the general areas, were picked by the researchers.

THE TEACHERS. Once the schools were chosen, the specific teachers were selected by the school administrators. In all three sites, primary grade teachers (i.e., teachers classified under such local categories as infant or junior level teachers in London, elementary level teachers in New York, and primary or therapeutic teachers in Vienna) were selected: 102 teachers in all, 50 in New York, 31 in Vienna, and 21 in London.

The teachers who were nominated were successful and highly experienced. Taking all three cities together, over 75 percent of the teachers had been on the job for five years or more at the time of their participation in the project (the Spring and Fall of 1988). More than 90 percent of the teachers were women (the sample contained just 4 men in New York, 3 in London, and 2 in Austria), a proportion that probably represents their percentages on the total school staffs. The teachers in the two European cities were white, with few exceptions, whereas the American sample was more diverse: 24 percent white and 76 percent Black or Hispanic.

*THE RESEARCH DESIGN.* The researchers asked participating teachers to recall, from the preceding fifteen days, two incidents, one which they thought they had handled competently and one where they felt they had not done as well. Each teacher was asked to provide two lengthy statements, one for each incident, reflecting on the personal and professional traits that had made the handling of one incident successful and the other one less so. We did not get the same quantity of descriptive material for the negative as for the positive incident. But even though the teachers in all three cities were much more eloquent on the traits that led to their successes than on the causes of their failures, we gathered a considerable amount of self-reflective information on the personal and professional characteristics our informants deemed relevant to their work.

Our information, then, comes directly from written or taped conversation with teachers. As such, it has the advantages and the shortcomings of self-reports.

The quantitative analysis involved a content analysis of topics covered by each respondent as the teacher reflected on the positive and negative experiences. Qualitatively, the researchers selected dominant themes, significant opinions, or interesting comments.

A coding manual containing 105 topics was developed for a systematic content analysis based on the teacher reports of relevant factors that affect success and failure in the teaching of minority children. Negative comments did not mean the teacher's attitude was malicious or prejudicial, but described an unresolved or otherwise unsuccessful experience. For example, the topic of children with special emotional problems was coded as negative because these characteristics are involved in many of the incidents that teachers think are not handled successfully.

The 105 topics were grouped into four categories or domains:

A.  Community characteristics
B.  Institutional characteristics
C.  Student characteristics
D.  Teacher characteristics

Domains A, B, and C were viewed as extrinsic to the teacher's classroom/ teaching concerns, while the latter (D) was intrinsic.

*THE COMMUNITY (Domain A)*. Teachers in New York regarded the cultural, racial, and linguistic characteristics of their children's communities in a positive light, a position with which their European counterparts concurred. But our respondents regarded many community factors as impacting negatively on their children and themselves. Teachers in New York, for example, mentioned with some frequency the high incidence of single parent households and drug addiction in the communities their children come from as a source of difficulty. Teachers in London expressed regret that standards of considerate behavior the school encourages are not reinforced at home.

*THE INSTITUTION (Domain B)*. As with community topics, institutional topics were mentioned infrequently, and were almost totally absent from the London responses. Teachers in New York positively mentioned the support they received from their colleagues, the training clinics, and the reading materials they obtained from District offices. They were extremely critical of mandated curricular programs and of pacing charts that dictated the timing of their lessons. In London, some respondents made negative mention of excessively large classes.

*THE STUDENTS (Domain C)*. Students with special emotional needs were the most frequently mentioned negative topic by teachers in New York; in Vienna, teachers who mentioned that they felt at ease when dealing with instructional tasks, called the emotional highlights of their work at school their work with problematic children.

*TEACHING RELATED CONCERNS*. Teachers in New York placed the highest importance on affective factors, covering both the personal qualities as well as the attitudes of the teacher; organizational skills, knowledge of the community and of the way children learn and develop, with a relevant but somewhat secondary role assigned to academic factors (a similar focus to the European teachers). In London, the skills that teachers stressed concerned the ability to "read" a situation; to understand, for example, how children feel when isolated or at odds with their surroundings; and to be able to initiate moves to restore the individual's self-esteem or the harmony of a class, so reestablishing the conditions in which children learn.

In both New York and Vienna, among the most frequently mentioned topics was the knowledge of how to work with individual children, and such topics as the commitment shown by donating extra time, and the ability to set up cooperative and sharing learning activities for children. There were also some important differences of emphasis. The abilities of being loving and intimate with children, and of being patient with them, were ranked much more highly in Vienna than in New York, while the ability to build self-esteem and pride in children was ranked more highly in New York than in Vienna.

## Qualitative Observations

The teachers' comments expand these findings. One respondent commented, "Teachers are of two kinds, some are just excellent academically and good in teaching techniques. These are only teachers. But there are those of us who have all that, and then put extra effort [into] those children who are in need. We care and give them love. It all has to do with the target population. In other districts, teachers may not have to be teachers, social workers, guidance counselors, but in this school you have to be all of the above."

Another teacher echoes her words: "I've given more attention to the affective part of teaching. Here, more than in a school of upper socioeconomic status, that is important. There are many societal problems. Children are abandoned in terms of the nurturing that once existed."

Successful teachers were confident of the children's ability to learn. They emphasized their willingness to depart from traditional authoritarian roles and to respect each child as an individual. One teacher commented, "...I listen to the kids, I listen to their complaints of fear, their uneasiness. I pick it up right away. I am good at picking up nonverbal communication that is often missed...I always hold my breath and listen to the kids. I give opportunity for them to work independently and for me to step back. I give time to the children."

Another teacher: "...Children were involved in the whole process [of resolving a situation]. Their ideas were considered and valued. When a problem arose on my part, the children were informed and included in identifying a solution. Honesty on my part in dealing with the children prevailed. I dealt openly with the children about my feelings and needs and what I felt capable of doing, and in turn, respectfully considered their feelings and needs too...In summary, I'd say the bottom line is to trust kids, give them credit. Praise and build their self-esteem continually. Build a relationship with them where both you and they can feel comfortable and safe in the classroom, safe to be who you are and all you can become."

Typical of these teachers was their intimate knowledge of the community in which they worked. For example, one teacher stressed her familiarity with the mores, culture, religion, ethnicity and language of the school community. Another said "...The important thing is to let parents teach you about them and their children, and respect all of them."

One majority culture teacher working in a predominantly Latino school recounted: "When I came to Jordan Elementary School, it was my first teaching experience where I was surrounded by a different language and culture. It was bad enough that I didn't speak Spanish, but it seemed to me that no one spoke English. Being constantly in the dark regarding what is being said around you is very nerve racking. Since I was a monolingual teacher, I thought I wouldn't have to deal with this in the classroom. I was wrong. Very often the children spoke Spanish. My reaction to this was to banish Spanish from the room. The change in the children was extreme. A noisy class suddenly became silent. If the children didn't know how to say something in English, they said nothing at all." This teacher and others reported that their classroom success increased when they learned how to be comfortable and at ease in the multilingual environment and acquired their students' native language which enabled them to communicate with parents, reinforce their relationship with children, and become involved with the community.

Teachers mentioned the importance of forging a link between the student's home and community experiences and the teacher's instructional practices. Among several such examples is the report of one teacher in London who described the following incident: "...A girl [newcomer to the class] from the Republic of Ireland had a pronounced Irish accent. The girl became very troubled and withdrawn when the class made fun of her speech and tended to shun her. [I] reinforced the confidence of the girl, discussed the problem of name calling with the class, and introduced a project on family trees (beginning with my own) to show the diversity of heritage in many people's family background." The teacher noted an improvement in class relationships and felt she had successfully met a challenge to utilize cultural diversity to improve instruction and rebuild a student's self-esteem.

Schools as well as individual teachers should make concerted efforts to incorporate the community into the instructional experiences of their students.

Another teacher recounted one successful learning situation where direct hands-on teaching proved successful: "The first step I took was to tell the students about the idea [concerning participation in a district science project] of working in small groups or committees and about the different projects that they were going to be involved with. I asked them to think about selecting an area of interest as I explained some of the activities that were going to take place in each group and the materials they would be working with. For example, in science we had been working in small groups, putting electrical circuits together; therefore, the students who were going to be involved in the Science Fair group were asked to create an interesting project using the materials and the knowledge they had obtained during the science hands-on activities they had been involved in...After a preview of the different projects, the students selected a project of their interest. We reviewed the rules of working in small groups...The next step was to find a large block of time in which the children could work without interruption. The furniture was arranged during this period to form different work areas to meet the needs of the different groups...The outcome of this situation was very positive. The students involved with the science project had the opportunity to participate in the school science fair. They demonstrated and shared with other classes in the school what they had learned about electricity."

In the above example the classroom and the school acted as an evaluative as well as an instructional setting, and what was learned was not only that one is evaluated, but also how to evaluate one's self and others (Jackson, 1968). While students may find themselves occasionally in a position to evaluate each other, the primary source of evaluation — praise or censure — is the teacher. Through this administration of praise or reproof the teacher assumes a position of a significant other. But as Giroux (1988) points out, what is significant is the manner in which this authority is used, and the kinds of social relationships it produces, values and influences.

In summary, these successful teachers were aware of their own and their students' culture, and were respectful of both; planned for the incorporation of the students' culture into classroom practices; linked the curriculum to student experience; maintained close contact with the students' family and community; and were extremely insightful in identifying individual student learning styles and motivational potentials. These findings and others under-score the importance of integrating the home and community experiences of students into the educative and evaluative processes of the school.

Since research has demonstrated that teachers as well as students are influenced by their culture, teachers' treatment of students, their evaluation of student performance and their organization of classroom activities must all be reconceptualized incorporating these cultural characteristics (Green, 1983). For example, observations of language use and communication patterns in classrooms by Erickson and Mohatt (1982), and Erickson, Cazden, Carrasco and Guzman (1978-1981) revealed that when teachers utilized their knowl-edge of the language patterns students used in their own cultural settings to organize and deliver instruction, students' learning experiences were more successful. In addition, teachers were more fluid in delivering pedagogy and more creative in the ways they managed the classroom. Similarly, Pierstrip (1973), Gumperz (1972), and DeStefano and Pepinsky (1981), found that students employed a culturally patterned discourse as they participated in reading exercises. When the discourse patterns used by the students were combined with those of the teachers who themselves were employing cultur-ally patterned discourse, communication was inhibited, which further com-plicated the teaching/learning process. These incompatibilities led to differ-ences in performance by students and, subsequently, to differential treatment and assessment by teachers.

A positive home, school and community relationship is viewed as a critical condition for a successful educational program for both educational institutions and the students they serve (Seeley, 1985). Utilizing the concept of "mediating structures" as a paradigm for determining the structural characteristics of education, Seeley identifies the family as the primary mediating structure which is augmented by other social institutions. The family screens, interprets, criticizes, reinforces, complements, counteracts, retracts and transforms other community-based institutions which can have a powerful influence on a child's education.

In effect, a more productive approach to establishing relationships for children is to understand that their socialization involves multiple influences from the nonacademic world. Therefore, if the teacher and the school are to be successful with the child, they must understand and incorporate the influences of the child's extended family, which may include the church, the ethnic group, and the neighborhood, as well as the immediate family, all of whom have a profound influence on the real world of the child.

On a more fundamental level, teachers can be trained to understand the prior knowledge and learning styles of their students, so that those characteristics may be built on or used to guide the selection of educational program elements to encourage academically appropriate behavior (Cole & Griffin, 1987; Jordan, 1985).

Apparently, successful teachers through experience, instinct and empirical trial and error develop instructional strategies which utilize their students' and their own cultural backgrounds. To make these approaches systemic, teacher preparatory institutions must carefully design and implement curricula focusing on the skills needed by teachers who are to work with multicultural populations.

## Implications for Teacher Training

As demonstrated in this paper, both researchers and successful teacher practitioners arrived at similar solutions for establishing educational equity and improving instruction for multicultural school populations. The teachers, who generally had more than five years of experience (and as many as fifteen years) and had developed and refined their classroom strategies, freely admitted to the confusion and failure they experienced during their learning period. Given this insight it is probable that without institutional help and support, even the most successful teachers flounder during their initial teaching years. This painful initiation period often contributes to early departure from the profession and may also prove educationally destructive for students. It is ironic that sincere teachers, inadequately prepared with theories and practices rooted in the past, are teaching growing numbers of multilingual, multicultural children for whom opportunities for educational success continue to diminish.

While the profiles of today's teachers may in large measure be similar to those of the past, today's student profiles are vastly different and require new approaches. If we are to successfully motivate and educate these new students, then we must reverse our currently failing system by devising new curricula and institutionalizing teacher training programs to incorporate preservice and inservice components which address the needs of multicultural student bodies. It is a responsibility of researchers and teacher training institutions to assist teachers to systematically investigate and appreciate the cultural orientations and influences of all children, and to understand the ways in which cultural orientation influences the child's perception of the world and the teaching and learning setting.

Currently, many teacher training institutions are engaged in honest debate about the reconstitution of curricula. Whatever course these redesign efforts may take, it is clear that the need to infuse awareness, knowledge and instructional behaviors appropriate for success with multicultural populations must be a requisite of such redesign. According to Gay (1983), teachers must be given the opportunity to develop three distinct types of process knowledge: they must develop the skills necessary to translate multicultural knowledge into programs, practices, and instructional behaviors; they must become competent at developing educational objectives, curriculum content and learning within the frame of reference and cultural backgrounds of all students, taking into account their perceptions, cognitive processes and linguistic skills; and they must be trained in adjusting their instructional methods to students' learning styles.

Although several successful teachers in the Beckum et al. study responded positively to the training they had received in college courses, they expressed particular enthusiasm about the opportunity to share knowledge and skills with their fellow teachers. One teacher speaking of another said, "Donna gave me my education." Another noted: "...When I want to seek information, I know where to get it. I go to classrooms to observe. I take initiative, I follow up, I bother other teachers." These teachers were lucky to find colleagues to support and nurture them and were self-motivated enough to seek their colleagues out.

Formal teacher training institutions would be wise to recognize such important networks and incorporate their strengths into the institutional training process. It is important for schools and colleges of education to initiate, foster and maintain ongoing relationships with the teachers they graduate including the granting of adjunct status, the establishment of teacher/faculty planning councils and involvement in the work of school-based management teams. The college faculty's expert knowledge of current research and effective pedagogy can, in turn, contribute to more effective decision-making.

Emphasis should be placed on the interaction between teachers' affective orientation, teacher behavior and the design of classroom environments, all of which contribute to student motivation and cognitive engagement in learning activities. (Blumenfeld and Meece, 1988). By providing a revised theoretical framework for teacher candidates, linked to preservice clinical experience and continuing inservice support, teacher training institutions can play a vital role in changing the face of schooling for large numbers of American children who are currently educationally disenfranchised.

To accomplish this task, we believe that teacher training institutions have to redesign their programs so that students will emerge with a professional diploma incorporating the bachelor's and the master's degrees. The new degree would provide opportunity to include cultural ethnography, child development, learning theory, emphasis on a second language, content and pedagogy, with each component linked to on-site work in a variety of schools. Like medical students, teacher candidates must begin clinical experience early in their preparatory careers if the theoretical basis of their knowledge is to become interactive with the reality of the classroom. Otherwise, we are perpetuating the process whereby only years in the classroom have value as the training ground for teachers, which leads to success for some and to mediocrity for too many others.

To continue the analogy with medical students, teacher candidates need to rotate through a number of school sites in order to ensure that they are exposed to several different cultures, since many schools reflect housing and social patterns which create majority/minority cultures in the school. These experiences, however, will be valid only if adequate support and supervision are provided.

Consequently, the role of the teacher educator has to be redefined. Both the college faculty member and the school practitioner must assume active roles in the educative process by discarding their hierarchical relationships and developing team approaches and responsibilities for preservice training. These new relationships also suppose that curriculum will be reconfigured, possibly involving both traditional and nontraditional distribution of college time and credits. Additionally, assessment would take place at both the school sites and at the college, lending itself to the exploration of a variety of assessment instruments for the measurement of student progress. For example, we visualize the development of a portfolio which might include research on learning styles, a series of lesson plans for different school populations utilizing learning style theory, videotapes of a series of lessons, self-evaluation of those lessons and, finally, shared perceptions of progress.

Simultaneously, the college faculty would be taking a more active part in school life through forming ongoing relationships with schools and their surrounding communities. This implies that faculty presence in schools would be a commonplace of school life, viewed not as an oddity but as part of the everyday effort of educating students. Thus, the expertise of the college faculty, in whatever the field — cultural ethnography, bilingual education, mathematical pedagogy or other disciplines — would represent a natural resource of the school, to be used according to need. In turn, practitioners would serve as instructors and consultants for college-based learning, more importantly providing an experiential resource for the college. Involving both college and school faculty in this manner should also have a systemic effect on the college curriculum, further encouraging linkages between what is taught at the college and the life of the schools.

It is clear that such reorganization will meet with resistance on the part of some college faculties and school level staff, often more interested in tinkering with change than in instituting encompassing reform. But if we return to our original premise that schools are failing to educate increasing numbers of students who are part of a multicultural population, then we must also take drastic steps to reorganize the way instruction is delivered and the ways teachers are trained. A teacher must be equipped as readily with the strategies necessary to function effectively in the multicultural classroom as with the strategies to teach reading. This awareness, sensitivity and knowledge must begin with the introduction to teaching as a profession and continue through the career of the teacher. For this to happen, the training institutions cannot remain isolated in academe, but are obligated to be on the frontlines of the evolution of teaching. Otherwise, they will be viewed as dinosaurs whose credentials are considered merely a visa to be obtained as painlessly as possible.

## CONCLUSION

The thrust of this discussion is to recognize that teachers can be trained to reorganize schools and classrooms and to reconceptualize classroom tasks to reflect an integration of the learner's cultural characteristics. This reconceptualization will result in improved instructional practices and better understanding and achievement by the learner (Cole and Griffin, 1987). The social organization of classrooms and the commitment to form school-community linkages are at the heart of creating more effective teaching and learning situations.

This discussion presents the view that the structure and organization of the classroom environment are properties of a culturally influenced system. A great deal of research remains to be done to provide a clearer understanding of how a particular instructional program interacts with students' racial or ethnic characteristics. However, it has long been recognized that the structure of the school environment impacts on the nature of classroom social relationships and task participation (Green, 1983; Jackson, 1968). The ways in which schools and classrooms are organized contribute to the development of a student ethos which may value individualism, competition or collective action (Giroux, 1988). Nevertheless, the schooling process is responsible for providing the maximum opportunity for students to grow and develop, regardless of which of these value orientations the student adopts. None of this can happen, however, if teachers are not trained to recognize these different orientations and to develop methodology which will be effective for each. If we are to succeed at our educational mission, we must be determined to create the strongest possible environment for all children, taking into account the cultural heritage which helps to define them, and integrating that rich diversity into the classroom.

## REFERENCES

Apple, M. A. (1979), *Ideology and curriculum*. London: R.K.P.

Beckum, L. C., Otheguy, R., Garcia, O., Zimny, A., Perry, P., Lord, E. and Rollett, B. (1988), *Moving towards developing a knowledge base for beginning teachers of multicultural, multilingual populations: an international study focusing on effective teacher behaviors*, unpublished paper for the Exxon Knowledge Base Task Force, New Jersey.

Bernstein, B. (1972), Social class, language and socialization. In Giglioli (Ed.), *Language and social context* (p. 57-178). Harmondsworth, Middlesex, England: Penguin.

Bernstein, B. (1961), Social class and linguistic development: A theory of social learning. In A. H. Halsey, J. Fland and C. A. Anderson (Eds.), *Education, economy and society*. New York: Free Press.

Blumenfeld, P. C. and Meece, J. L. (1988), Task factors, teacher behavior, students' involvement and use of learning strategies in science, *The Elementary School Journal*, 88 (3), 235-250.

Brophy, J. and Good, T. (1985) Teacher behavior and student achievement, In M. Wittrock (Ed.) *Handbook of research on teaching* 3rd ed. New York: Macmillan.

Byalick, R. and Bersoff, D. N. (1974), Reinforcement of black and white teachers in integrated classrooms. *Journal of Educational Psychology* 66: 473-480.

Cole, M. and Griffin, P. (Eds.) (1987), *Contextual factors in education: Improving science and mathematics education for minorities and women*, Madison, Wisconsin: Wisconsin Center of Education Research, School of Education.

Cole, M. and Scribner, S. (1974), *Culture and thought: A psychological introduction*, New York: Wiley.

Cornbleth, C. and Korth, W. (1980), Teacher perception and teacher-student interaction in integrated classrooms. *Journal of Experimental Education*,48 (4):259-263.

Cummins, J. (1984), *Bilingualism and special education: Issues in assessment and pedagogy*. England: Clevendon, Multilingual Matters, Ltd.

DeStefano, J. and Pepinsky, H. (1981), *The learning of discourse rules of culturally different children in first grade literacy instruction*. (NIE G-79-0032), Washington, D. C.: National Institute of Education.

Doyle, W. (1977), Learning the classroom environment: An ecological analysis. *Journal of Teacher Education*, XXXIII (6): 51-55.

Erickson, F. (1987), Transformation and school success: The Politics and culture of educational achievement. *Anthropology and Education Quarterly*, 18: 335-355.

Erickson, F. (1986), Culture differences and science education. *The Urban Review*,18 (2), 117-124.

Erickson, F. (1986) Tasks in times: Objective of study in a natural history of teaching. In K. K. Zumwalt (Ed.), *Improving teaching*, p. 131-149, Alexandria, Va.: Association for Supervision and Curriculum Development Yearbook.

Erickson, F., Cazden, C., Carrasco, R., Gozman, A. (1978- 1981), *Mid-quarter reports for social and cultural organization of interaction in classroom of bilingual children project*, (NIE G-78-0099). Washington, DC: National Institute of Education.

Erickson, F. and Mohatt, G. (1982), Cultural organization of participations structures in two classrooms of Indian students. In G. Spindler (Ed.), *Doing the ethnography of schooling*, New York: Holt, Rinehart and Winston.

Gay, G. (1983), Why multicultural education in teacher preparation programs. *Contemporary Education* 54:79-85.

Ginsburg, H. P. (1987), *Assessing the arithmetic abilities and instructional needs of students*. Austin, Texas: The PRO-ED Assessment Series.

Ginsburg, H. P. (1986), The myth of the deprived child: New thoughts on poor children. In U. Neisser (Ed.), *The School achievement of minority children: New perspectives*. New Jersey: Erlbaum.

Giroux, H. A. (1988), *Teachers as intellectuals: Towards a critical pedagogy of learning*, Mass.: Bergin & Garvey Inc.

Goldenberg, C. N. (1988), Methods, early literacy and home-school compatibilities: A response to Sledge et al. *Anthropology and Education Quarterly* 19: 425-432.

Green, J. (1983), Exploring classroom discourse, *Linguistic Perspectives on Teaching-Learning Processes*,18 (3), 180-199.

Green, M. (1987), Education adequacy: A philosophical approach. Unpublished paper.

Gumperz, J. J. (1972), *Verbal strategies in multilingual communication*, Georgetown Roundtable on Languages and Linguistics 1970, (p. 129-147) Washington, D. C.: Georgetown University Press.

Harnischfeger, A. and Wiley, D. (1985), The origins of "active learning time," In C. Fisher and D. Berliner (Eds.) *Perspective on instructional time*, New York: Longman.

Heath, S. B. (1983), *Ways with words: Language, life and work in communities and classrooms*, Cambridge: Cambridge University Press.

Heath, S. B. (1982), Questioning at home and at school: a comparative study. In G. Spindler (Ed.), *Doing the ethnography of schooling: Educational anthropology in action*, (p. 103-129) New York: Holt, Rinehart & Winston.

Heath, S. B. (1982), What no bedtime story means: Narrative skills at home and school, *Language in Society*, 11:49-76.

Jackson, P. (1968), *Life in classrooms*, New York: Holt, Rinehart and Winston.

Jackson, G. and Cosca, C. (1974), The inequality of educational opportunity in the southwest: An observational study of ethnically mixed classrooms. *American Educational Research Journal*,11: 219-229.

Jordan, C. (1985) Translating culture: From ethnographic information to educational program. *Anthropology and Education Quarterly*, 16 (2): 105-123.

LaBelle, T. J. (1972), An anthropological framework for studying education. *Teachers College Record*, 73 (4), 519-538.

Mercer, J. R. (1989), Alternative paradigms for assessment in a pluralistic society. In J. A. Banks and C. A. McGee Banks (Eds.) *Multicultural education: Issues and perspectives*. Massachusetts, MA: Allyn and Bacon.

Moll, L. and Diaz, S. (1987), Change as the goal of educational research, *Anthropology and Education Quarterly*, 18, 300-311.

Nyiti, R. M. (1982), The validity of "cultural differences explanations" for cross-cultural variations in the rate of Piagetian cognitive development. In D. A. Wagner and H. D. Stevenson, *Cultural perspectives on child development*, (p.146-165).

Ogbu, J. (1985) Research currents: Cultural-ecological influences on minority school learning. *Language Arts*, 62 (8): 860-869.

Ogbu, J. (1982), Cultural discontinuities and schooling, *Anthropology and Education Quarterly*, 13 (4): 290-307.

Pierstrip, A. (1973), *Black dialect interference and accommodation of reading instruction in first grade* (Monograph No. 4) Berkeley, California: Language Behavior Research Laboratory, University of California.

Ramirez, A. G. (1985), *Bilingualism through schooling: cross-cultural education for minority and majority students*, Albany: State University of New York Press.

Rist, R. (1970), Student social class and teacher expectations: The self-fulfilling prophecy in ghetto education, *Harvard Educational Review*, 51, 261-269.

Scribner, S. and Cole, M. (1981), *The psychology of literacy*, Cambridge, Mass.: Harvard University Press.

Seely, D. S. (1985), *Education through partnership*. Washington, D.C.: Publication of the American Enterprise Institute for Public Policy Research.

Sivan, E. (1986), Motivation in social constructivist theory. *Educational Psychologist*, 21 (3), 209-234.

Smith, C. H. (1972), Teaching in the inner city: Six prerequisites to success, *Teachers College Record* 73 (4): 547-558.

Sprinthall, R. C. and Sprinthall, N. A. (1977) *Educational Psychology: A developmental approach*, Menlo Park, Cal.: Addison-Wesley.

Truebe, H. T. (1988), Culturally based explanations of minority students' academic achievement, *Anthropology and Education Quarterly* 19: 270-287.

Vogt, L. A., Jordon and Tharp, R. G. (1987), Explaining school failure, producing school success: two cases. *Anthropology and Education Quarterly*, 18: 276-286.

Vygotsky, L. S. (1978), *Mind in society: The development of higher psychological processes*. Cambridge, Mass.: Harvard University Press.

Vygotsky, L. S. (1962), *Thought and language*, Chicago: MIT Press.

Wertsch, J. V. (1985), *Vygotsky and the social formation of mind*, Cambridge: Harvard University Press.

Wiederholt, J. L. (1987), *Assessing the reading abilities and instrumental needs of students*. Texas: PRO-ED, Inc.

Witkins, H. A., Moore, C. A., Goodenough, D. R., & Cox, P. W. (1977), Field-dependent and field-independent cognitive styles and their educational implications. *Review of Educational Research*, 49, 1-54.

# Culture Building for Diversity and Excellence:

*Changing Instructional Methods, Roles, Regularities and Relationships*

# Chapter 10
# Changing Instructional Methods and the Culture of the School

*by Shlomo Sharan, Tel Aviv University, and Yael Sharan*

## INTRODUCTION

### Some features of Israel's schools and of schools almost anywhere

In 1976, we undertook to introduce cooperative learning in small groups into three elementary schools in Israel. The instructional change project followed two years of work as consultants to the Israel Center for Educational Television, during which time a series of films on cooperative learning was produced for in-service teacher training. The films were based on principles presented in a book we had written at that time (Sharan and Sharan, 1974). Following the production of the films, the Center wished to learn about their potential effectiveness, and the change project was conceived. Funds for the project were granted by the Ministry of Education, on condition that the project would be carried out in schools whose populations consisted of children from a lower class, "culturally deprived" background. In anticipation of the difficulties reported in the literature about introducing change in school cultures, planning for the change project was based on guidelines found in the current literature on school change, including publications from the Rand Corporation's assessment of educational change projects in the United States (Berman and McLaughlin, 1978; Bushell and Rappaport, 1971; Sarason, 1971).

Subsequent to the first change project that we and our colleagues carried out from 1976 to 1978 (Sharan and Hertz-Lazarowitz, 1981), we continued to work on a series of extensive and fairly long-term experiments in schools directed at assessing the effects of cooperative learning on teachers and pupils in Israel's elementary and secondary schools (Sharan, Kussell, Hertz-Lazarowitz, Bejarano, Raviv and Sharan, 1984; Sharan and Rich, 1984; Sharan and Shachar, 1988).

More recently, we have begun a new set of projects designed to implement participative management in schools. In this latest series of projects, the goal is to have the teaching staff establish a number of committees that identify school problems and serve as problem-solving and decision-making groups (Sharan and Shachar, 1990). The greater our experience, the more we learn about the nature of the difficulties that confront us in attempting to implement innovative instructional methods in classrooms or deal with teachers' work relationships at the level of the school as an organization.

What impediments to change did we expect to find even before we began our first project? Both of us had more than a passing acquaintance with the school system, Yael as a teacher, teacher trainer and remedial reading specialist; Shlomo as a former supervisor of school psychologists in various townships in Israel and as an instructor in the Department of Psychology at Tel-Aviv University, responsible for training school psychologists. (Later he began teaching in the Department of Education.) Our colleagues had similar backgrounds and training. We knew that Israel's schools displayed a remarkable degree of uniformity in instructional method, at least in classrooms above the third grade.

Some changes in the direction of less structured modes of learning began to penetrate the first two or three grades of elementary school in the middle of the 1970's. But as a general rule, instruction throughout the country's educational system through the 12th grade was notably uniform, regardless of the background or interests of the students.

Typically, teachers presented academic material verbally or with the use of a few simple aids (visual or other), pupils made copious notes or filled out worksheets and did mountains of homework (mostly of a rote nature). They were frequently called upon to recite verbally in the classroom and were tested often. In more reverent moods we called this the "presentation and recitation" method. More frequently it was dubbed "ping-pong." In Israel this instructional strategy is generally known as "frontal teaching," a description that applies to most secondary schools. It is found to a lesser degree in kindergarten and the first three or four years of Israel's elementary schools. In those grades definite progress has been made over the past decade to develop more progressive methods of instruction.

Israel is one of the smallest nations in the world, and hence it is possible to make some tentative generalizations about schooling that contain more than a kernel of truth. However, given the vastly different scale of schooling in the U.S., it seems unrealistic to make any generalizations about how classroom instruction is actually carried out. It is improbable that anyone knows how teachers actually teach in most classrooms in any country. Yet, the impression received from reading the professional literature (e.g., Goodlad, 1984; Heckman, 1987; Sarason, 1983) is that in the majority of cases, U.S. schools rely heavily on the presentation-recitation method.

Recently, the first author spent a year teaching at a university in the western United States. He participated in an undergraduate class for teacher trainees on methods of instruction. There were 180 students in the class conducted in a large auditorium. The instructor deftly used a combination of slides, films and lectures during classroom instruction. Nevertheless, toward the middle of the semester he felt constrained to confess sadly that he hoped the students would teach in their classrooms in the ways he was *telling them about* and not in the way he was actually teaching them. Nor did our sporadic visits to secondary schools in the immediate neighborhood reveal any surprises: Instruction was exclusively by the frontal expository method. Herbert Thelen seems to be quite accurate when he calls this approach to classroom teaching the "cultural archetype" that "acts as a force to restrain change and to secure order. It is at once the guardian and avenging angel of every classroom" (Thelen, 1981, p. 5). There is consensus among students of planned change in education that schools have a "culture of resistance" to change (Heckman, 1987).

## Behavioral regularities in school cultures

The traditional expository teaching method can certainly be viewed as constituting one of the prime examples of what Sarason (1982) called "the behavioral regularities" that typify schooling the U.S. and in Israel, and probably in most western countries and Eastern Europe. Anyone who sets out to change this archetypal pattern undertakes a struggle with a mighty opponent who possesses an awesome power to transform opposition into an image of itself, bereft of any distinguishing characteristics. It appears certain that the large majority of classroom practitioners take this pattern for granted, perhaps even considering it to be inviolable. Furthermore, in the opinion of many university professors of education as well as teachers, changing teaching methods does not contribute to improving student achievement. These authorities provide the educational system with "scientific" legitimation for eschewing change. The change agent has the burden to prove that alternatives are appropriate, feasible and productive. No wonder the image of the consultant is quickly transformed into religious missionary or dragon killer rather than psychologist or educator.

The second major "behavior regularity" we encountered in school cultures which similarly presented a formidable bulwark against change, was the teaching schedule that regulated the work of the teachers and the whereabouts of the students. In Israel, full-time teachers have two hours a week free from classroom instruction which must be spent in the school. Apart from these two hours, all of the teachers' time in school is scheduled for classroom teaching. Thus, the space-time allocation of teachers to classrooms consumes all but two hours a week: There is no paid time set aside for the school to function as an organization, such as teachers' meetings, committee meetings, consultation with individual students, meetings with parents, etc. Of course, all schools hold teachers' meetings, usually once every three weeks, in the evening or late afternoon, when teachers return to the school. (School in Israel is usually in session from 8:00 A.M. to noon in the elementary grades, or to 2 P.M. in secondary schools, six days a week, Sunday through Friday.)

We found very little, if any, systematic committee work in schools where teachers examined the curriculum, determined school policy, made decisions about instruction, etc., apart from school parties and trips. The principal made most if not all of the important decisions. Many schools had what is called "an administrative team," consisting of three or four faculty members appointed by the principal. This group often functioned as a governing committee, but without involving the rest of the teaching staff in the process of decision making. Even the decision of whether to enter into an instructional change project was not made by the teachers. They were not empowered to determine what they would like to learn (Huberman and Miles, 1984).

One of the main consequences of this form of organization is that school cultures have little or no organizational flexibility needed for self-examination, self-renewal, or even self-regulation. If a principal became interested in adopting new forms of instruction or new instructional materials, he or she had to rely on the teachers' willingness to devote their own free time to in-service training courses with very little compensation. Schools generally allocated little or no working time to teachers to deal collectively with plans for improving instructional practice. The absence of such organizational flexibility needed for committee meetings or other non-instructional staff activities also sustained teacher isolation and insulation from collegial inter-action, as so many observers have noted about schools in the United States (Goodlad, 1987; Lieberman and Rosenholtz, 1987; Lortie, 1975; Sarason, 1982).

Since this interaction was not built into the school's work schedule, effecting change in a school became a truly Herculean task. All these phenom-ena: the unseen walls erected by the schedule, in addition to the real walls that separate teachers in a school building (according to the principle of "one class, one teacher"), the lack of clear ties between means and ends, all accompanied by the absence of a coherent school policy in most realms of the school's instructional operation (aside from the distribution of students to grades and classes) — all of these have been subsumed under the concept of "schools as loosely coupled organizations" (Corbett, Dawson and Firestone, 1984).

In short, investment of teachers' time and energies were totally dictated by their teaching schedules. It is almost unreasonable to expect people in their situation to display exuberance over some outsider's suggestion that they learn new methods and change their ways of practicing their profession. As we shall see, these outsiders rarely went to schools in response to an invitation from their would-be clients, but more likely because of events completely beyond the ken of the schools.

Another factor which inhibits new learning in a school is the built-in perpetuation of established patterns of behavior which Argyris (1982) attrib-uted to "limited-learning systems." Teachers and principals indeed detected many "errors" in their organization. Generally school cultures, like so many other organizational cultures, are not designed to correct these "errors." Schools as organizations and teachers as individuals often adopt new pro-grams and curricula in an attempt to change situations that cause dissatisfac-tion. But these changes frequently do not truly transform the school's under-lying assumptions and goals. As a result, the impact of these changes is temporary and limited in scope. Sooner or later the causes of dissatisfaction reappear, indicating that no real change occurred.

Despite all these constraints and limitations, it must be pointed out that large numbers of teachers in Israel participate regularly in in-service courses, and they frequently come to school for various kinds of activities without expecting any compensation. Teachers desperately want to succeed and to fulfill their professional self-image as people devoted to their students' academic and social development and welfare. Teachers constantly seek help for dealing with the challenges of classroom teaching, challenges with which they can barely cope and for which they are given precious little assistance by the school system. Most of the in-service training opportunities, designed by persons in central offices of the Ministry of Education or in various universities, are unrelated to the needs of specific schools. These training opportunities do not seem to alleviate teachers' concerns or provide practical means for solving the manifold problems teachers confront. The answer to this question lies beyond the scope of this chapter.

## Changing instructional methods: What's so hard about that?

In the early stages of the first project it became clear that classrooms as social systems played a powerful role in the change effort. The various features or components of this social system were interrelated so that change in one part implied or required change in most if not all of the other parts as well. One can easily identify four major components of classroom life related to instruction, namely:

1. The role of the teacher
2. The role of the students
3. The organization of the students in the classroom
4. The design of the learning task.

If anyone seeks to introduce a new set of procedures that are intended to affect any one of these four components, failure to take into consideration the other three components is likely to impede or even prevent the implementation of the change (Sharan, Hertz-Lazarowitz and Hare, 1981).

For example, if a learning task calls for students to perform an experiment in small groups, obviously students must be organized in the room differently than if they were expected to watch a slide presentation. The students' role also changes, but contrasts with their role in the "frontal" classroom, from one of listener or note taker, to one of an active agent collaborating with their peers in the performance of the task. The teacher's role is no longer to be stationed at the head of the class expounding information and asking questions, but to walk around to each of the groups, offering help where needed and generally overseeing the activities of this collection of small groups in the class. Finally, since one goal of cooperative learning is to allow everyone in the small group to participate and not just have one student take over while all the others stand by and watch, the design of the task must provide an opportunity for each group member to make a contribution (Sharan and Sharan, 1974). If the task fails to do this, most of the students will not participate and, for all intents and purposes, the group will cease to function. Hence, all four components of the classroom learning process are interdependent.

Clearly, each teaching method presents its own special requirements in terms of these four elements. We have observed many classrooms where teachers organized the students in small groups sitting around a table because it was a trend to do so. But lacking any systematic training in or knowledge of cooperative learning, they did not make the necessary adjustments in relation to other instructional decisions. This was particularly true with respect to teachers who seated students around tables, yet continued to lecture to them from the front of the room. The organization of the students into small groups was the only element that was changed. This made it appear as if they were engaged in cooperative learning. Also, quite often the teachers continued to design tasks that required students to fill out individual worksheets, further precluding any need for direct interaction among groupmates. The result was what was commonly known in Israel as the "stiff-neck syndrome," where students must constantly turn their heads to see and hear the teacher. The lack of congruity among the four basic elements of classroom learning impeded its proper implementation. When the results were disappointing, teachers typically expressed their disillusionment with cooperative learning as a potentially effective form of instruction.

At least three out of the four components of classroom learning that we mentioned (obviously there are more), namely, classroom organization, and the teachers' and students' roles, constituted fundamental "behavioral regularities" or archetypal features of classroom cultures. Hence, it comes as no surprise that any attempt to introduce instructional practices that run counter to these deeply rooted habits of teacher and student behavior will encounter resistance. Even if the teachers remained verbally congenial and cooperative during the in-service training project, implementation of the new teaching method in actual classroom practice proceeded at a snail's pace simply because it was hard to change these socially and institutionally sanctioned habits.

Imagine then how different cooperative learning is from accepted traditional instruction in terms of all of the basic behavioral regularities that characterize the different methods.

Apart from the obvious difference in classroom seating arrangements between traditional and cooperative learning, the latter approach seeks to have students engage in a great deal of direct conversation among members (up to 5) of the small groups. Just think of the hum of conversation in the class instead of the mandatory silence demanded by most schools. Students also get up and walk around when necessary. Frequently, though not always, groups undertake to study different topics, departing from the typical uniformity of the learning task for the entire classroom. Moreover, the students participate in planning what and how they will study, at least within the general parameters set by the teacher.

Teachers must keep tabs on each group, help them overcome obstacles both in their peer relations within groups and in terms of their study of the academic material. To do so, teachers must circulate often among the groups and offer the appropriate amount of direction without interfering in the group's progress and without doing the work for them. Moreover, teachers must be prepared to allow students to pursue subtopics that they select, some of which the teacher may not have planned for in advance. This generates uncertainty that many teachers find anxiety provoking because they are accustomed to exercising complete control over the material studied in the classroom. Finally, the groups prepare a presentation from which their classmates are expected to learn something about the work of each group and the conclusions they reached. In a sense, the students assume the role of seekers, synthesizers and presenters of knowledge rather than one of listeners and absorbers of knowledge. The pursuit of knowledge is accomplished through cooperation, rather than by competition with one's peers. In all of these manifold ways, cooperative learning creates a classroom society fundamentally different from the traditional classroom. How could teachers, hitherto unexposed to cooperative learning, be expected to welcome these changes without prolonged adaptation to its benefits and potential contribution to them, to their students' education and to the school as a whole?

## Sources of resistance

Assessments of educational change programs have noted that trivial changes are less likely to mobilize the teaching staff to concentrate its energies on the change program than complex changes (Berman and McLaughlin, 1978). Complex projects seek to change the nature of the behavioral regularities found in classrooms and/or school-wide norms of behavior of the teachers and pupils, as distinct from relatively simple changes in curricular contents, textbooks, etc. On the other hand, some investigators have claimed that too complex an innovation will likewise fail (Corbett, Dawson and Firestone, 1984, p. 8). Fullan (1982) argued that the perceived importance of the problem being addressed, the resources made available to implement the change and the way in which the change is carried out are more critical determinants of success in implementation than the question of the scope of the proposed change. Changing teachers' instructional behavior from expository teaching to cooperative learning is obviously a complex change and requires a significant investment of resources (e.g., prolonged assistance by project consultants). As Fullan would predict, implementation of cooperative learning in the schools we worked in was slow and incremental, even with all of the steps taken to facilitate adoption of the new teaching method. We describe these steps in detail later in this chapter. The relatively slow adoption of cooperative learning was to be expected since it required changes in the most fundamental behavioral regularities of classroom instruction found in the schools where we worked.

We did not come to schools seeking to change the content of the curriculum. Yet, that is precisely what the teachers expected from us. When we were not forthcoming with newly prepared material for the various subject areas taught in school, the teachers and principals were somewhat bewildered and disillusioned. It seemed to us that one reason for this confusion was that educators, at least in Israel, ordinarily associated change in education with change in the substantive *content* of the instruction. The process or method of teaching was not generally perceived by many teachers as having an existence of its own apart from the content. Form must have content in order to exist, as teachers commonly assert, and teachers are expected to devote their energy to content (preparation time, planning, etc.), not to process. School consultants who focus on the process without changing the content accordingly leave teachers' expectations largely unmet. It is the content of the various academic disciplines that teachers need for their everyday classroom work, not knowledge of how to organize and foster the process of learning. The latter is perceived as esoteric or peripheral in assisting teachers to cope with the relentless press of work. Thus, change in the behavioral regularities of schooling is not what educators generally want from consultants.

There is still another source of resistance to change that surfaced in the projects we conducted, and which must not go unmentioned. The in-service training projects we conducted were not offered in response to an invitation by the teachers based on their felt needs. They were offered to the school by the school's supervisor, the principal and the project team.

Typically the sequence of events was as follows: The principal investigator would receive a grant either from a major granting institution, such as the Ford Foundation, or from the Israel Ministry of Education. These grants specified the exact duration of the project or experiment (usually one or, at most, two years) before it was known in which schools the project would be implemented or how long it would take to implement cooperative learning in those particular schools. Therefore, recruitment of schools always came after the funds were made available and without any reference to a particular site with special needs. Strangely enough, our impression is that our experience was typical for Israel, namely, that supervisory personnel are approached by professors or other agents who have been funded to try out their preferred methods or innovations. The schools are then contacted upon advice of the supervisor. Rarely does a school identify its problem first and then search for a consultant to help cope with their problem. This may not be the case in other countries where there is a large number of private consulting firms which offer their services to the school system and where schools have budgets for engaging such consultants. In Israel there are three such firms known to us, and schools are neither accustomed to, nor do they have independent sources of funds available for, engaging consultants to help them with specific problems. However, Huberman and Miles (1984) in their study of a series of educational change projects in the United States noted that, in the majority of cases, the change project was accepted by teachers because they felt constrained to do so by their superiors, not necessarily out of personal choice.

Of course, once a school was recommended by a supervisor, we appeared at a teachers' meeting to present a detailed description of the project, its potential benefits and the demands it would make on the teachers' time and energy. We tried to answer all questions the teachers asked, and we tried to convince the teachers that we were sincere when telling them that they were completely free to decide to accept or reject our proposal. In light of their past experience with the introduction of change projects, it is doubtful they believed us. Given the rather authoritarian system they work in, the teachers probably thought they had little choice because they could not displease their principal or supervisor. In fact, in all the projects we conducted, only once did the teachers vote to reject the project. On the other hand, most often we had to spend a lot of time convincing the principal that cooperative learning was worth the effort. And so, we began our long-term projects with teaching staffs who seemed to agree to participate of their own free will. Without the teachers' initial agreement, we would never have entered the school, despite the agreement of the supervisor and principal.

Yet, we could not avoid reaching one of two conclusions: Teachers' agreements were merely pro forma, made under conditions of intimidation by their superiors, as some investigators found (Huberman and Miles, 1984). We asked them to make a "free, informed choice" when they weren't used to doing so. Or, the "culture of resistance" that is endemic in schools in light of their organizational norms is in conflict with the verbal commitments made prior to the time teachers actually experience the nitty-gritty of change. It is, of course, entirely possible that both explanations have partial validity and operate simultaneously. It is also the case that teachers have little or no tools for coping with the conflict between their professional preferences and school organizational regularities. Nor are they accustomed to airing and clarifying negative feelings and criticism of the school's organizational function (Argyris, 1982; Fullan, 1982; Sarason, 1983).

## Designing ways of coping with resistance

In order to counteract prevailing school norms about classroom teaching and other forces of resistance that we anticipated—and we were far from being aware of all of them—our project staff, whose mandate was to retrain teachers in cooperative learning in schools serving lower-class populations, employed several strategies found to be potentially successful in facilitating the process of change (Sharan and Hertz-Lazarowitz, 1982). These were:

1. Training sessions were simulations of teaching with cooperative small groups, thus forming a "temporary system" in which the method was the message (Miles, 1964). Lectures were avoided as much as possible, and the workshops focused on teachers experiencing the required skills for teaching in small groups. Teachers also planned the classroom application of the various cooperative learning methods they learned.

2. The participants were a majority of the members of a given school staff (in elementary schools) or most of the teachers of specific subjects (in a particular secondary school), not an ad hoc collection of teachers from different schools. Limiting the workshop to members of the same teaching staff was intended to generate school-wide support for and acceptance of new norms of teachers' instructional behavior.

3. The principal had to agree to attend the training sessions, or most of them, to lend official sanction to the adoption of these new norms.

4. We set up small self-help teams numbering three or, at most, four teachers,

who would act as mutual-assistance units in the school. These teams were to plan together the content and process of specific lessons, formulate a small number of criteria by which to judge if the plan was in fact implemented, observe each other's classroom teaching in light of the predetermined criteria, and give each other feedback based on their observations. None of this information was to be transmitted to anyone outside the team: It was intended exclusively for purposes of professional growth of the team members in the use of cooperative learning methods.

5. Last, but not least, was the relatively long duration of the change agents' contact with the teaching staff and the extent of this contact. We planned to conduct at least ten, if not more, workshops of two-and-a-half hours each. In other words, the teachers participated in over 25, and often more than 30, hours of workshop sessions. Also, project team members visited the teachers' classes when they were invited and offered specific assistance to teachers about all aspects of using cooperative learning in the classroom in a given content area. The workshop sessions, coupled with classroom "coaching" by the project staff as well as by colleagues working together in the mutual-assistance teams, provided as strong a support system as we could devise and deliver with the resources available.

In the two-year projects, teacher training occupied most of one academic year. In the one-year projects, the workshops and classroom coaching were "squeezed" into the first semester of the academic year with meetings held three times a month.

Of course, all this is easier said than done. Some of the very steps designed to neutralize those aspects of the school's organizational culture that impeded the acquisition and adoption of new teaching methods, such as teachers' isolation and lack of systematic interaction with peers, had their own built-in impediments. For example, the project staff thought that teacher self-help teams would counteract resistance and provide a source of support for teachers trying out new ways of teaching. However, as we shall discuss in greater detail later in this chapter, having teachers observe each other's actual teaching behavior in itself proved to be such a radical departure from accepted school norms that it aroused considerable anxiety and resistance in some teachers. To have other adults, and colleagues at that, present in the room while a teacher was conducting a lesson was an invasion of the teacher's privacy and autonomy that conveyed unforeseen and undesirable connotations. Later we understood that it was also experienced as depriving teachers of one of their most reliable defenses, which is the opportunity to tell colleagues about their classroom experiences without anyone being able to ascertain the degree to which these "war stories" bore any resemblance to observable events. Again, we failed to appreciate the extent to which teachers had learned to camouflage dissatisfaction with what happened in their classrooms. The very act of raising problems is perceived as casting some doubt on their competence, since there is no norm for openly discussing these problems (Argyris, 1982).

We do not intend to imply that teachers purposely distort their accounts of what occurs in their classrooms. We refer primarily to the well known phenomenon that it takes painstaking training or unusual talent to relate complex behavioral events with a high degree of accuracy, i.e., in the same way that several observers could identify. It is natural for people to relate events with a great deal of personal meanings and unconscious alterations stemming from their unique perspective. Teachers are confronted by such a myriad of acts occurring almost simultaneously in the classroom that only a battery of video cameras could record them all. Unless a teacher agrees in advance with some outside observer to focus on a specific set of events, two people sitting in the same class at the same time are likely to "see" different events. If, as we have asserted, teachers are not trained in their professional education to focus on interpersonal processes in the classroom, and concentrate primarily on the subject matter they are required to teach, it should come as no surprise that their reports of classroom behavioral events related to the instructional process do not reflect a high degree of reliability.

Some of the measures we employed to assist teachers in implementing cooperative learning also required a period of learning and adjustment, quite apart from teachers' adjustment to the cooperative learning methods themselves. Also, the use of mutual assistance teams required the principal to free teachers from some classroom teaching hours in order to observe their colleagues, requiring substitute teachers. The constraints of school scheduling and minuscule resources imposed severe limitations on the extent to which any organizational procedure could be invoked to sustain the innovation in instruction (Corbett, Dawson and Firestone, 1984; Fullan, 1982).

The "one class, one teacher" axiom, upon which rests the entire organizational structure of the school, is not only a behavioral regularity deeply ingrained in teachers' and principals' concepts of school organization. It is also a bedrock economic reality from which there is little room for appeal. Without resources for hiring substitute personnel, even if the participants in the change project are teachers from the same school who have free time now and then, it is nearly impossible to sustain mutual assistance teams over more than a few meetings. Once teachers retreat again "behind the classroom door," and their classroom teaching behavior is not exposed to or supported by other colleagues, implementation of new teaching methods becomes more dependent upon the teachers' personal characteristics than upon school policy and school culture. This too is a feature of the school's "loosely coupled" organization.

## Teachers' reactions to the change project: Innovators and resisters

Sharan and Hertz-Lazarowitz (1982) presented data about the teachers who participated in an instructional change project to implement cooperative learning in three elementary schools. We cannot review here all of the findings reported in that study. In addition to those data, several qualitative analyses were done of the extensive interviews conducted with all of the teachers at the conclusion of the project.[1] The interviews provided insight into the thoughts and feelings of the teachers in these schools, as well as much information about their perceptions and responses to the change project. What follows expands on the quantitative results reported earlier.

Interviews lasting between one and two hours were conducted with each of 34 homeroom teachers in three elementary schools in Israel. The tape-recorded sessions were subjected to a series of content analyses that yielded both quantitative and qualitative results. During the two years, the teachers had participated in 18 workshops devoted to cooperative learning in small groups. They also participated in self-help teams to provide support to the teachers for planning and implementing the new teaching method, and classroom coaching was made available to the teachers by members of the project team. It should be noted that only two of the 34 teachers were college graduates, the others being graduates of teacher training institutes that grant a teaching diploma (for two or three years of post-high school study). All the homeroom teachers were women with a median age of 34 years (ranging from 22 to 55 years of age) and with a median of 14 years experience in classroom teaching. This group constituted the majority of the homeroom teachers in the three schools. The schools were identified by the area school supervisor as serving a lower socioeconomic level population, in accordance with the mandate given us by the Ministry of Education that funded the project.

The conclusions to be reached from a close study of these interviews referred to two distinct levels of the project's impact: The level of the teaching staff as a whole, as members of a given organizational environment, and the level of the individual. The interviews indicated the teachers' reactions were far more positive in a variety of ways than negative. There was a "school-level impact" that was critical for insuring that the change project made progress. When we looked closely at how each individual evaluated her experiences as part of this project, we found that the teachers responded in radically different ways. Some praised particular activities or features of the project as being highly effective, beneficial and supportive, while others, even in the same school, viewed the very same events in a singularly negative light, almost diametrically opposed to what other teachers claimed. That fact alone is a very sobering phenomenon. It emphasizes that agents of planned change in schools can have a wide range of different impacts on the teachers in a given school, and that a staff of teachers is not likely to react uniformly to an attempt to change their professional behavior. One can see responses to the change efforts as more or less typical of a given school, but that central tendency also obscures a variety of individual coping patterns that form a complex mosaic

---

[1] The interviews with the teachers in this project were conducted as part of an M.A. dissertation by Yehudit Lichtensohn at the School of Education, Tel-Aviv University, under the guidance of Shlomo Sharan and Rachel Hertz-Lazarowitz (of Haifa University). The original version of the qualitative analyses presented here appeared as a chapter by Sharan, Hertz-Lazarowitz and Lichtensohn in the volume called: *Changing Schools: The Small Group Teaching Project in Israel* (in Hebrew), Ramot - Tel-Aviv University, 1981, edited by Shlomo Sharan and Rachel Hertz-Lazarowitz.

in the school culture. Taken alone, that conclusion borders on the trivial, despite the fact that this conclusion expresses a truth frequently ignored. How this conclusion manifested itself in the interviews will provide it with more meaning.

Study of the interviews led to the identification of three major themes:

1. Teachers' sense of control over events in their classrooms as a function of participation and of employing cooperative learning;

2. The relative efficiency of cooperative learning for teaching subject matter and for contributing to the personal and educational development of the students;

3. The impact of the project on the professional growth of the teachers and on their professional satisfaction or disappointment, particularly in respect to their intensified contact with colleagues in the school.

## Students' learning and behavior

Research on teachers and teaching (Fuller and Brown, 1975; Lortie, 1975) documented the fact that teachers' locus of concern was, first and foremost, anchored in the students, their progress in learning and their behavior in the classroom. Classroom behavior is a source of considerable anxiety, particularly in terms of the teachers' ability to control events in the classroom and to ensure orderly progress in the pursuit of learning, as they understand it. Students' progress is the main source of teachers' professional satisfaction. This combination of heightened anxiety over classroom control, coupled with the need to derive professional gratification from student progress in learning, seems to provide the basis for the overdetermined investment of emotional attachment teachers develop to relatively strict control over students' interactions in the classroom.

We divided the 34 teachers into two groups, innovators (N=22) and resisters (N=12), based on careful classroom observations on several occasions. The precise content of these observations and their quantitative findings appear elsewhere (Sharan and Hertz-Lazarowitz, 1982). The teachers who adopted cooperative learning perceived the effects of the new method on their students quite differently from those teachers who did not implement it systematically in their classes. The innovators related in their interviews that their students appeared to be much more relaxed, less tense and more confident while pursuing their work than they were in the frontal classroom. Students concentrated more on the task at hand even though there was more noise than usually permitted, and they appeared to enjoy their work. They took a great interest in how their groupmates proceeded in implementing their task.

Most of the innovating teachers noted that the slower learners spoke up and were not as lost in the crowd as usual. They also enjoyed greater trust by their peers than was noticed earlier. When small groups of students presented their work to the class as a whole, the groups went out of their way to ensure that the presentation involved everyone in the class in some activity. Finally, the teachers noted that the nature of their own interaction with the students underwent significant positive change. They presumed this was a result of the decided relaxation in classroom discipline (e.g., teachers stopped reprimanding students for talking) that occurred almost naturally in the cooperative learning classroom (see Hertz-Lazarowitz and Shachar, 1990).

The teachers who resisted implementation of cooperative learning claimed that the "weaker" students exploited the opportunity to remain silent and not participate, a phenomenon that social psychologists have called "social loafing" or "the free rider effect" (Kerr and Bruun, 1983; Latane, Williams and Harkin, 1975). Teachers of English as a second language asserted that students were unable to function in small groups that were not led by a teacher because of lack of knowledge or because they would hear too many mistakes. Still others related that the students themselves said they found cooperative learning very tiring and requested time off to rest. Finally, some teachers reported that groups were unwilling to admit or cooperate with problematic students who remained rejected and uninvolved.

According to their testimony, the threat of loss of control over the class as a result of its division into small groups brought on depression in some teachers. It seems, however, that the depression stemmed as much from the challenge of change itself, with all its uncertainty, as from the anticipated loss of control over students' behavior in the classroom.

## Efficiency in teaching subject matter

Both the innovators and resisters claimed that cooperative learning required more time than frontal instruction, so that teachers were able "to cover" less material with the cooperative learning approach. In the teachers' perception (not always confirmed by Ministry officials or field supervisors), they are required by the Ministry of Education to cover a given amount of subject matter during given periods of time. Hence, except on relatively rare occasions, they cannot afford the luxury of employing any instructional method that is more time consuming than the "rapid delivery" afforded by direct frontal teaching.

The project staff ascertained that even if it were demonstrated to the teachers that their perceptions of the curricular requirements were exaggerated, teachers had internalized the demand for racing against the clock in order to cover the material. They would feel frustrated if they could not act in accordance with their own inner pressures to present large quantities of subject matter at a relatively rapid pace. When circumstances of any kind, originating in the children themselves or in external sources, required that teachers slow down, they felt that their work was disrupted or even that they were professionally cheated. Of course, students who require additional assistance or more time, thereby slowing the pace of instruction, are quickly branded as slow learners or as deserving of even less flattering titles.

Observers of schools can testify that whether the pressure to cover material is internalized by teachers or not, principals and supervisory personnel, and particularly the universities in Israel, frequently put pressure on schools and teachers to present ever greater amounts of subject matter to students, at the secondary level in particular. Hence, it is not merely the teachers' illusion that they are subject to severe role conflicts related to conflicting goals. On the one hand, they wish to engage students in meaningful learning, and on the other, they feel constrained to present large quantities of material that students must grasp quickly. The school system communicates double messages to teachers that are at cross purposes. Change agents striving to introduce innovative instructional practices in schools become caught in this cross fire. They, too, are forced to concede that adoption of the innovation is unlikely unless the overriding goals of the system are altered, and that change is beyond their powers to effect at the level of the school.

All of the above does not negate the fact that, at least as far as the teachers who were innovators are concerned, the students acquired important skills from their experiences with cooperative learning. Most obvious was the fact that they learned much about "how to learn." Difficult material was perceived by the students as a challenge that they had to cope with and plan how to overcome, rather than complaining how hard it was or showing signs of apathy. Formal evaluation showed that the students in the cooperative learning classes achieved as much or more than their peers in the traditional classes (Sharan, Hertz-Lazarowitz and Ackerman, 1980).

But results from external evaluation aside, the teachers perceived students were making strides in learning which the teachers had not anticipated or expected from children from "culturally deprived" backgrounds. Students were seen planning learning activities cooperatively and following their plan. They conducted discussions in small groups without wandering off the subject; they learned to listen to one another, and they expressed their own ideas in the group. They referred to a variety of sources—books, newspapers, films, interviews, etc.—to obtain the information they sought, without having it delivered to them prepackaged by the teacher. Progress of this kind, however, is not regularly or easily measured by formal tests, and, consequently, teachers' testimony in these matters frequently is discounted by the authorities as not constituting bona fide learning.

## Impact on the teachers

The most complex and, at times it seems, painful impact of the change project was on the teachers themselves, as we anticipated. Teachers occupy a relatively modest place in educational psychology research, the main attraction being "the child." In the project we described here, the teachers were the main focus of our study. And the teachers, when asked, had a great deal to say about themselves and how they were affected by this project, only some of which can be presented here.

Many teachers were aware of the fact that the project ostensibly was directed at classroom instruction. But considerable time and energy were invested toward developing school-wide procedures and practices. They knew the entire staff was the object of our efforts, and not the individual teacher. Most teachers expressed great satisfaction with the forms of collegial collaboration introduced into the three schools. They perceived this collaboration as a source of welcome support in their work, whether they adopted cooperative learning or not. Other teachers also conveyed their gratitude to the project for generating changes in the teachers as individuals, even though these changes often entailed some initial discomfort. They felt they were more able to lead a class now than ever before, more capable of carrying out the role of instructor than they had been, and were less bored with their job.

Their rejection of the idea of being observed by colleagues was, more often than not, supplanted by genuine enthusiasm for having other teachers in the classroom during a lesson. Teachers appreciated hearing constructive comments about their work and learned to accept them without succumbing to resentment, fear of failure and antagonism. The teacher self-help teams legitimated the open clarification of classroom teaching problems that were previously considered to be taboo as topics of public discussion. For some, the teacher self-help teams became the most important component of the project.

Many teachers commented about the importance of having most of the teachers in the school participate in the project, although as we will note soon, the absence of even a few teachers created many unforeseeable complications. The point was made many times during these interviews that the project imparted to the teachers a new sense of belonging to an entire school. Common problems encountered when trying to implement cooperative learning brought teachers together to try and find solutions. Teachers praised the relatively long duration of the project (2 years), which made it possible to implement and practice specific techniques with the help of the project consultants. Equally important for many teachers was their perception of the systematic fashion in which the project progressed, as well as the fact that it provided direct assistance to the teachers in the classroom.

Many of the same points that were considered to be the project's more positive features by some teachers were the foci of criticism for others. We shall begin with the teacher self-help teams that stimulated so much praise and satisfaction from the majority of the teachers. Some teachers felt that the self-help teams aroused competition among teachers. A relatively new teacher on the staff of one school said the presence of other teachers in her class made her fearful that her fellow teachers would be less inclined to accept her than when she was not scrutinized so closely. We were told that some teachers emphasized that in their school everyone was an individualist. Collaboration with others became, for some teachers, a new source of concern that they could be manipulated, that teachers would take from them what they invented by themselves without giving them due credit, or that they could be made to take the blame for failures that were not their doing. Moreover, the principal was not always supportive in this new venture, so that adopting cooperative learning could place a teacher at risk for breaking the rules or angering colleagues.

Nor were all the teachers prepared to accept their colleagues' comments as potentially constructive feedback. Some questioned the right of teachers who were their "equals" to say anything about the way they performed their job. What gave other teachers in the school the knowledge or authority to voice an opinion about what their colleagues did, is a question we heard voiced several times in the interviews. One teacher, on the verge of tears, said, "I had a really positive self-image about my teaching, and suddenly I got a slap in the face."

Indeed, some teachers, albeit only two or three, said bluntly that they lacked any motivation to join the project. The reason they went along with it was because they did not wish to appear in a negative light in the eyes of their colleagues who accepted the project. They had no interest in the new teaching methods, and, for that matter, they cared little for teaching in general. They taught because they wanted to work, and teaching from 8 A.M. to noon or 1 P.M. was convenient for them. To begin learning new methods now was too much trouble and would not improve their working conditions. On the contrary, the need to constantly find imaginative and exciting learning tasks for the children, instead of simply relying on the textbook that had been in use for years, imposed additional burdens that they and other teachers were unhappy about. Admittedly, the children became more involved with their learning, but some of the teachers were put out by the extra work involved. Together with the challenge of acquiring competence in a new method, the change project seemed to hold little attraction for one small group of teachers. The fact that a project could potentially cause teachers more work than their accepted routine has often been found to be sufficient reason for rejecting a project or initially accepting and then later transforming or distorting it (Huberman and Miles, 1984).

## Proposed stages in the adoption of cooperative learning

Analysis of the interviews led to the formulation of a series of stages, or, more correctly, of phases in the teachers' adoption of cooperative learning. Obviously, the teachers who rejected the project and the new teaching methods did not proceed very far along this road, so that the complete set of stages was experienced only by the innovators, not by the resisters. It should be noted that an ad hoc construction of a 5-stage model such as this one has no claim to validity beyond the confines of the present study and the data it generated. If other teachers in other places and circumstances experience a similar set of stages in their adoption of an instructional innovation, that would lend some support to our conclusions. Not much research of that nature is available to date, and we hope that more knowledge on this subject will be forthcoming (Hall, George and Rutherford, 1979; Huberman and Miles, 1984; Zaltman, Florio and Sikorski, 1977). In the meantime, we offer these observations with all of the appropriate caveats.

Stage 1: *Initial attitudes toward change: Acceptance or rejection*
>Upon learning of the proposed change project, teachers are asked to express their perception of the change and their willingness or unwillingness to proceed. Their response is based on personality characteristics, on prevailing norms and expectations of the school culture, earlier experience with change, and on their limited knowledge

about the nature of the change ("initial size-up of the innovation," Huberman and Miles, 1984, p. 61).

Stage 2: *The need to act in light of increased awareness of the change*
As the teachers participate in the training workshops, their awareness of the new method's potential increases and with it the inclination to apply their knowledge. The first resistance to change has diminished, gradually replaced by information and motivation to change.

Stage 3: *Encounter with cooperative learning as a set of skills*
Teachers begin to implement cooperative learning in small doses, and, at times, with frustrating consequences. They develop strategies for coping with problems. Initial successes pave the way for continued implementation.

Stage 4: *Evaluating the change*
After some successful experiences in implementing cooperative learning, the teacher begins to gain awareness of the personal and professional change that is occurring. Teachers begin to evaluate the meaning of the change for themselves.

Stage 5: *Internalizing and transferring the change*
Teachers understand the change intellectually, they incorporate it, each according to his/her style, in their behavioral repertoire and adjust to it on an emotional-value level. Moreover, they begin to employ their new skills in new classroom situations.

## CONCLUSION

For all the resistance, conflicts, ambivalence and frustration that accompanied this instructional change project, the reader might register some surprise at the claim that, on the whole, we consider the project to have been largely successful. With two-thirds of the teachers implementing cooperative learning at a level of between 25-30% of instructional time as recorded by observers, we felt that our investment yielded positive results. Was the extent of our investment in time and energy out of proportion to the extent of the visible results? Since we did not engage in a cost-effectiveness analysis of this project, that direction of questioning is beyond our scope.

The emphasis in this chapter on individual teachers' reactions to the change project should not obscure the *school-wide organizational character of the change process*. Were it not for the direct involvement of the principal and of the majority of the teachers in each school in the acquisition and implementation of cooperative learning, it is doubtful that any significant change would have occurred. Subsequent attempts of other groups of change agents in Israel to bring about similar changes in the instructional behavior or teachers have not yielded remarkable results. Even though the educational system has been talking about cooperative learning for close to 20 years, it is still rare to find it practiced with any degree of competence. Our view is that change efforts have not encompassed the organizational level of the schools or a substantial majority of the teaching staff in any given school. Rather, they have continued to direct their efforts at subgroups of teachers within the schools, and have consistently failed to provide the needed support systems and classroom guidance necessary for real change in instruction. The relative lack of results was predictable.

What we wished to highlight here was that, above and beyond the change that did occur in the particular project described here, and despite the considerable effort that was invested in the teaching staff as a whole, some teachers perceived the change efforts very differently from what the change agents intended or could imagine in advance. This message should alert instructional change agents to the need to be sensitive to the forces of resistance operating in any staff of teachers. It might be advisable to try to clarify with the resisters the nature of their objections during the conduct of the project and not wait until the project has been concluded. We admittedly failed to do that, and our present understanding of what occurred is the wisdom of hindsight. Of course, one impediment to realizing this suggestion is that the resisters often refuse to identify themselves, and any attempt to do so may be met with denial or be perceived as an insult or a threat. The oft-repeated maxim that "you have to crack an egg to make an omelet" cannot be applied naively to mean that some teachers' feelings must unavoidably be hurt in order to foster change. Contrary to our intention, it might seem as if we were in fact saying just that throughout this chapter.

Another topic mentioned in this chapter that deserves additional comment is the resistance to change presented by some of the school's behavioral regularities and professional norms. For example, the teachers' felt need to "cover the material" which, some said, virtually precluded their adoption of cooperative learning because it consumed more time than traditional expository teaching. It could be that, in the long run, this prevailing norm for presenting fairly large amounts of subject matter within given time limits in lecture form will prove more potent as a resister of change than any effort made by change agents operating in a few schools. The data we gathered testify to the adoption of cooperative learning by two-thirds of the teachers we worked with. It reflected the condition of instruction in the schools immediately following the formal conclusion of the change project. We were never funded to return to the schools after the lapse of a year or two to observe or study how instruction proceeded in those schools at that time. Hence, we do not really know if our change efforts had staying power much beyond the departure of its advocates. Data about change over the long term can be obtained only under unusual circumstances (see Solomon, Watson, Schaps, Battistich and Solomon, 1990).

One school about which we do have information proved that, given the proper administrative support, cooperative learning could survive in a school over the long term. The year following the formal conclusion of the project, one project staff member, in the employ of the Ministry of Education, continued to serve as a consultant to the school. She worked with the teachers but invested much effort in expanding the principal's knowledge and understanding of cooperative learning. He, in fact, became his school's expert and continued to guide his teachers in implementation of cooperative learning after the conclusion of the consultant's year of work in his school.

Perhaps long-lasting change in many schools can come only when supported by legislation that mandates specific changes so that the majority of teachers are constrained by the authorities to perform their duties in a different way. It is doubtful that such legislation is forthcoming in an era that insists that it does not know how to identify the preferred modes of instruction in public schools. It appears that educational change will continue into the near future, at least to be a school-by-school affair, with all of the complexities that we and other investigators have tried to document.

# REFERENCES

Argyris, C. *Reasoning, learning and action.* San Francisco: Jossey-Bass, 1982.

Berman, P. and McLaughlin, M. *Federal programs supporting educational change.* Santa Monica, CA: Rand Corporation. Vol. 1. *A model of educational change,* 1974. Vol. 2. *Factors affecting change agent projects,* 1975. Vol. 3. *The process of change,* 1975. Vol. 4. *The findings in review,* 1975. Vol. 5. *Executive summary,* 1975. Vol. 6. *Implementing and sustaining Title VII bilingual projects.* Vol. 7. *Factors affecting implementation and continuation,* 1977. Vol. 8. *Implementing and sustaining innovations,* 1978.

Bushnell, D. and Rappaport, D. *Planned change in education.* New York: Harcourt, Brace, Jovanovich, 1971.

Corbett, H.D., Dawson, J. and Firestone, W. *School context and school change.* New York: Teachers College Press, 1984.

Fullan, M. *The meaning of educational change.* New York: Teachers College Press, 1982.

Fuller, F. and Brown, O. Becoming a teacher. In *Teacher education 1975.* 74th Yearbook of the National Society for the Study of Education. Chicago: The University of Chicago Press, 1975.

Goodlad, J. *A place called school.* New York: McGraw-Hill, 1984.

Hall, G., George, A. and Rutherford, W. *Measuring stages of concern about the innovation.* Austin, TX: The Research and Development Center for Teacher Education, The University of Texas, 1979.

Heckman, P. Understanding school culture. In J. Goodlad (Ed.), *The ecology of school renewal.* 86th Yearbook of the National Society for the Study of Education. Chicago: The University of Chicago Press, 1987, 63-78.

Hertz-Lazarowitz, R. and Shachar, H. Teachers' verbal behavior in cooperative and whole-class instruction. In S. Sharan (Ed.), *Cooperative learn-*

*ing: Theory and research.* New York: Praeger Publishing Co., 1990, 77-94.

Huberman, A. and Miles, M. *Innovation up close.* New York: Plenum Press, 1984.

Kerr, N. and Bruun, S. Dispensibility of member effort and group motivation losses: Free rider effects. *Journal of Personality and Social Psychology, 44*, 1983, 78-94.

Latane, B., Williams, K. and Harkins, S. Many hands make for light work: The causes and consequences of social loafing. *Journal of Personality and Social Psychology, 36*, 1975, 886-893.

Lieberman, A. and Rosenholtz, S. The road to school improvement: Barriers and bridges. In J. Goodlad (Ed.), *The ecology of school renewal.* 86th Yearbook of the National Society for the Study of Education. Chicago: The University of Chicago Press, 1987, 79-98.

Lortie, D. *Schoolteacher.* Chicago: The University of Chicago Press, 1975.

Meyer, J. and Rowan, B. The structure of educational organizations. In J. Meyer and W.R. Scott (Eds.), *Organizational environments: Ritual and rationality.* Beverly Hills: Sage Publications, 1983, 71-97.

Miles, M. On temporary systems. In M. Miles (Ed.), *Innovation in education.* New York: Teachers College Press, 1964, 437-490.

Sarason, S. *The culture of the school and the problem of change.* Boston: Allyn and Bacon, 1971. 2nd revised edition, 1982.

Sarason, S. *Schooling in America: Scapegoat and salvation.* New York: The Free Press, 1983.

Sharan, S. and Hertz-Lazarowitz, R. (Eds.) *Changing schools: The small-group teaching project in Israel.* Tel-Aviv: Ramot—Tel-Aviv University, 1981 (Hebrew).

Sharan, S. and Hertz-Lazarowitz, R. The effects of an instructional change project on teachers' behavior, attitudes and perceptions. *Journal of Applied Behavioral Science, 18*, 1982, 185-201.

Sharan, S., Hertz-Lazarowitz, R. and Ackerman, Z. Academic achievement of elementary school children in small groups versus whole class instruction. *Journal of Experimental Education, 48*, 1980, 125-129.

Sharan, S., Hertz-Lazarowitz, R. and Hare, P. The classroom: A structural analysis. In S. Sharan and R. Hertz-Lazarowitz (Eds.), *Changing schools: The small-group teaching project in Israel.* Tel-Aviv: Ramot - Tel-Aviv University, 1981, 21-53.

Sharan, S., Kussell, P., Hertz-Lazarowitz, R., Bejarano, Y., Raviv, S. and Sharan, Y. *Cooperative learning in the classroom: Research in desegregated schools.* Hillsdale, NJ: Lawrence Erlbaum, 1984.

Sharan, S. and Rich, Y. Field experiments on ethnic integration in Israeli schools. In Y. Amir and S. Sharan (Eds.), *School desegregation*. Hillsdale, NJ: Lawrence Erlbaum, 1984, 189-217.

Sharan, S. and Shachar, H. *Language and learning in the cooperative classroom*. New York: Springer Publishing Co., 1988.

Sharan, S. and Sharan, Y. *Small group teaching*. Tel-Aviv: Schocken Publishing House, 1974. English language edition: Educational Technology Publications, Englewood Cliffs, NJ, 1976.

Solomon, D., Watson, M., Schaps, E., Battistich, V. and Solomon, J. Cooperative learning as part of a comprehensive classroom program designed to promote prosocial development. In S. Sharan (Ed.), *Cooperative learning: Theory and research*. New York: Praeger Publishing Co., 1990, 231-260.

Thelen, H. *The classroom society. The construction of educational experience*. London: Croom Helm, 1981.

Weick, K. *The social psychology of organizing*. Reading, MA: Addison Wesley, 1969.

Zaltman, G., Florio, D. and Sikorski, L. *Dynamic educational change*. New York: The Free Press, 1977.

Chapter 11
# Teacher Leadership:
# Ideology and Practice

*by Ann Lieberman, Ellen R. Saxl, and Matthew B. Miles,*
*Teachers College, Columbia University*

The "second wave" of school reform has been characterized by much talk of
restructuring schools and professionalizing teaching. Commission reports
from business, education, and statewide policy groups are calling for major
changes in the ways schools go about their work and the ways teachers are
involved in their decision-making structure (Darling-Hammond, 1987). There
is clearly an attempt to change the organizational culture of schools from one
that fosters privatism and adversarial relationships between and among
teachers and principals to one that encourages collegiality and commitment
(Lieberman & Miller, 1984; Little, 1986; Lortie, 1975; Rosenholtz, in press). On
the political level, some states and school districts are creating new roles and
new structures in an attempt to change the social relations of the people who
do the work at the school level. The leap from report to reality, however, is a
difficult one, for there are few precedents, few models, and no guidelines. We
are literally learning by doing. What is needed then, is a beginning description of this work and some understanding of the people involved — what
they know and do, what the dynamics of their interactions look like — as these
new forms come into being. What are these new structures? What can we
learn about the meaning of these new roles for teachers? What is teacher
leadership? What actually happens when teacher-leaders help other teachers? Our purpose here is to understand some of these new roles and begin to
answer some of the questions now being raised as we look at a particular
group of successful teacher-leaders in a major metropolitan area. We consciously use the term *teacher-leader* to suggest that there is not only a set of
skills that are teacherlike, but a way of thinking and acting that is sensitive to
teachers, to teaching, and to the school culture.

## THE SKILLS OF TEACHER-LEADERS

From 1983 to 1985 we had a unique opportunity to study 17 former teachers
who played leadership roles in a variety of schools in a large eastern city (see
Miles, Saxl, & Lieberman, in press). (We have continued to work with some
of them for an additional two years.) Within that time, we were able to collect
a great deal of information about who these people were, what they had
learned in their new roles, what they did in the context of their school, and
even, in their own words, their view of being teacher-leaders. The 17 teacher-
leaders worked in three different programs, and all were considered successful in the work they did within their schools. The criteria for success varied,
depending on the context, all the way from creating a healthy climate, to

making organizational change, to raising achievement scores.

The programs represented three different approaches to working with school people. The first was based on the "effective schools research," the second had as its major strategy the formation of a large school site committee with a broad constituent group, and the third utilized an organic approach to working with teachers on a one-to-one as well as a group basis — providing support and expanded leadership roles for teachers. Despite the differences in strategy, we looked to see if there was a core of skills that was common to these people in their roles as teacher-leaders. (Skills to us meant knowing how to do something rather than knowing that something was appropriate to do. Our focus was on the *capabilities* of these people to activate strategies for change.) We reasoned that, as leaders, these people had to have or develop both process and content skills and that they had to be able to adapt to different contexts and different situations. It is important to note that although these people were very experienced, they learned from both their new role and the context of their particular program.

First, it was necessary to separate out what these teacher-leaders knew when they came to the job from what they had learned while on the job. This gave us not only a sense of the possible criteria that were used in choosing these leaders, but what their new learnings had been as they worked to create these new roles and structures. Ultimately, we were looking for what skills would be teachable to new teacher-leaders in the future.

## Entry Characteristics

We found that these leaders had a broad range of skills, abilities, and experience, which included teaching children at several grade levels as well as adults. They were truly "master teachers." In addition, many had been involved in *curriculum development* in the past, as well as having held positions that enabled them to teach new curriculum to others. Their enthusiasm for learning was made manifest by an impressive array of *academic pursuits* and accomplishments. They held many academic degrees, as well as having attended a broad spectrum of courses, conferences, and workshops on topics as diverse as conflict resolution, teacher effectiveness, and adult development. They came to their work knowledgeable about schools, the change process, and how to work with adults. Most had held positions in which they had gained experience in *administrative and organizational skills* and had learned something about the complexity of school cultures. They were knowledgeable about community concerns as well as schools, some having served as school board members, community organizers, and in a variety of support positions in schools.

These leaders were risk-takers, willing to promote new ideas that might seem difficult or threatening to their colleagues. Their *interpersonal skills* — they knew how to be strong, yet caring and compassionate — helped them legitimate their positions in their schools amidst often hostile and resistant staffs.

## On-the-Job Learning

In spite of this impressive array of skills and abilities, it was significant that these leaders had so much to learn to cope with their new positions. Where before, working in a variety of roles, they had been sensitive to individual personalities and perspectives, now they had to be aware of the interests of teachers, principals and the community as a whole. These new conditions made it necessary for them to seek new ways of working, which, in turn, led them to find new sets of learnings. They found that what had worked in more narrowly defined positions would not work in the pursuit of a larger, common vision.

*Learning about the school culture.* Without exception, these leaders learned about the school culture as if it were a new experience for them. They saw how isolated teachers were in their classrooms and what this isolation did to them. They realized how hard it would be to create a structure to involve them, to build trust within the staff, and to cut through the dailiness of their work lives. They were confronted with the egalitarian ethic held by most teachers — the belief that teachers are all alike, differing only in length of service, age, grade level, or subject matter, rather than function, skill, advanced knowledge, role, or responsibility (Lortie, 1975). They saw that, while some principals understood the need for teacher involvement in their own growth and for allocating time during the school day for reflection and adult interaction, other principals pressed for "outcomes" — with or without a structure or process for teachers to learn being in place. In some schools, they saw literally no one supporting anyone. It came as no surprise then that some of these leaders said that the school climate and the administrator's style were the two most critical components of the school culture.

*New skills and abilities.* All of these leaders learned a variety of techniques for gaining acceptance by teachers and principals. They learned to break into the everyday activities and provide hands-on experiences to get teachers interested. They provided new environments and activities in which people could communicate with one another and learn how to facilitate both group and individual learning and involvement. They learned to be part of the system, but not get co-opted by it — a difficult but essential ability. They struggled with the collegial/expert dichotomy, one that clearly contradicts the egalitarian ethic that was being disrupted. In working with adults, they tried hard to listen more and suggest less and to resist jumping in with too many solutions. In spite of a high self-regard, several reported that they had not realized how much they did not know (Goodwin & Lieberman, 1986).

These new leadership roles tend to expose the powerful infantalizing effects on teachers of the existing structure of most schools. It is not that no one is in charge, or that people are inherently distrustful, but that the structure itself makes it difficult for adults to behave as adults. Rather than work collectively on their problems, everyone must struggle alone. This ubiquitous isolation dramatizes what "restructuring schools" means. New organizational forms enabling people to work together are certainly necessary, but in order for them to be established, the teachers must be organized, mobilized, led, and nurtured, with the principal's support, participation, and concern and the support and concern of all who share in the life of the school.

*Self-learning.* In addition to the techniques, skills, abilities, and new understandings that these leaders learned in their schools, they strongly expressed the feeling that they had learned a great deal about themselves as well. Many spoke of a new confidence that they felt in their own abilities. Some thought that they had acquired a more complex view of how to work with people. One said, "I can't believe I have learned to motivate, to lead, to inspire, to encourage, to support, and yes, even to manipulate." Assuming leadership in schools, then, may provide the means for greatly expanding one's own repertoire. Providing and facilitating for other people in the school offers opportunities for learning how to work with others, how to channel one's time, how to develop one's own abilities — to stretch both intellectually and personally.

It is paradoxical that, although teachers spend most of their time facilitating for student learning, they themselves have few people facilitating for them and understanding their needs to be recognized, encouraged, helped, supported, and engaged in professional learning. Perhaps this is what we mean by "professionalizing" teaching and "restructuring the work environment" of teachers. Maybe the opportunities for participating in the leadership of schools, and the structures created as a result, are the means to break the isolation of teachers and engage them in collective efforts to deal with what surely are large and complex problems.

## BUILDING COLLEAGUESHIP — A COMPLICATED PROCESS

Researchers have found the building of collegiality to be essential to the creation of a more professional culture in schools (Little, 1986; Rosenholtz, in press). They have also documented that norms of collaboration are built through the interactions created by the principal's facilitation of collegial work. In her now-classic study, Little describes how these norms were built as daily routines of isolation were replaced by talking, critiquing, and working together. In Rosenholtz's study, schools were differentiated as being of two kinds — "collaborative" or "isolated." In "collaborative settings" teachers perceived the principal to be supportive, concerned with treating any problems as collective schoolwide opportunities for learning; in "isolated settings" teachers and principals were alienated, with teachers feeling that any requests they made threatened the principal's feelings of self-esteem.

Since our study focused on the introduction of a new role that expanded the structure of leadership in a school, we were looking for the kinds of skills, abilities, and approaches that these leaders utilized in building collegiality in schools. In our search to understand how these teacher-leaders worked, we created sets of clusters, each cluster representing different skills, abilities, and approaches to building collegiality among the faculty. Although their contexts and styles were different, the similarity of the ways these leaders worked has added to our understanding of the complexities involved in changing a school culture when the leadership team is expanded beyond the principal.

The clusters were drawn from 18 different skills that were manifested by these leaders (Saxl, Miles, & Lieberman, in press). They include:

Building trust and rapport

Organizational diagnosis

Dealing with the process

Using resources

Managing the work

Building skill and confidence in others

## Building Trust and Rapport

A very important cluster, this set of skills appears early in the development of the work of all teacher-leaders. We found that these leaders did a variety of things to gain the trust of the people in their buildings and that, even when the person was previously known to all the teachers, the same kind of work was still necessary. Because these leaders, in every case, did not have a teaching load, they were immediately suspect: "How come this person doesn't have a class load like me? What are they supposed to be doing anyhow?" Thus the first problem to be faced was how to clarify the expectations of their role for the teachers in the school.

To begin with, the leaders had to figure out for themselves what they could realistically do in the school. Then, they tried to explain to the teachers what they were going to do, describing in a broad way why they were there and what might be the effects of their work. In some ways, perhaps, it is like the beginning of school, where the students want to know what kind of teacher this is, what will be expected of them, and what will go on in the classroom. The relationship here is similar, in that these expectations are negotiated over time, but different, in that the adult culture in schools is not kind to newcomers, especially those of their own rank. The image and the reality of a new role (a teacher without a class) is not the norm, and it is often easier to use a new person as the source of one's frustrations rather than to accept her or him as a helper, go-between, or leader of a different kind.

Just as in the teacher/class relationship, the leader must come to be seen by the teachers as legitimate and credible. They try to accomplish this by finding various ways to demonstrate their expertise and value to the teachers. For some, it is giving a make-or-break workshop — one that they know will either give them immediate credibility if it is successful or set them back for months if it fails. For others, it means becoming a "gofer" and providing resources: going to the library, bringing new materials, keeping the coffee pot going and the cookie jar filled. Somehow they have to do enough to show the staff that they are "good" — experts and helpers, important enough to belong in "their" school. It is at this point that these leaders must learn to deal with *addressing resistance*, for they are coming into a social system with well-developed formal and informal ties. Sometimes this resistance is based on old disappointments and unfulfilled promises from past years. Other times a newcomer takes the brunt of all kinds of existing tensions in a school, caused by everything from lack of adequate communication to complaints about space, resources, time, and so forth.

*Engaging in open supportive communication* is part of building trust. These leaders found ways of working with teachers and proving to them that they were capable of being open without betraying trust — that they were there for the staff in a helping, nonevaluative way. As they worked with the teachers, they began to *build a support group*, people who came to see that they could work together, struggle collectively, and feel comfortable working as a group rather than alone. For many leaders this meant finding teachers who could be experts in their own right, teachers who could teach other teachers things that they had learned. In the process of facilitating for others, the leaders began to *develop shared influence* and shared leadership. The idea that there are problems common to teachers and problems in a school that can be addressed collectively began to take hold, and teacher-leaders began to build a set of *productive working relationships*.

The abilities mentioned above appear to be necessary to the building of trust and rapport, which are the foundation for building collegiality in a school. Regardless of the size or complexity of the school, the age or experience of the staff, or the differences in the programmatic thrust, the same kinds of skills were used to legitimate the leadership role.

## Organizational Diagnosis

This set of skills — an understanding of the school culture and the ability to diagnose it — is crucial if a leader is to have the basis for knowing how and where to intervene to mobilize people to take action and begin to work together. Leaders did this in very different ways. Some people had an intuitive awareness of the formal and informal relationships in a school, while others consciously worked out strategies to help them collect data to help them better understand the school social system.

Depending on the specifics of the program, the methods of collection ranged from a formal needs assessment that asked teachers what they would find useful, to an informal collection of information about the principal, curriculum, resources, and so on. However it was accomplished, some initial *data collection* gave teacher-leaders a beginning awareness of the school environment. All were involved in picking up cues from staff, bulletin boards, teachers rooms, principals, parents — anyone who could provide information.

> In the beginning ... I had to overcome my own personality — the tendency to move too quickly and speak out.

> When you are a teacher, you only know your classroom problems. Now I look at the whole system... When I was in the classroom, I controlled it; the higher you go, the less control you have.

As we can see, collecting information while being conscious of one's self within the larger system was a strategic part of the teacher-leaders' way of working. Either as an insider or as one who came to a school with a leadership role, these people came to form some kind of a conceptual scheme in their minds — a map of what the school looked like, whom one might work with, where the trouble spots were, who was open to thinking about working on schoolwide problems. As they collected information about the school by being there, hanging around, talking to people, and so on, they began to get enough information to *make a diagnosis*.

If action and change were what their diagnosis called for, these leaders had to find ways to engage key school people with their observations, to *share the diagnosis* with them to see if it was theirs as well. This series of steps, not always consciously thought out, formed the basis for action plans for the school. We begin to see a process: understanding the school, collecting information about the people and how they work, constructing a valid picture of the organization, sharing the picture with others and planning a strategy for action.

## Dealing with the Process

Critical to the work of teacher-leaders were their understanding of and skill in managing the change process. Since this meant, among other things, promoting *collaborative relationships* in schools where people had little experience in working together, it involved the use of *conflict mediation* and *confrontation skills*. They soon learned from the realities of their work that, when one tries to get people to work together where they have previously worked alone, conflicts arise, and that their job was to find the means to deal with them. As they worked in their schools, building and modeling collaborative work, they were called upon to weave their way through the strands of the school culture. This involved many types of interactions with teachers, staff members, and administrators.

The relations with the principal varied according to the style of the principal and the structures for collaboration that were being created. When the structure called for working as a team and the principal had been accustomed to working alone, the teacher-leader had to show the principal the benefits to the school of shared decision making. Where a teacher center had been created, the principal had to learn to give support for teachers to work independently without feeling that the existence of this room threatened her or his perceived role as "instructional leader." The tact, skill, and understanding of the teacher-leader were crucial to the involvement of the principal in supporting these new modes of collaboration.

Sometimes the school was in conflict from the start: "The first mission was to bring teachers together to talk to each other. There was a general distrust of the administration by the teachers." Sometimes the job entailed helping the faculty work through conflicts. "At committee meetings, many conflicts come up. He helps us talk them out... We ventilate and direct our energy in a specific way."

Collaboration does not come as a natural consequence of working in a school. It must be taught, learned, nurtured, and supported until it replaces working privately. There were times when these teacher-leaders were the ones who had to confront negative information and give feedback where it was appropriate. Where conflicts appeared as a result of personal incompatibilities or differing interests, their job was not merely to smooth them over, as had often been the case in the past, but to find areas of agreement based on a larger view of the school and its problems.

They worked hard to *solve these problems* by making decisions collaboratively. This was a key skill: Who will do what, how will we do it, when will we make it happen, and how will we come to agree? They found that it took more than a vote to build consensus. It was always necessary to be alert to discontent and to practice and work on being open, communicating together, and finding ways to bring people, as individuals, to think of themselves as part of the group with group concerns.

## Using Resources

The fourth cluster of skills involved the use of resources. This refers to people, ideas, materials, and equipment — all part of the school, but often not utilized in the pursuit of collective goals. The teacher-leaders found themselves engaged in providing material things for teachers that helped to link them to the outside world.

> I'm a reader. I need follow-up materials from the literature to find out about good ideas.

> They needed a lot of resources.

> I would attend conventions, day and weekend seminars and collect handouts.

> I keep on tops of things. What texts are good?

They did workshops for teachers, demonstrated techniques, and provided follow-up. They also looked inside the school to plug people in to what was already there and, where appropriate, to link people together.

In the process of finding resources and using existing staff to help, these teacher-leaders also began to build a *resource network*, which included developing active linkages between teachers and other members of the school community. It was not just knowing where or whom to go to for help, but choosing the right person or right thing at the right time. Matching local needs and capabilities became the key skill.

Finally, it was necessary to help people make good use of the resources.

Just getting the "stuff" there was not enough. The leaders had to perform a brokerage function and then follow-up to see that the resources were being used. As we observed, this cluster of skills is part of a complicated process: from finding people and materials, both inside and outside the school, to building networks with these resources, to seeing that whoever, whatever, and wherever they were, they were available and utilized.

## Managing the Work

The teacher-leaders worked hard to maintain a balance between the process of getting people to work on collective problems and providing the content or substance around which they worked. Managing this work required a subtle blend of skills, including managing time, setting priorities for work, delegating tasks and authority, taking initiative, monitoring progress, and coordinating the many strands of work taking place in their schools. (It should be noted that these leaders differed in the amount of time they spent in a school. Some spent four days a week in one school, while others spent one day a week in four schools.)

*Administrative/organizational skills*, although part of their qualifications, were far more complex in these roles than the teacher-leaders had faced before. Time was a persistent problem. How much time does one spend with people having difficulties, or getting resources, or making arrangements for workshops, or demonstrating, or troubleshooting? This proved to be a formidable task, with the successful teacher-leaders we studied gaining great skill in allocating their time as they became experienced in their role.

*Managing and controlling skills* were needed to organize and manage the work. The teacher-leaders had to learn to move from thought to action. Some used charts to keep track of their activities; some did not. But all of them had to learn how to mobilize the staff and coordinate the many activities, while walking the fine line between exerting influence and "overmanaging" the process of change.

Although contexts differed, these leaders shared the skill of being proactive, that is, having a bias for action. This included modeling specific new techniques as well as promoting a general vision of more productive ways of working. Maintaining momentum in their work, without usurping the authority or the prerogatives of other leadership in the school, required them to take initiative while negotiating their way through the delicate yet tough relationships between and among teachers and principal.

## Building Skill and Confidence in Others

The last cluster of skills involved the continuous monitoring and *individual diagnosis* of teachers' communication needs and concerns, while attending to the general organizational health of the school. Working for several years in the same schools, these leaders tried to make normative the notions that it was both legitimate to have technical assistance and necessary to have in place some structure for problem solving. They were attempting to socialize a whole staff to have individual teachers look at themselves critically and take action on their own behalf, while continuing to build supportive structures to better carry out the work as a whole.

They tried to involve as many people as possible in leadership roles by institutionalizing a process or mechanism for dealing with improvement goals, at the same time trying to make sure that constructive changes occurred that would be visible to the whole school. They were concerned with building a support network for the school community, based on commitment and involvement, that was sensitive to individual teachers and other members of the community and, at the same time, promoted organizational change. This required constant vigilance: building networks for support, continuously recognizing and rewarding positive individual efforts that improved the school, helping to create short-term goals, and always working to institutionalize individual and collective efforts at improvement so that they would become "built into the walls."

# TEACHER-LEADERS IN THE CONTEXT OF THEIR SCHOOLS

The skill clusters we have been describing are based on interview and observational data from the 17 teacher-leaders we studied from 1983 to 1985. We can get another view, perhaps more integrated and dynamic, by being there, by seeing these people in their own contexts. We did several case studies of these teacher-leaders in 1985 and 1986. The following summary of two of them will help round out the picture we have drawn thus far (Miles, Saxl, James, & Lieberman, 1986).

## Urban High School

Urban High is a large comprehensive high school that also serves as the special education center for the entire area. It is in a blighted area in a large urban city. There are 3,500 students in the school, 62 percent Hispanic and 30 percent black. Achievement is low overall. The majority of the students (2,000) are enrolled in general education. Reading, math, and writing scores are low. The principal is young, energetic, and extremely receptive to innovative ideas and any means to improve the school. He is very concerned with raising the level of instruction and increasing the professionalism of teachers through staff development and increased teacher control of the curriculum.

In March 1985, a teacher center opened in the school. Brenda C., a former English teacher at Urban, became the teacher-specialist — a full-time teacher-leader hired to run the teacher center and work with the staff. Because the school was in the process of reorganizing from departments to clusters, experienced teachers were becoming the coordinators or heads of special projects, causing them to leave teaching and move to these new positions. (Given the harsh conditions of the school context — crime, purse snatchings, noise, pitted chalkboards, lack of necessary supplies, prisonlike rooms, and other difficult teaching conditions — it is not hard to see why teachers would want these positions.) When they left new teachers replaced them.

Brenda wanted to do three things during her first year: improve morale, facilitate communication between the various groups in the school, and encourage the staff to utilize the center for professional growth. Subtle resistance plagued her efforts in the beginning. There was the natural resistance to being "improved," as well as the notion that being a high school teacher — a subject-matter specialist — somehow made one already expert.

She began, during her first month, by just offering free coffee and refreshments to the teachers. (The principal had supplied a large room and the coffee.) She spent a great deal of time and money (her own) buying materials that would be of interest to the teachers. She tried hard to get materials that would engender self-help as much as possible, attempting to be sensitive to the sensibilities of her peers. She spoke at department meetings to advertise the availability of these materials to the teachers.

Little by little the teachers began to come to the center. At first they came only for coffee. Brenda wrote personal notes to people to encourage them to come back and to participate in other activities. To enhance communication, she formed a site committee made up of representatives from the various cluster groups. (Finding a common meeting time for everyone was impossible, so staggered meetings went on during the day.)

With encouragement from the director of the teacher center consortium, Brenda helped create a workshop, given after school was over in June, to teach teachers about the latest research on classroom management, mastery learning, and learning styles. The workshop was planned in such a way that the teachers had an obligation to attempt one or more of the ideas in their classrooms in the fall. In this way, Brenda hoped to begin to build a core group of teachers, encourage professional development in the center, and work on greater communication among the teachers.

The impact of these efforts, and others, has been to draw more and more teachers to the center. They read the bulletin boards, look at materials, use the machines, plan lessons, talk together, and work with Brenda. Informally, teachers come for afterschool courses from other schools, which indicates that the center is reaching out to a larger network in the district.

Teachers from the site committee have been instrumental in disseminating information about the center to other teachers. New teachers have talked about being offered nonjudgmental assistance by Brenda in the center. Experienced teachers have spoken about the amenities that make their life easier: a quiet place to work, rexograph machines, and new materials and supplies. All of this has greatly increased the morale of the staff. (An indication of the center's growing popularity was the success of a party for the staff that was given at the end of June. Almost all the teachers came — a highly unusual occurrence.)

Brenda, who has been a teacher at Urban High for 23 years and knows the social system of her school as an insider, has been using this knowledge to create an "oasis in the desert." We see the special role that a teacher in a leadership position can play — encouraged and supported by a sensitive principal — as she gently and cautiously plans for and takes on the function of building morale and professionalism among the staff. She helps alleviate the tensions of a large, experienced staff trying to deal with the tremendous problems that exist in a school in a depressed community. She builds trust among the faculty, recognizing not only the classical resistance to new ideas, but also the special nature of high school teachers (subject-matter specialists with advanced degrees who have their own special reasons to resist being "improved"). Although just a beginning, Brenda's leadership has begun to fill in the tremendous gap between a professional environment and the bare level of subsistence in a complex, difficult high school.

## Parkridge Elementary School

At Parkridge Elementary School, Andrea G., a teacher-leader who came from another part of the city, also runs a teacher center. She has been at her school for four years. Her school has always been known as the showcase school of the district. It is a school with 1,500 children. The ethnic mix of the neighborhood has changed over time from Jewish and Italian to Hispanic and black, with a small percentage of Caucasian children.

The school has many fine teachers, many of whom have been there since the 1960s, when additional resources were given to particular schools, including this one, to help with their special problems. These teachers were attracted to the school because of the supply of specialists and the support they would be given. They came because they felt it would be a good place to teach. To this day, the school is still quite special for the area, but it is manifesting problems that are eroding the quality of the program. (Because of the positive reputation of the school, many parents want to send their children there; as a result, the school is suffering from serious overcrowding.) The principal is known to be a real "professional." He is very hard working and the school is remarkably stable. The principal has been there for fifteen years, which is almost unheard of in this area.

Andrea, unlike Brenda, came from the outside to work at Parkridge, but, like Brenda, she, too, had the problem of legitimatizing her presence to the teaching staff. Because the staff was large, and because many had been there for a long time, there were numerous cliques among the teachers. There was also a group of eight new teachers who had taken over classrooms with little preparation for the job. (There was a massive teacher shortage in this city at the time.) An all-day kindergarten program had just been implemented, and the district had called for the school to involve the parents in working with their children at home.

In looking over this situation and figuring out her goals for the year, Andrea decided that the new teachers would be a focus for her work. She also decided to take on the responsibility for working with the parents of the kindergarten children to facilitate better understanding of what the school was doing and what the parents could do to reinforce student learning. In addition, she continued to maintain the teacher center; although it was a small, crowded room, teachers would know that at least there was a place to come where they could give and get help, put their feet up, and share some hot soup from the corner deli.

Everyone speaks of Andrea as the "glue" of the school: "She has made the school a family. Everyone feels a sense of gratitude and loyalty to her." Because she is a very giving person, her mere presence and her way of working fill a great void in this large, three-story building. Her first words are always, "How can I help you?" An hour and a half with her illustrates the point.

> On this day Andrea arrives at the center at 8:15 A.M. She is immediately involved in a "major" problem. One of the teachers, who has a refrigerator in his room, is complaining that because people leave food in it his room smells, thus disturbing him and the students. Andrea gets into the conversation to try to sort out who is responsible for cleaning the refrigerator and what needs to be done to get it cleaned. (This may seem like an insignificant problem, but no problem is insignificant. The message to the teachers is that all problems can be worked on in the center.)
>
> Andrea goes downstairs to the auditorium. She is due to hold a meeting there to teach parents how to provide for reading-readiness activities for their children. When she gets there she finds someone else is rehearsing a play.
>
> Instead of complaining that the auditorium was reserved for her, she quickly negotiates with the teacher to use his room and runs to the front door to alert the parent sitting there to tell the parents what room to go to. Stopping off at the photocopy room to see that the materials are being run off for the parents, she finds a paraprofessional having trouble with the photocopy machine and also with someone in the office. Andrea helps her fix the machine and then intervenes to ease the problem with the staff person. She then makes her way to the new room, where several parents are waiting, and quickly makes arrangements for one of the parents to translate for one who does not understand English.

In this one-hour period, Andrea has already made four interventions that do not go unnoticed. She has helped a teacher (with the smelly refrigerator), changed her room (by negotiating with the teacher in the auditorium), helped the paraprofessional with the photocopy machine (and a small problem with an office person), and provided for a translator (so that her work with the parents could go on in two languages). Such sensitivity does not go unnoticed, even in a faculty of this size. As a matter of fact, it turns out to be a mode of leadership that is felt by everyone. The principal is extremely respectful of Andrea's good work with the faculty. The supervisors find her presence welcome, since she helps them with their work without overstepping her authority. The specialists know that Andrea and the teacher center can support their work and also help them deliver services. And the new teachers come to the center because they know they can get help and support from both Andrea and other teachers who serve as a support group for them.

## THE TEACHER-LEADER AS LEARNER

From this initial look at teacher-leaders, we see that they are not only making learning possible for others but, in important ways, are learning a great deal themselves. Stepping out of the confines of the classroom forces these teacher-leaders to forge a new identity in the school, think differently about their colleagues, change their style of work in a school, and find new ways to organize staff participation. As we have documented, it is an extremely complicated process, one that is intellectually challenging and exciting as well as stressful and problematic. Changing the nature of an occupation turns out to have the possibilities for both "high gain and high strain" (Little, Chapter 5 of this volume). The gain is mostly in the personal and professional learnings of the leaders themselves: the technical learnings about teachers, instruction, and curriculum; the social learnings about schools as social systems, including how to build collegiality and manipulate the system to help teachers do a better job; the personal learnings about their own professional competence as they learn new skills and abilities and find new approaches to being a leader among their peers; and even, in some cases, the satisfaction of learning how to create structures that alter the culture of the school.

But the strain is there, too. Building trust among teachers, who have long felt that they have little or no voice in choosing what is best for their students or themselves, is not easy. Initial hostility and resistance are always there, and it is hard not to take some of it personally. (What works with students does not necessarily work with adults.) Dilemmas of being a colleague and also being an "expert" are not easily negotiated. Being nonjudgmental and helping are often in conflict with making value judgments that affect the priorities for one's work. Listening to teachers — rather than giving advice — and working with them on their terms is sometimes in conflict with personal style. Learning to negotiate from a position of leadership — in a school where there is little precedent for teacher leadership — without threatening those in existing administrative positions takes skill, courage, and nerve. Teacher-leaders have to learn that these tensions and dilemmas are an inevitable part of the drive to professionalize schools and of the change process itself.

## THE TEACHER-LEADER AS PROFESSIONAL MODEL

Part of the ideology developed in these new roles is the belief that there are different ways to structure schools and different means to work with teachers and other members of the school community. This involves such characteristic themes as:

Placing a nonjudgmental value on providing assistance

Modeling collegiality as a mode of work

Enhancing teachers' self-esteem

Using different approaches to assistance

Building networks of human and material resources for the school community

Creating support groups for school members

Making provisions for continuous learning and support for teachers at the school site

Encouraging others to take leadership with their peers.

We are only beginning to understand the nature and impact of these new roles in schools and the subtleties of fashioning new ways of working with the school community. From studying these teacher-leaders, we see that some sort of team, teacher center, or site committee — a structural change — appears necessary to the creation of collegial norms in a school. More cooperative work, increased interaction across department lines, and support groups for new teachers require new modes of collaboration to replace the existing isolated conditions prevailing in most schools.

What we have, then, is a new leadership role that can help in the creation of new collaborative structures. It appears that a combination of these new roles and structures is necessary to professionalize the school culture and to bring a measure of recognition and respect to teachers — who may be, in the final analysis, the best teachers of teachers as well as children.

# REFERENCE

Darling-Hammond, L. (1987). Schools for tomorrow's teachers. *Teachers College Record, 88*(3), 354-358.

Goodwin, A., & Lieberman, A. (1986, April). Effective assistance personal behavior: What they brought and what they learned. Paper presented at the annual meeting of the American Educational Research Association San Francisco.

Lieberman, A., & Miller, L. (1984). *Teachers: Their world and their work.* Alexandria, VA: Association for Supervision and Curriculum Development.

Little, J.W. (1986). Seductive images and organizational realities in professional development. In A. Lieberman [Ed.), *Rethinking school improvement: Research, craft, and concept* (pp. 26-44). New York: Teachers College Press.

Lortie, D. (1975). *School teacher.* Chicago: University of Chicago Press.

Miles, M., Saxl, E., James, J., & Lieberman, A. (1986). *New York City Teacher Center Consortium evaluation report.* Unpublished technical report.

Miles, M., Saxl, Lieberman, A. (in press). What skills do educational "change agents" need? An empirical view. *Curriculum Inquiry.*

Rosenholtz S.J. (in press). *Teacher's workplace: A social-organizational analysis.* New York: Longman.

Saxl, E.R., Miles, M.B., & Lieberman, A. (in press). *ACE — Assisting change in education.* Alexandria, VA: Association for Supervision and Curriculum Development.

# Chapter 12
# Staff Development, Innovation and Institutional Development

*by Michael G. Fullan, University of Toronto*

It has been well known for at least 15 years that staff development and successful innovation or improvement are intimately related. However, even in the narrow sense of successful implementation of a single innovation, people have underestimated what it takes to accomplish this close interrelationship more fundamentally. I argue later in this chapter that we must go beyond the narrow conception of staff development to consider how it relates to instructional development of schools.

Staff development is conceived broadly to include any activity or process intended to improve skills, attitudes, understandings, or performance in present or future roles (Little, Sparks, and Loucks-Horsley (in press).[1] Despite the fact that we know a great deal about what effective staff development looks like, it is still not well practiced. There are at least major and often mutually reinforcing reasons for this. One is technical—it takes a great deal of wisdom, skill, and persistence to design and carry out successful staff development activities. The other is political. Staff development is a big business, as much related to power, bureaucratic positioning, and territoriality as it is to helping teachers and students (see Little in press, Paris 1989, and Pink 1989).

The problem of harnessing staff development is compounded by its increasingly sprawling prominence. On the one hand, it is correctly seen as the central strategy for improvement. On the other hand, it is frequently separated artificially from the institutional and personal contexts in which it operates.

The purpose of this chapter is to provide some clarity concerning the different ways in which staff development and innovation are related. Putting staff development in an innovation perspective should help us in sorting out where and how to put our energies into approaches that will have both specific and lasting effects. I examine three different innovation perspectives. The first is "staff development as a strategy for implementation," and the second is "staff development as an innovation" in its own right. "Staff development as institutional development" is the third and more fundamental perspective. I conclude by claiming that the first two perspectives are useful for certain limited purposes but that only the third approach promises to make continuous staff development and improvement a way of life in schools.

---

[1] Thus the terms "staff development," "professional development," "inservice," and "assistance" are used interchangeably in this chapter.

## Staff Development as a Strategy for Implementation

In an earlier review, Pomfret and I established beyond doubt that staff development and effective implementation of innovations were strongly interrelated (Fullan and Pomfret 1977). The logic and evidence were fairly straightforward. Effective implementation consists of alterations in curriculum materials, practices and behavior, and beliefs and understandings by teachers vis-a-vis potentially worthwhile innovations (regardless of whether the innovations were locally or externally developed). Put more simply, successful change involves learning how to do something new. As such, the process of implementation is essentially a learning process. Thus, when it is linked to specific innovations, staff development and implementation go hand in hand.

At the time (1977), in gross terms we learned that staff development should be innovation-related, continuous during the course of implementation, and involve a variety of formal (e. g., workshops) and informal (e. g., teacher-exchange) components. We also confirmed that most innovation attempts did not incorporate these characteristics. There were two things we did not know. First, we needed to identify some of the subprocesses of staff development/implementation success experienced by teachers. Second, although we could demonstrate that staff development and classroom implementation were closely linked, there was little evidence that these in turn were related to student achievement.

Since the earlier review, we have obtained further confirmation and additional insights into the link between staff development and implementation. Huberman and Miles (1984) put the case best in their detailed examination of 12 case studies of innovation:

> Large-scale, change-bearing innovations lived or died by the amount and quality of assistance that their users received once the change process was under way ... The forms of assistance were various. The high-assistance sites set up external conferences, in-service training sessions, visits, committee structures, and team meetings. They also furnished a lot of ongoing assistance in the form of materials, peer consultation, access to external consultants, and rapid access to central office personnel. ... Although strong assistance did not usually succeed in smoothing the way in early implementations, especially for the more demanding innovations, it paid handsome dividends later on by substantially increasing the levels of commitment and practice mastery (p. 273).

Huberman and Miles, along with others, also contributed new insights into the process of teacher learning, which included the universal presence of early implementation problems in all cases of success, the role of pressure and support, the way in which change in practice frequently preceded change in beliefs and understanding, and the time-line of two or more years of active assistance during implementation.

The link between staff development and school achievement was not systematically demonstrated until recently. Stallings (1989) provides a precise response to this question. In several settings using different designs, Stallings and her colleagues set out to improve teaching and student achievement relative to reading practices in secondary schools. Stallings identified research findings on effective reading practices (i. e., the innovation), as well as research on critical factors related to effective staff development. Relative to the latter, Stallings states that teachers are more likely to change their behavior and continue to use new ideas under the following conditions:

1. They become aware of a need for improvement through their analysis of their own observation profile;

2. They make a written commitment to try new ideas in their classroom the next day;

3. They modify the workshop ideas to work in their classroom and school;

4. They try the ideas and evaluate the effect;

5. They observe in each other's classrooms and analyze their own data;

6. They report their success or failure to their group;

7. They discuss problems and solutions regarding individual students and/or teaching subject matter;

8. They need a wide variety of approaches: modeling, simulations, observations, critiquing video tapes, presenting at professional meetings;

9. They learn in their own way continuity to set new goals for professional growth (Stallings 1989, pp. 3-4).

The cornerstones of the model, according to Stallings, are:

• Learn by doing — try, evaluate, modify, try again.

• Link prior knowledge to new information.

• Learn by reflecting and solving problems.

• Learn in a supportive environment — share problems and successes (p.4).

Over the years, Stallings was able to compare the effects of three different training designs; the question was, what would the effect be on secondary students' reading scores...

1. If only reading teachers were trained and their students tested?

2. If all language arts teachers and reading teachers in a school were trained—hence reaching all students—and all students are tested?

3. If all teachers in a district were trained...over a three-year period, what would be the effect on the school district's level of reading at the end of ninth grade? (pp. 1-2).

Without going into all the details, the first design involved 47 teachers in seven districts, along with a control group. Teachers in the treatment group, compared with the control group, changed their behavior in the classroom and their students gained six months in reading scores over the control group. In the second design, all teachers in two schools were trained and compared with a control group of two schools. The differential gain in reading scores was eight months. In the third study, all teachers in the district were provided with the training, with no control group. Each group of 9th grade students across three years of testing steadily improved their reading scores.

These impressive results demonstrate the power of a carefully designed staff development strategy for implementing single innovations.[2]

Joyce et al. (1989), in their recent work in Richmond County, Georgia, provide further confirmation of the link between staff development, implementation, and student outcomes. After 18 months of intensive training and follow-up with teams of teachers focusing on models of teaching, Joyce and his colleagues were able to claim considerable (but variable) implementation in the classroom, which in turn was related to a dramatic impact on student achievement and student promotion rates.

It is worth emphasizing that both the Stallings and Joyce initiatives required considerable sophistication, effort, skill, and persistence to accomplish what they did. Most staff development activities do not measure up to these standards, as Pink's (1989) review of four change projects illustrates. He found 12 barriers to innovation effectiveness that were common to all four projects. Paraphrased, they are as follows:

1. An inadequate theory of implementation, including too little time for teachers to plan for and learn new skills and practices

2. District tendencies toward faddism and quick-fix solutions

3. Lack of sustained central office support and follow-through

4. Underfunding the project, or trying to do too much with too little support

5. Attempting to manage the projects from the central office instead of developing school leadership and capacity

6. Lack of technical assistance and other forms of intensive staff development

7. Lack of awareness of the limitations of teacher and school administrator knowledge about how to implement the project

8. The turnover of teachers in each school

9. Too many competing demands or overload

10. Failure to address the incompatibility between project requirements and existing organizational policies and structures

---

[2] In a later section, I indicate how limiting this strategy is in the long run, but it does produce short-term results.

11. Failure to understand and take into account site-specific differences among schools

12. Failure to clarify and negotiate the role relationships and partnerships involving the district and the local university — who in each case had a role, albeit unclarified, in the project (Pink 1989, pp. 22-24).

In short, staff development, implementation of innovation, and student outcomes are closely interrelated, but because they require such a sophisticated, persistent effort to coordinate, they are unlikely to succeed in many situations. Any success that does occur is unlikely to be sustained beyond the tenure or energy of the main initiators of the project.

## STAFF DEVELOPMENT AS AN INNOVATION

A second useful, but still limiting perspective is to consider major new staff development projects as innovations in their own right. In particular, new policies and structures that establish new roles, such as mentors, coaches, and the like, are and can be considered as innovations in the states and districts in which they are adopted. The question is whether our knowledge about the do's and don'ts of introducing curriculum innovations is applicable to introducing new mentoring and coaching practices. This section provides some support for the notion that the establishment of new staff development roles or projects would benefit from knowledge of implementation theory.

In a recent review, Judith Little (1989) has applied such a perspective to the evolution of the mentoring phenomenon. As Little states: "Those who would implement mentor roles are confronted with a two-part challenge: to introduce classroom teachers to a role with which they are unfamiliar; and to introduce the role itself to an institution and occupation in which it has few precedents" (pp.7-8). In reviewing empirical studies, Little identified three implementation problems: the pace of implementation, lack of opportunity to carry out the role, and precedents that constrain mentors' performance.

It is well known that major policy initiatives are often introduced mentors' performance rapidly, with little thought or time given to consider implementation (Fullan 1982). Among other studies, Little cites California's Mentor Teacher Program:

> California launched a precipitous schedule of implementation....A schedule of implementation limited to the state's fiscal year propelled them toward quick decisions about the form it would assume. The result was a pervasive effort to bring the definition of the mentor role within the boundaries of familiar roles and functions. Based on nine case studies and a summary of 291 districts, Bird (1986) concludes that, "a good deal was lost, and little or nothing gained, by haste in implementing the mentor program" (Little 1989, pp.9-10).

---

[3] In the following paragraphs, I concentrate on the mentor rather than the mentor-inductee pair. For reviews involving the latter, see Huling-Austin (in press), and Kilcher (1989).

Rapid starts involving complex innovations often result in simplifying and reducing the intended scope of the change. Little notes Huberman and Miles' observation based on their 12 case studies of innovation:

> Smooth early use was a bad sign. Smoothly implementing sites seemed to get that way by reducing the initial scale of the project and by lowering the gradient of actual practice change. This "downsizing" got rid of most headaches during the initial implementation but also threw away most of the potential rewards; the project often turned into a modest, sometimes trivial enterprise (p.273).

A second problematic area of implementation relates to selection criteria, preimplementation training for mentors, and support during implementation, which Little sums up under the general label of opportunity. She starts with selection criteria, indicating the importance of basing selection of mentors on their expertise and credibility — both as classroom teachers and as colleagues who had track records of working successfully with other teachers. Little also found that preimplementation training for mentors was variable, often focusing only on general process skills. Relative to post-selection support, Bird and Alspaugh (1986) found that 40 percent of districts participating in the first two years of California's mentor program allocated no resources to support mentors during implementation.

The lack of precedents for the mentor role, combined with the previous two factors, frequently resulted in the mentor role's being played out at the lower and sager limits of its potential. The ambiguity of the role often left mentors to "invent their roles as they went along" (Hart 1989 cited in Little 1989a). According to Little, this permissive stance tends to produce a low rate of direct teacher-to-teacher involvement of the very sort needed to make the role credible and effective. Little concludes that lack of precedence for these new roles is a major normative barrier to their implementation.

Coaching faces similar implementation problems, but not on the same scale because, unlike mentoring, coaching projects have tended to be less formal (e.g., not involving legislation or formal policy), more voluntary, and smaller in scale. Coaching projects, perhaps because of these characteristics, have proliferated at a rapid rate. Many so-called coaching projects, as we shall discuss in the next sections, appear to be superficial. Even if we assume rigorous coaching designs, the innovation perspective is instructive.

We can take, as an example, Joyce and Showers' (1989) work because it is more developed and available in the literature. According to Joyce and Showers, coaching programs represent powerful strategies for implementing instructional improvements that impact on student learning. In their work coaching is (a) attached to training, (b) continuous, (c) experimental in nature, and (d) separate from supervision and evaluation. It involves theory-demon-stration -practice-feedback-and follow-through support.

The innovation perspective is revealing because it starts with the question, "In what respects is coaching an innovation?" Joyce and Showers' work implies at least three types of innovations for school systems. First, it represents a change in the technology of training. Coaching leaders have to learn and carry out a sophisticated training program over a period of time. Second, it involves organizing study groups of teachers at the school level. This entails restructuring the workplace in a more collegial mode. Third (and related but more fundamental than the previous point), coaching implicitly raises questions about the deeper collaborative work cultures of schools and the role of teachers as professionals.

Joyce and Showers have effectively tackled the first problem. They are able to implement the training model with desired effects. They are in the midst of working on the second problem — organizing study groups at individual schools within a district (Joyce et al. 1989) The third problem — how to change the culture of the organization — remains unaddressed.

The implications of this analysis are quite profound. While most districts do not provide the training support, the problem is much deeper than that. Even if districts were to address the training and study group issues, coaching as an innovation would be short-lived. It would be just another ad hoc innovation that has a short half-life. The danger is that coaching, which has powerful potential, will be trivialized, because the organizational necessities and cultural change implied by coaching will be missed altogether, or addressed superficially.

At this time, we will not take up further the problem of achieving cultural changes the schools. The main point is that mentoring and coaching projects would benefit if guided by innovation models. Miles (1986), for people, identified 14 key success factors across the three well-known phases of change projects:

Initiation
- Linked to high profile need
- Clear model of implementation
- One or more strong advocates
- Active initiation

Implementation
- Coordination
- Shared control
- Pressure and support
- Ongoing technical assistance
- Early rewards for teachers

Institutionalization
- Embedding
- Links to instruction
- Widespread use
- Removal of competing priorities
- Continuing assistance

The factors and processes of implementation can be used to analyze staff development projects and to guide implementation planning and monitoring. Those involved in coaching projects would be well advised to approach their work with some model of change in mind, which would enable them to take into account organizational factors known to affect implementation success (Fullan 1982, 1987; Huberman and Miles 1984). Although this will not be sufficient to achieve cultural change at the school level, it would provide more effective beginnings toward that goal.

It should be obvious that I am not advocating that coaching or mentoring projects become innovations as ends in themselves. Many such projects, for example, do not appear to be focused or clear about their pedagogical and student learning objectives. Joyce and Showers (1988), contrary to popular belief, have never advocated coaching per se. Rather, "the major purpose of peer coaching programs is implementation of innovations to the extent that determination of effects on students is possible" (p. 83). In pursuing this goal, I have suggested that it is important to consider coaching and mentoring as innovation, which they are, provided that one does not stop there.

Although mentoring and coaching have great potentials as long as they are treated as innovations or projects or even as strategies, their impact will be superficial and short-term and will be confined to a few participants. It is the ultimate thesis of this chapter that our attention must shift explicitly to how staff development fits into long-term institutional purposes and development of schools.

## STAFF DEVELOPMENT AND INSTITUTIONAL DEVELOPMENT

By institutional development, I mean changes in schools as institutions that increase their capacity and performance for continuous improvements. The domain is the culture of the school as a workplace (Little 1982; Rosenholtz 1989, Sarason 1982). I want to start by examining the relationship between the culture of the school and the two perspectives just considered. This will amount to a critique of the imitations of the two perspectives. Second, it will pave the way for describing what it means to focus directly and more systematically on institutional development. I will provide an example from my current work. Finally, three major implications for staff development will be outlined.

To start with the "strategy for implementation" perspective, teacher collegiality and other elements of collaborative work cultures are known to be related to the likelihood of implementation success (Fullan and Pomfret 1977; Little 1982). Thus, all other things being equal, schools characterized by norms of collegiality and experimentation are much more likely to implement innovations successfully. The first point to be made is that those using staff development for implementation should take into account the nature of teacher collegiality that exists in the schools with which they intend to work. For example, as impressive as Stallings' (1989) staff development design is, there is no mention of these school level variables, which must have had effects that remain unknown on implementation and institutionalization. In other words, staff developers must work with schools as organizations as much as they work with individuals or small groups of teachers.

The second point to be noted is that even when teacher collegiality is taken into account, it is usually treated as a contextual factor or as a given; that is, it is used to explain differences in implementation more or less along the lines that some schools happen to be more collegial than others.

Third, it can be argued, at least hypothetically, that solid staff development projects, like that of Stallings, in addition to having a positive impact on change in teacher practice and student achievement, can also have a spin-off or residual impact on increasing collegiality among teachers. Put another way, since good staff development practices always incorporate teacher-teacher sharing and interaction, they could, if successful, demonstrate the value of new norms of collegiality. At a minimum, it would seem that people using the staff development for implementation strategy should explicitly concentrate on the dual goals of implementing a project successfully and influencing the collegial climate of the school as an organization. This would be a useful contribution, but I am afraid that the culture of the school is much too strong to be influenced for any length of time (or at all in some cases) by single, passing projects—no matter how well designed.

The coaching and mentoring phenomenon is much more intriguing. On the surface, it looks like these strategies are indeed tantamount to attempting to change the collaborative culture of the school. In fact, they are not.

Coaching is particularly instructive for examining the underlying issues. There are at least three basic problems: (1) the relationship of coaching to the culture of the school; (2) the form and content of coaching; (3) the need for a more objective and balanced appreciation of the complex relationship between autonomy and collaboration. In effect, these problem areas amount to cautioning advocates of coaching and collaboration against assuming that working toward increased interaction among teachers is automatically a good thing

## Coaching and the Culture of the School

As we have seen, coaching, mentoring, and other similar arrangements usually involve pairs or small groups of teachers working together. As such they represent only a small subpart of the total culture of the school. Thus, whether or not a particular coaching project finds itself in an hospitable environment (i.e., a school in which a collegial climate predated the coaching initiative) is a very important variable. Seller and Hannay (1988) examined a well-designed coaching project in two high schools and found that the pre-existing climate of collegiality explained whether or not the project was successful. At a minimum, the advice to those advocating coaching is to take into account the total culture of the school before deciding to proceed. One can also infer that even good coaching programs do not alter the culture of the school. Although coaching can be intentionally designed as a strategy for increasing the collaborative work culture of the school, there is no evidence that this by itself will work. Normative cultures are not that easily influenced.

## Form and Content

Little (1989b) has provided the clearest exposition of the importance of considering variations in the form and content of collegiality. Form involves the degree and type of collaborating relationship. She suggests that there are at least four types of relationships ranked along an interdependence continuum: storytelling and scanning for ideas, aid and assistance, mutual sharing, and joint work. In Little's words:

> The move from conditions of complete independence to thorough-going interdependence entails changes in the frequency and intensity of teachers interactions, the prospects for conflict and probability of influence. That is, with each successive shift, the warrant for autonomy shifts from individual to collective judgment and preference (p. 5).

Little claims that the first three forms represent "weak ties" of collegiality. Little (1989a, 1989b) cites evidence that most coaching and mentoring projects are of this relatively superficial, safe, inconsequential variety, and hence have little impact on the culture of the school.

For Little, joint work involves:

> encounters among teachers that rest on shared responsibility for the work of teaching... collective conceptions of autonomy, support for teachers' initiative and leadership with regard to professional practice, and group affiliations grounded in professional work. Joint work is dependent on the structural organization of task, time, and other resources in ways not characteristic of other forms of collegiality (pp. 14-15).

Little does not assume that joint work is more appropriate, only that it is much more demanding psychologically and organizationally to bring about and is more consequential for better or for worse. Thus, the content, not just the form of collaboration, is also critical:

> The content of teachers' values and beliefs cannot be taken for granted in the study or pursuit of teachers' collegial norms of interaction and interpretation. Under some circumstances, greater contact among teachers can be expected to advance the prospects for students' success; in others, to promote increased teacher-to-teacher contact may be to intensify norms unfavorable to children (1989b, p. 22).

Further, Little asks:

> Bluntly put, do we have in teachers' collaborative work the creative development of well informed choices, or the mutual reinforcement of poorly informed habit? Does teachers' time together advance the understanding and imagination they bring to their work, or do teachers merely confirm one another in present practice? What subject philosophy and subject pedagogy do teachers reflect as they work together,

how explicit and accessible is their knowledge to one another? Are there collaborations that in fact erode teachers' moral commitments and intellectual merit? (p. 22).

## Autonomy and Collaboration

We cannot assume that autonomy is bad and collaboration is good. One person's isolation is another person's autonomy; one person's collaboration is another person's conspiracy. Flinders (1988) speaks to the former:

> The teachers I observed not only accepted their relative isolation but actively strove to maintain it. At those points in the day when teachers had the greatest discretion over their use of time (during lunch breaks and preparation time), they typically went out of their way to avoid contact with others...Teachers used their classrooms as sanctuaries during breaks as well as before and after school, remaining alone in their rooms to prepare lessons instead of working in their department offices where collegial interaction would have been more available (p. 23).

Flinders claims that for many teachers isolation is a strategy for getting work done because "it protects time and energy required to meet immediate instructional demands" (p.25). Flinders observes that most of us seek periods of independent work in order to meet obligations:

> It is not uncommon to respond to increased job demands by closing the office door, canceling luncheon appointments, and "hiding out" in whatever ways we can. We do not attribute our motives for such behavior to naturally conservative personality traits or to malevolent or unprofessional regard for our colleagues. On the contrary, it is professional norms that dissuade us from sacrificing our commitments to job responsibilities even when such a sacrifice can be made in the name of collegiality (p.25).

None of this is to gainsay that isolation can be a protection from scrutiny and a barrier to improvement, but it does say that we must put the question of autonomy and collaboration in a perspective conducive to assessing the conditions under which each might be appropriate.

Hargreaves (forthcoming) formulates a useful typology for considering school cultures. He suggests that there are four types: fragmented individualism, Balkanization, contrived collegiality, and collaborative cultures. The first two are well known. Fragmented individualism is the traditional form of teacher isolation so clearly depicted by Lortie (1975). Balkanization, often found in high schools, consists of subgroups and cliques operating as separate subentities, often in conflict with each other when major decisions have to be made.

The designation contrived collegiality is new:

> [It] is characterized by a set of formal, specific bureaucratic procedures...It can be seen in initiatives such as peer coaching, mentor teaching, joint

planning in specially provided rooms, formally scheduled meetings
and clear job descriptions and training programs for those in consulta-
tive roles (p.19).

Contrived collegiality can ignore the real culture of the school and lead to a
proliferation of unwanted contacts among teachers that consume already
scarce time with little to show for it (see also Hargreaves 1989).

Hargreaves and Dawe (1989) elaborate on the problem of contrived
collegiality by claiming that many forms of coaching are too technical,
narrow, and short-term in focus. Hargreaves and Dawe argue that the current
move away from teacher isolationism is locked into a struggle involving two
very different forms of collegiality:

> In the one, it is a tool of teacher empowerment and professional
> enhancement, bringing colleagues and their expertise together to gen-
> erate critical yet also practical grounded reflection on what they do as
> a basis for wiser, more skilled action. In the other, the breakdown of
> teacher isolation is a mechanism designed to facilitate the smooth and
> uncritical adoption of preferred forms of action (new teaching styles)
> introduced and imposed by experts from elsewhere in which teachers
> become technicians rather than professionals exercising discretionary
> judgment (p. 7).

True collaborative cultures, according to Hargreaves (in press), are deep,
personal, and enduring. They are not "mounted just for specific projects or
events. They are not strings of one-shot deals. Cultures of collaboration rather
are constitutive of, absolutely central to, teachers daily work" (p. 14).

In short, collegially oriented staff development initiatives either fail to
address the more basic question of school culture, or vastly underestimate
what it takes to change them. There is also evidence that collaborative
cultures, when they do occur, are achieved through the extraordinary efforts
of individuals. Often, such efforts either cannot be sustained over time or are
vulnerable to the inevitable departure of key individuals (Hargreaves 1989,
Little 1989b). In other words, what is at stake are basic changes in the
professional institution of schooling.

## An Illustration

The main implication of this chapter is to refocus staff development so that it
becomes part of an overall strategy for professional and institutional reform.
We provide here one illustration taken from our current work in The Learning
Consortium. Although we do not claim that it represents a full-blown
example, it reflects movement toward the type of comprehensive conception
and strategy required for substantial institutional development of schools.
Space permits only a brief description of the framework (see Fullan, Rolheiser-Bennett, and Bennett 1989 for more information).

The Learning Consortium is a three-year partnership among four major
school districts and two higher education institutions in the greater Toronto

area. There are two overriding assumptions in the Consortium. One is to design and carry out a variety of activities that make the professional and staff development continuum a reality (from the Bachelor of Education through preservice, induction, and career-long developments). The second major assumption is that classroom and school improvement must be linked and integrated if serious improvements are to be achieved.

We will not describe the various activities here, but they involve Summer Institutes and follow-up, cadre staff development and support, leadership inservice, team development in schools, and the like. They focus on instructional improvements like the use of cooperative learning strategies, as well as on school-wide changes involving greater collaboration.

Our goal is to understand and influence both classroom improvement and school improvement through identifying and fostering systematic links between the two. The framework for analysis and action we are developing is contained in Figure 1.1 (p. 18).[4] For classroom improvement, we and others have found that teachers must work simultaneously (but not necessarily at the same pace) on all four subcogs. For both teachers and students, the combined capacity to manage the classroom, the continuous acquisition of proven instructional strategies and skills, and the focus on desired educational goals and content are essential.

The subcogs in the far right of Figure 1.1 relate to school improvement. There is considerable evidence, we think, that the more basic features of school improvement (as distinct from a list of effective school characteristics) are the following four. Schools improve when they have, or come to have, (1) a shared purpose, (2) norms of collegiality, (3) norms of continuous improvement, and (4) structures that represent the organizational conditions necessary for significant improvement (Little 1987 Rosenholtz 1989). Note that these are not individual characteristics. They are discrete and measurable features of collectivities — in this case, people in schools.

It is necessary to comment on the interrelationship of the school improvements cogs. Shared purpose includes such things as vision, mission, goals, objectives, and unity of purpose. It refers to the shared sense of purposeful direction of the school relative to major educational goals. Shared purpose is of course not static, nor does it arise by itself. The other three cogs in interaction constantly generate and (re)shape purpose. Norms of collegiality refer to the extent to which mutual sharing, assistance, and joint work among teachers is valued and honored in the school. As stated earlier, there is nothing particularly virtuous about collaboration per se. It can serve to block change or put down students as well as to elevate learning. Thus, collegiality must be linked to norms of continuous improvement and experimentation in which teachers are constantly seeking and assessing potentially better practices inside and outside their own school (and contributing to other people's practice through dissemination). And, as the framework depicts, commitment to improving student engagement and learning must be a pervasive

---

[4] The following paragraphs are adapted from Fullan, Rolheiser-Bennett, and Bennett (1989).

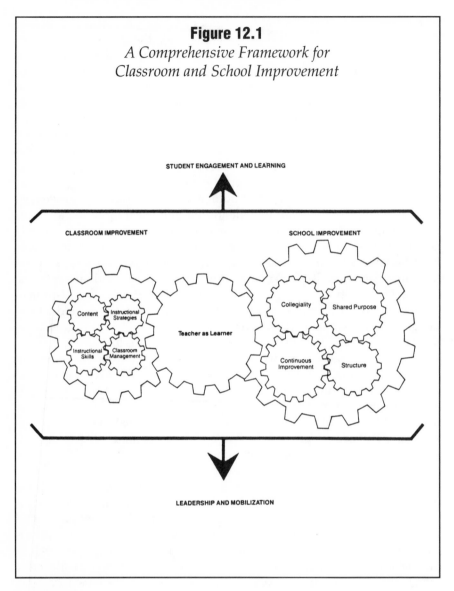

**Figure 12.1**

*A Comprehensive Framework for*
*Classroom and School Improvement*

STUDENT ENGAGEMENT AND LEARNING

CLASSROOM IMPROVEMENT                    SCHOOL IMPROVEMENT

Content    Instructional Strategies

Instructional Skills    Classroom Management

Teacher as Learner

Collegiality    Shared Purpose

Continuous Improvement    Structure

LEADERSHIP AND MOBILIZATION

value and concern.

We use structure in the sociological sense to include organizational arrangements, roles, and formal policies that explicitly build in working conditions that, so to speak, support and press for movement in the other cogs. Time for joint planning, joint teaching arrangements, staff development policies, new roles such as mentors, and school improvement procedures are examples of structural change at the school level that is conducive to improvement.

The centerpiece, or bridge, linking and overlapping classroom and school improvement in Figure 1.1 is the teacher as learner. Figure 1.2 elaborates on this concept. There are two absolutely critical features of this

**Figure 12.2**

# *Teacher as Learner*

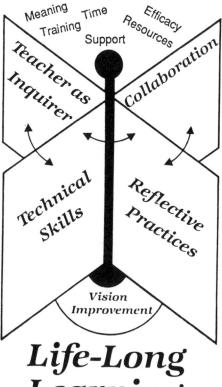

From Fullan, Rolheiser-Bennett, and Bennett 1989

component of the framework. First, the four aspects of teacher as learner —
technical, reflective, inquiry, and collaborative — must be seen in combination. Each has its separate tradition of research and practice, and each has
made important contributions in its own right. The mastery of technical skills
increases instructional certainty; reflective practice enhances clarity, meaning, and coherence; inquiry fosters investigation and exploration; collaboration enables one to receive and give ideas and assistance.

Although many approaches address aspects of all four features of the
teacher as learner in one way or another, all models to this point have a central
tendency to stress only one or two of the four. Rarely (and we would say never
in a fundamental sense) have all four received intensive attention in the same

setting. It is easier said than done. The question is, how can the strengths of each of these four traditions be integrated and established in the teacher as learner?

The second critical feature is to distinguish between specific and generic levels of development of the teacher as learner. By specific we mean how particular improvements are experienced and designed. For example, one can start with a technical instructional innovation, such as cooperative learning, and find that it has consequences for all four aspects of the teacher as learner (which is in fact how we started). Similarly, one could begin with any of the other three subcogs—an action research project, for example—and proceed to incorporate the development of technical instructional skills, reflective methods, and so forth. We do not know enough yet about the very difficult conceptual and strategic questions of whether it is better to start with a single teacher-learner dimension (and if so, which one), or to work on all four equally.

A more fundamental point at this time is the recognition that teachers (remember that we are still talking about the teacher as individual learner) can come to develop the generic capacity to function on all four cylinders. In this case, it is not just being good at cooperative learning but mastering an array of instructional models; it is not just being involved in a reflective practice project but being a reflective practitioner; it is not participating in an action research investigation but conducting constant inquiry; it is not being part of a peer coaching project but being collaborative as a way of working. In short, teachers come to internalize these ways of being to the point where it becomes second nature to be a perpetual learner.

Now it is precisely when every teacher in the school develops this "generic capacity" to learn that classroom improvement and school improvement entirely overlap. Such an ideal will never be achieved, of course, but one can immediately see how powerful the bridge can become when a school experiences a significant increase in the proportion of staff who are learners as we have defined the term.

Two final aspects of the framework revolve around the singularly important question of what drives the framework. It is, after all, not self-generating. One of two key driving factors is the presence of student engagement and learning as a pervasive preoccupation. We propose that the impact on all students be front and center for every cog and interrelationship among the cogs. Constant valuing and attention to student engagement and learning can be a powerful motivating force if it is integrated with movement in the cogs. The second agent of change is leadership and mobilization. We explicitly rejected the idea that leadership be a particular component of the framework. Leadership can, does, and must come from a variety of different sources in different situations (and different sources in the same situation over time). Leadership for success variously comes from the principal, key teachers, the superintendent, parents, trustees, curriculum consultants, governments, universities, and so on. As the list reveals, the driving force for change can initially come from inside or outside the school and from a variety of different roles. Once the model is fully functioning, leadership does indeed come from multiple sources simultaneously

The Learning Consortium has been operating for a little more than a year. It has been successful in mobilizing a great number of people to action which they and others agree has resulted in improvements in classrooms and schools. We do not think that The Learning Consortium, as much as it is becoming integrated into the lives of the institutions involved, will end up deeply affecting collaborative work cultures in the sense that Hargreaves and Little use the term. Nias' (1989) study illustrates how rich and complex collaborative cultures really are.

We do see very clearly, however, that the multilevel and multifaceted staff development activities that occur in all large school districts are, in the case of The Learning Consortium, being harnessed and interrelated in a more coherent and synergistic manner. There are still dilemmas between autonomy and collaboration, but staff development in these districts is becoming less fragmented and desultory, more purposeful, and more linked to classroom and school development as defined by teachers and principals.

## IMPLICATIONS

Staff development will never have its intended impact as long as it is grafted onto schools in the form of discrete, unconnected projects. The closer one gets to the culture of schools and the professional lives of teachers, the more complex and daunting the reform agenda becomes. More powerful strategies are needed for more powerful changes. At least three strands of the problem require radical rethinking and integration, namely, the individual, the school, and the district.

First, those involved in staff development must think and act more holistically about the personal and professional lives of teachers as individuals. As we have seen, many staff development projects provide temporary resources and incentives for particular changes (e.g., Stallings 1989) but do not amount to much in the bigger scheme of teachers' lives (Smylie 1988). Huberman's (1989) research clearly shows the importance of recognizing career and life cycle experiences of teachers. What is at stake is the reconceptualization of the professional role of teachers (Fullan and Connelly 1989). Staff development in this view becomes the sum total of formal and informal learning experiences accumulated across one's career. The agenda then is to work continuously on the spirit and practice of lifelong learning for all teachers.

The second element involves working more organically with the school as an organization. This is turning out to be both complex and powerfully resistant to influence. It is not at all clear how autonomy and collaboration should be balanced. We do know, however, how powerful the school culture is. For example, despite massive effort and support over eighteen months, and despite some remarkable success in student achievement, Joyce et al. (1989) comment on the fragility of their accomplishments: "It depends on about forty teachers—only ten percent of the total" (p. 15).

We have seen that many of the reform efforts actually work at cross-purposes to intended directions by creating unnecessary status differences, role ambiguities, and superficial, inefficient relationships (Hargreaves and Dawe 1989, Little 1989a, and Smylie and Denny 1989).

There are endemic difficulties to establishing and maintaining collaborative work cultures. Nias (1989) found that teachers had great difficulty collaborating even when they wanted to work together. When collegiality is achieved, it is often short-lived because the social organization of the workplace is not conducive to maintaining collaboration in the long run (Hargreaves forthcoming, Little 1989b, Smylie 1989). Restructuring schools is complex and unclear (Elmore 1988a, 1988b) and will involve a long-term effort led by those within schools (Fullan 1989, Fullan and Hargreaves forthcoming). Finally, the centralization of policymaking and resources for staff development must be reconfigured. Little's (forthcoming) examination of district policy for staff development in California reveals the problem. Central office administrators and staff development specialists designed and delivered over two-thirds of the staff development experienced by teachers across 30 districts. "Leader time" was one of the highest cost items, more so than costs for time allocated to support learners (teacher participants). Many of the studies of mentoring reviewed by Little (1989a) also documented the centralization of staff development resources, which were devoted to supporting activities directed outside rather than inside schools. In the area of curriculum change, Paris (1989) chronicles the struggle between increased curriculum control at the district level and the uphill battle of one innovative school.

Neither centralization nor decentralization has worked in achieving educational reforms. The lines of development involving individuals, schools, and districts will require close collaboration between those inside and outside schools. Staff developers have a much bigger role to play in teacher development than hitherto realized.

# REFERENCES

Bird, T (1986). "The Mentor's Dilemma." Unpublished paper. San Francisco: Far West Laboratory for Educational Research and Development.

Bird, T, and D. Alspaugh. (1986). *1985 Survey of District Coordinators for the California Mentor Teacher Program.* San Francisco: Far West Laboratory for Educational Research.

Elmore, R. (1988a). "Contested Terrain: The Next Generation of Educational Reform." Paper prepared for the Commission on Public School Administration and Leadership, Association of California School Administrators.

Elmore, R. (1986). "Models of Restructured Schools." Stanford, Calif.: Center for Policy Research in Education.

Flinders, D. (1988). "Teacher Isolation and the New Reform." *Journal of Curriculum and Supervision* 5, 4: 17-29.

Fullan, M. (1982). *The Meaning of Education Change.* New York: Teachers College Press.

Fullan, M. (1987). "Implementing Educational Change: What We Know." Paper prepared for The World Bank. Washington, D.C.

Fullan M. (1988). *What's Worth Fighting for in the Principalship?* Toronto: Ontario Public School Teachers Federation.

Fullan, M., and F.M. Connelly (1989). *Teacher Education in Ontario.* Final report to the Teacher Education Review Committee: Ontario Ministry of Education, Toronto.

Fullan, M., and A. Hargreaves. (In press). *What's Worth Fighting for in the School.* Toronto: Ontario Public School Teachers Federation.

Fullan, M., and A. Pomfret. (1977). "Research on Curriculum and Instruction Implementation." *Review of Educational Research* 5, 47: 335-397.

Fullan, M., C. Rolheiser-Bennett, and B. Bennett. (1989). "Linking Classroom and School Improvement." Paper presented at the annual meeting of the American Education Research Association, San Francisco.

Hargreaves, A. (1989). "Teacher Development and Teachers' Work: Issues of Time and Control." Paper presented at the International Conference on Teacher Development in Toronto, Canada.

Hargreaves, A. (forthcoming). "Cultures of Teaching." In *Teachers' Lives New York,* edited by I. Goodson and S. Ball. Boston: Routledge & Kegan Paul.

Hargreaves, A., and R. Dawe. (1989). "Coaching as Unreflective Practice." Paper presented at the annual meeting of the American Educational Research Association, San Francisco.

Hart, A. (1989). "Role Politics and the Redesign of Teachers' Work." Unpublished manuscript. Salt Lake City: University of Utah.

Huberman, M. (1989). "Teacher Development and Instructional Mastery." Paper presented at the International Conference on Teaching Development in Toronto, Canada.

Huberman, M., and M. Miles. (1984). *Innovation up Close.* New York: Plenum.

Huling-Austin, L. (forthcoming). "Teacher Induction Programs and Internships." In *Handbook of Research on Teacher Education,* edited by Houston. New York: Macmillan Publishing and the Association of Teacher Educators.

Joyce, B., and B. Showers. (1988). *Student Achievement Through Staff Development.* New York: Longman.

Joyce, B., C. Murphy B. Showers, and J. Murphy (1989). "Reconstructing the Workplace: School Renewal as Cultural Change." Paper presented at the annual meeting of the American Educational Research Association, San Francisco.

Kilcher, A. (1989). "Mentoring Beginning Teachers: A Review of Theory and Practice." Paper prepared for The Learning Consortium in Toronto, Canada.

Little, J. (1982). "Norms of Collegiality and Experimentation: Workplace Conditions of School Success." *American Educational Research Journal* 5, 19: 325-340.

Little, J. (1989). "The 'Mentor' Phenomenon and the Social Organization of Teaching." *Review of Research in Education* 5, 16. Washington, D.C.: American Educational Research Association.

Little, J. (1986). "The Persistence of Privacy: Autonomy and Initiative in Teachers' Professional Relations." Paper presented at the American Educational Research Association.

Little, J. (In press). "District Policy Choices and Teachers' Professional Development Opportunities." *Educational Evaluation and Policy Analysis.*

Lortie, J. (1975). *Schoolteacher.* Chicago: University of Chicago Press.

Miles, M. (1986). "Research Findings on the Stages of School Improvement." Conference on Planned Change, The Ontario Institute for Studies in Education.

Nias, J. (1989). *Primary Teachers Talking: A Study of Teaching as Work.* London: Routledge & Kegen Paul.

Paris, C. (1989). "Contexts of Curriculum Change: Conflict and Consonance." Paper presented at the annual meeting of the American Educational Research Association, San Francisco.

Pink, W (1989). "Effective Development for Urban School Improvement." Paper presented at the annual meeting of the American Educational Research Association, San Francisco.

Rosenholtz, S. (1989). *Teachers' Workplace.* New York: Longman.

Sarason, S. (1982). *The Culture of the School and the Problem of Change,* 2nd edition. Boston: Allyn & Bacon.

Seller, W, and L. Hannay (1988). "The Influence of School Climate on Peer Coaching." Paper presented at the annual meeting of the American Educational Research Association, New Orleans.

Smylie, M. (1988). "The Enhancement Function of Staff Development: Organizational and Psychological Antecedents to Individual Teacher Change." *American Educational Research Journal* 5, 25:1-30.

Smylie, M. (1989). "Teachers' Collegial Learning: Social and Psychological Dimensions of Helping Relationships." Paper presented at the annual meeting of the American Educational Research Association, San Francisco.

Smylie, M., and J. Denny (1989). "Teacher Leadership: Tensions and Perspectives." Paper presented at the annual meeting of the American Educational Research Association, San Francisco.

Sparks, D., and S. Loucks-Horsley (In press). "Models of Staff Development." In *Handbook of Research on Teacher Education*. New York: Macmillan Publishing and the Association of Teacher Educators.

# Chapter 13
# Challenging the Regularities of Teaching Through Teacher Education

*by Richard I. Arends, University of Maryland, College Park*

## INTRODUCTION

The concept of culture is normally used to explain how members of social groups or societies think about their world and how these views lead to behavioral regularities. Ways of behaving in a particular culture become familiar and are taken for granted by insiders; to outsiders those same behaviors appear strange. Just as we can think about societies and communities having cultures, so too can we think about school and classroom cultures. Teaching behavior in schools and classrooms are informed and guided by strong cultural norms that persist over time. Just as most adults learn the preferred child-rearing practices of their society by participating in the culture as children and by watching parents and other adults behave in regular and predictable ways, so do teachers learn to teach (initially at least) by participating in the culture of classrooms as students and by watching teachers behave in culturally prescribed ways.

On the surface, this situation would appear to make *learning to teach* a rather straightforward proposition. Unlike most other jobs in complex societies, where youth get few opportunities to observe adults doing their work, students get to observe teachers every day for most of their lives. Indeed, a quick calculation would show that upon graduation from college, a teacher candidate would have observed their teachers at work for at least 16,000 hours, not including formal field experiences or practice teaching. One could conclude that this amount of observation would make it quite easy for prospective teachers to pick up the conventions of appropriate teacher behavior and become effective teachers. This situation could also be used to support a belief held of many that they could teach effectively without training (if only given the opportunity), and of lawmakers in several states who conclude that formal preparation for teachers is an unwarranted luxury.

These conclusions, unfortunately, are spurious and dangerous. It is true that previous school experiences have a strong and powerful impact on prospective teachers' conceptions of teaching and learning and their subsequent teaching behaviors. If these traditional behaviors were believed to be effective, and if important stakeholders, such as parents, citizens, and students were satisfied with the schools as we know them, this situation would be ideal. This is not the case, however, evidenced by the fact that between 1983 and 1990, over one thousand reports on education were issued by various groups in the United States. All criticize education in general and teaching specifically. This suggests rather deep dissatisfaction with schools and teaching as we know them today.

In this chapter, I develop the thesis that one of the major reasons schools and teaching are so severely criticized decade after decade is that the reforms deemed important are never realized because they require substantial change in the ways teachers teach. The practices used by many teachers are those patterns of teaching and learning that have been established by tradition. They are not necessarily those practices known to be most effective. They are the practices Courtney Cazden (1986) has labeled the "default option." They persist, in part at least, because the preparation of teachers is simply too weak to overcome important cultural regularities of teaching thoroughly learned by teacher candidates in their "apprenticeship-of-observation" (Lortie, 1975). After discussing the nature of these regularities, I illustrate how teacher education fails to challenge their persistence over time and conclude with a proposal for correcting this situation.

## Two Persistent Behavioral Regularities of Teaching

Two patterns of teaching and teachers' lives persist in American schools, as well as in schools in many other countries. The first, *recitation teaching*, stems from the culture of the classroom where strong and persistent norms regulate the discourse pattern among teachers and students. The second, *teacher autonomy*, exists within the culture of the school and the teaching profession itself where norms regulate the ways teachers relate to one another and play out their professional lives. Both are believed by most informed observers (and buttressed with considerable research evidence) to have negative effects on student learning and achievement. Both have been the targets of most educational reform initiatives over the past century.

## Recitation Teaching

Since the turn of the century, major educational reform efforts have strived to make classrooms more student centered, to get teachers to abandon didactic-recitation forms of teaching and to embrace more inquiry-oriented, open pedagogy. Dewey built his work on these pedagogical premises; they were reflected in the curriculum development work of the early progressives; they were embraced quickly by curriculum reformers during the post-Sputnik era, as well as those advocates of open education. Manifestations of these reforms are found today in programs advocating higher level thinking skills (Resnick, 1987), cooperative learning, (Sharan, Kussell, Hertz-Lazarowitz, Bejarano, Raviv & Sharan, 1984; Slavin, 1983) and reciprocal teaching (Palincsar and Brown, 1984). They are also high on the list of most major studies of school reform, including *A Place Called School* (Goodlad, 1984), *Tomorrow's Schools* (Holmes, 1986), and *Teachers for the 21st Century* (Carnegie, 1986).

These reforms have been widely endorsed by legislative and policy groups who have provided rather extensive funding during the past thirty years to encourage student-centered classrooms and inquiry-oriented pedagogy. They have been supported by teachers' professional organizations, including the NEA, the AFT, by numerous subject-specific professional societies, and, for the most part, by university-based teacher educators responsible for the initial preparation of teachers. For instance, many of the attempts to develop inquiry-oriented curricula stemmed from scholars working in universities. Small-group teaching and cooperative learning have long histories of advocacy by individuals in higher education starting with John Dewey, and continuing through Herbert Thelen (1956; 1960), and Robert Slavin (1983). A quick review of content included in contemporary textbooks on educational psychology and pedagogy will, in every instance, find chapters on inquiry and discovery teaching and on cooperative learning. No major textbook can be found today that advocates the effectiveness of the teacher-centered classroom or recitation teaching.

This presents a particularly puzzling situation. On the one hand, it appears that a consensus about what constitutes effective practice has existed for almost one hundred years by many of the major stakeholders in education. On the other hand, preferred practices do not seem to filter down to the classroom. Those who study classrooms and teaching have found that teacher-centered and didactic pedagogy persists and that even heroic efforts in the past have produced only piecemeal and shortlived change.

Larry Cuban (1981; 1984) has studied constancy and change in classrooms using five major indicators: ratio of teacher-to-student talk, use of groupings for instruction, use of interest centers, use of classroom space, and availability of student movement. He concluded that none of these features of classrooms and teaching has changed significantly since the turn of the century. Teachers talk most of the time to fairly large groups of students. They use mainly didactic methods rather than relying on small-group instruction or interest centers, and little substantive inquiry-oriented discourse can be found.

In the early 1980s, John Goodlad (1983) and his colleagues visited over 1,000 classrooms in the United States. They report finding a few exemplary and innovative classes. For the most part, however, they found pedagogical conformity. "Teachers lectured and questioned, students listened..." (p. 247). When Courtney Cazden reviewed the extensive literature on classroom discourse for the third edition of the *Handbook of Research on Teaching* (Wittrock, 1986) and again with Hugh Melan for the *Knowledge Base for the Beginning Teacher* (Reynolds, 1989) they, like others before, pointed out how discourse patterns in contemporary classrooms are characterized by an "unfolding series of initiations-reply-evaluation sequences" (p. 50). In other words, recitation teaching where "teachers elicit information through questioning from students about topics for which the teachers already have the answer" (p. 50).

Finally, Richard and Patricia Schmuck (1989) have uncovered evidence that recitation teaching is very much alive in the rural schools of America. In the spring of 1989, the Schmucks visited and collected information on rural schools and classrooms in the United States. Over a period of 6 months, they visited 25 school districts in 21 states. They interviewed 212 teenagers about their school experiences, and they observed lessons in 30 high school class-rooms. In 75 percent of the classrooms, they reported seeing mainly recitation teaching with teachers who talked over three-fourths of the time. Only twice did the Schmucks observe students talking in pairs, and only four times did they observe small group or cooperative learning strategies being used.

## Teacher Autonomy

Just as there have been reform efforts aimed at changing the way teachers teach within their classrooms, so too have there been proposals for school-wide reform. Historically, these reform initiatives have focused on the ways teachers relate to one another. They have taken the form of advocating less teacher autonomy and isolation and more interdependence and collegial problem solving. However, like recitation teaching, teacher autonomy and isolation persist because they are governed by two strong norms. The "autonomy norm" prescribes in most schools (not all) that it is okay for teachers to do pretty much what they want once they are inside their classrooms, while the "hands-off norm" makes it unacceptable for teachers to ask for or provide professional advice, help, or assistance in the most important aspects of their work—classroom management and pedagogy—particularly at times when serious difficulties are being experienced. The norms supporting teacher autonomy and noninterference have been de-scribed and criticized consistently for over 50 years. They were observed by Waller (1932) and by Sarason (1971; 1982), labeled by Lortie (1975), and analyzed thoroughly by numerous observers of schools (Feiman-Nemser & Floden, 1986; Joyce, McKibbon & Hersh, 1983; Lieberman & Miller, 1984). The concept of collegiality is again at the center of current reform efforts aimed at the empowerment of teachers, as it was early in this century from Dewey (1916) through Counts (1932).

Reformers want to change this behavioral regularity for several good reasons. Teacher autonomy prevents active participation in school-wide efforts (e.g. adoption of school-wide goals), a feature found important for overall well-being and academic performance of students. Lack of collegial interaction prevents teachers learning from one another as practitioners do in other professions (e.g. physicians who can't diagnose a problem ask for a consultation from another physician; lawyers and architects who are stumped with a particular situation ask for help from colleagues) and from using and applying the knowledge base on teaching and learning that exists today. It has also been argued, even by teachers themselves (Welsh, 1989), that lack of collegial interaction makes teaching a lonely job, leading to low morale and high turnover.

Proposals for school reform, thus, have been consistent over time—make pedagogy more open and inquiry oriented and help teachers relate to one another in more cooperative and collegial ways. Yet, solutions offered for most of this century have had little enduring impact. When observers visit schools they can find only isolated instances of serious departures from the basic patterns. The obvious question to ask is, "how can this be?"

Numerous explanations have been offered. It has been argued that the existing patterns persist because they "fit the environmental demands of the classroom" (Feiman-Nemser & Floden, 1986). The way schools were originally conceived (grade level groupings, carnegie units, cellular structures) created organizational arrangements that keep practices deemed undesirable alive (Joyce, McKibbon & Hersh, 1983; Lortie, 1975; Huberman and Miles, 1984) as do the demands placed on teachers to cover vast amounts of materials quickly. Others have used the social class backgrounds and conservative nature of teachers and teacher educators to explain resistance to change (Lanier & Little, 1986; Lortie, 1975). Cuban (1984) has provided a more global and historical interpretation: "the classroom is anchored in the particular history and culture of a society and its organizational imperatives, producing a setting in which traditional practices and beliefs change very slowly indeed" (p. 387).

All of these explanations hold some truth and each helps us understand the problem and its complexity. Nonetheless, we remain perplexed. Certainly, societal imperatives and cultural regularities change slowly, but in most other areas of our lives they do change. For instance, the historical time span in which we have tried to change recitation teaching has seen significant alterations in the basic patterns of other aspects of life. Within the 40 years since World War II, we have observed the complete reorganization of life in Eastern Europe, first its collapse from what it had been and now a second rebuilding likely to lead to new economic, and perhaps, different political structures and processes. Similarly, it is hard to imagine a person in the United States today denied the right to vote because of race, while this was not so 30 years ago. We have all made fundamental and lasting changes in our family lives and our child-rearing practices as careers outside the home for women became the norm. The point is that during a period of time in history when almost every other aspect of our lives has changed, and in some instances dramatically so, the basic patterns of teaching and schooling have remained fixed. Without discounting other explanations for the persistence of the regularities of teaching and schooling, a substantial portion of the problem *rests in the ways teachers are trained initially*, a topic explored in the next section.

## The Weaknesses of Professional Preparation

Recently, educational historian William Johnson (1989) made the observation that, unlike other fields (law, medicine, architecture) where university-based professional schools revolutionized both training and practice, the professional schools which train teachers have failed to find a paradigm that has transformed either educational practice or the education of teachers. Teacher preparation, as historically conceived and practiced, has not been powerful enough to provide teacher candidates with alternative ways of thinking about teaching and learning or with alternative ways of behaving. It has had low impact. It has left beginning teachers without a vision of teaching, beyond their own personalistic views, and without sufficient repertoire to challenge the traditional regularities they have learned so well as students. To correct this situation requires strong measures on the part of teacher education. It requires a stronger intervention than currently exists, one that is conceptually and procedurally designed to combat directly existing behavioral regularities of teaching. It must be built on the preconceptions of teaching teacher candidates bring with them; and, it must incorporate the rather extensive knowledge base we now have about how professionals learn the art and science of their practice.

## Those Who Choose to Teach

Obviously, the characteristics of those choosing to teach influences training efforts. Prior knowledge about anything acts as a significant filter through which new ideas must flow. The conventional wisdom about prospective teachers that has received the most attention has been a belief that they are, as a group, academically weak. If this proposition is accepted, the obvious solution is to find way of attracting more talented people into teaching. During the past few years, however, evidence is beginning to accumulate showing that prospective teachers are not as academically weak as previously believed, but that other characteristics they possess influence their professional training significantly. Two particular lines of inquiry are illustrative.

*CULTURAL INSULARITY.* During the past five years a team of researchers working under the auspices of the American Association for the Colleges of Teacher Education (AACTE) has been studying teacher education programs and students in the 700 plus institutions that make up the Association's membership. Known as the Research About Teacher Education (RATE) study, researchers annually survey a random sample of ninety institutions stratified by types (small liberal arts colleges, medium size regional colleges, and large research universities). This work has produced information on over 3,000 teacher candidates and over 100 teacher education programs. (See Galluzzo & Arends, 1989; Howey, 1989; and Zimpher, 1989).

Data from the RATE studies afford a rather complete portrait of persons preparing to teach, nationwide. This portrait does not show that teacher candidates have low academic abilities and records, as some earlier studies have suggested (Schlechty & Vance, 1982, for instance). Instead, persons preparing to teach, as a group, have slightly above average abilities and their performance in high school and college classes is also slightly above average. Although this is good news, other aspects of the portrait are important when considering the redesign of teacher education to challenge the existing regularities of teaching.

Essentially, those preparing to teach present a group portrait that Zimpher (1989) has described as *culturally insulated*. The large majority of teacher candidates in the RATE studies reported they had selected their teacher training institution not for its reputation for preparing excellent teachers, but for its "proximity to home and because it was accessible and affordable" (p.

29). Most reported they planned to stay close to their institutions or to their home town to teach. They preferred to teach normal students and middle-income students and had little interest in special education instruction or working with culturally diverse schools. Teacher candidates were filled with idealism and eager to enter the profession for the purpose of helping children grow and learn—a trait similar to one described by Lortie (1975) almost two decades ago. They were predominately white, with fewer than five percent black and two percent Hispanic. Less than one third reported any familiarity with a second language, and only 15 percent reported themselves fluent.

This portrait is both promising and challenging. On the one hand, it is good to know that people with average to above average talents are choosing teaching. The teaching profession of the next century will not be filled with the illiterates that some predict. The challenge, however, is to find ways of working effectively with the cultural insularity of this cadre of prospective teachers and to help them expand existing conceptions they bring with them about life and about teaching.

*UNREALISTIC OPTIMISM.* Over the past several years, Carol Weinstein at Rutgers University has been studying teacher candidates' expectations about their abilities as future teachers and about the beliefs they hold toward teaching. In two different studies (1988; 1989), she asked teacher candidates to rate their future teaching performance compared to peers in their teacher education program, and to provide information about their views of the ideal teacher.

Weinstein found that teacher candidates, even as early as their sophomore year in college, were extremely optimistic about their abilities to be good teachers. On a seven-point scale (with "1" meaning well below average and "7" much above average) the mean rating of 131 teacher candidates surveyed in one study was 5.4. In fact, nearly 85 percent of the students perceived their future teaching performance would be above average or better. Only 1 subject out of the 131 rated himself/herself as slightly below average. This optimism even extended to the areas of teaching documented for years to be the most troublesome for beginners. Weinstein reports that the candidates in her study were confident, for instance, in their abilities to teach students from different cultures and backgrounds, to maintain discipline, to establish and enforce class rules and procedures, to relate to parents, to respond effectively to misbehavior, and to deal with individual differences" (p. 54).

Weinstein also asked teacher candidates to record the attributes of "a really good teacher" and to rate themselves on these attributes. Teacher candidates' perceptions of a good teacher emphasized interpersonal relationships such as caring, warmth, patience, enthusiasm, and ability to relate. What is most interesting, however, is Weinstein's finding that candidates who perceived themselves as having a particular attribute, (patience, for instance) "tended to rate it more important for teaching" than an attribute that they perceived they didn't possess. Weinstein's conclusion from this phenomenon was that "it would appear that in the absence of a clear ... consensus about good teaching, students are free to construct 'mini-theories' about teaching that devalue attributes that they do not themselves possess" (p. 58). We might add that it also allows them to hold on to their individualistic and traditional conceptions of teaching.

The RATE studies have uncovered a similar phenomenon among teacher candidates. Candidates were asked to rate their readiness to teach on 12 facets of teaching: planning instruction, using proper teaching methods, evaluating student learning, working with other teachers, using materials properly, responding to student differences, managing classrooms, developing materials, diagnosing learner needs, dealing with misbehavior, developing curriculum and using computers. For all of the facets, except using computers, over two-thirds of the students in their junior year (close to the beginning of most teacher education programs) reported that they already had a "high level" of readiness to teach (AACTE, RATE II, 1988). In a later study, students were asked how confident they were that their teacher education program had adequately prepared them to teach. Almost all (97 percent) reported that they believed they were "adequately" or more than adequately prepared to begin teaching (AACTE, RATE III, 1989).

This situation, labeled "unrealistic optimism" by Weinstein, describes teacher candidates, then, who enter teacher education with high levels of confidence and "the conviction that they possess the characteristics needed for teaching." And, although in many instances confidence is a good thing, Weinstein warns that teacher candidates "who hold unrealistic optimism about their own success may devalue the need for professional preparation..." (p. 59). This situation becomes particularly serious and troublesome when we link it to the portrait of cultural insularity and with the fact that teacher candidates are carrying around in their minds the outmoded patterns of teaching they have observed so long as students.

## What is Taught and How

Teacher education, as designed today, is simply too weak either to produce a paradigm shift for teacher candidates or to provide them with a sufficient repertoire to make serious departures from what they think they already know and can do well.

*TIME IS A FACTOR.* Information collected in the RATE studies shows that the average secondary teacher candidate's teacher education program consists of 26 semester hours of work—two methods courses, three courses in educational foundations, one early field experience and student teaching. The course of study for elementary teachers is pretty much the same except that they are required to take 6 or 7 methods courses, making their total program about 50 semester hours. This training, in well over 90 percent of the institutions, is spread out over 3 years, making the amount of attention focused on professional knowledge at any particular time, except during student teaching, a very small portion in relation to other studies and activities that consume the lives of undergraduate college students. These findings are consistent with others who have counted the amount of time teacher candidates spend in preparation (Conant, 1963, AACTE; 1976; Kerr, 1983). Additionally, this time frame has remained remarkably constant since 1920. If anything, it has decreased slightly (about 2 percent) according to Kerr (1983) in the 50-year period between 1929 and 1979. This contrasts sharply with the increase of professional training in every other field during the same 50-year period (see Kerr, 1983).

*SPRINKLING THEM LIGHTLY.* Time is not the only factor which causes teacher preparation to be a weak intervention. What is taught and how it is taught are equally important. Observers for three decades (AACTE, 1976; Conant, 1963, Holmes, 1986; Joyce et. al., 1977; Kerr, 1983) have reported consistently that teacher education is characterized by a number of college courses being taught in rather traditional and individualistic ways without thematic structures and without tight connections between college course-work and clinical field experiences. What is most striking is that programs across all kinds of institutions are essentially alike and contain the same inadequacies. When we probe more deeply into these assertions, we find a situation where students are introduced to many important pedagogical topics, but in such a "shotgun" manner it becomes a very mild intervention in comparison to the very strong interventions required to challenge existing knowledge structures.

Over the past three years a colleague and I (Christensen, 1990; Arends, 1989) have been studying the content in textbooks used in colleges classes on pedagogy and collecting and analyzing syllabi of courses in education. We find that several alternatives to recitation teaching are introduced to teacher candidates and faculty advocate their use in most programs. For instance, no science methods text existed that did not have a chapter on inquiry or discovery teaching. No social studies methods text was found without a chapter on the use of role playing and simulation. Every educational psychology text had information about cooperative learning. Prospective teachers, thus, are introduced to countervailing ways of teaching but not in a powerful enough way to insure their use later. Probing a bit more deeply into this assertion and analyzing a sample of course syllabi illustrates why.

One course that captured our interest was called "teaching strategies" or "general methods of teaching." This is a three- hour course required almost everywhere for prospective secondary teachers and in many places for elementary as well. From our analysis of 43 course syllabi (31 nationwide and 12 from the state of Maryland) several conclusions can be made about this course and the experiences it provides for teacher candidates.

The goals for the teaching strategy course vary widely and the topics covered are numerous. The set of topics listed below, from one course syllabus, illustrates what is covered in this 15-week course at one institution:

| | |
|---|---|
| Introduction to Teaching | Group and Discussion Methods |
| The School | Inquiry and Discovery |

The Student and How They Learn

Motivation

Classroom Management

Discipline

Objectives

Planning for Teaching

Lesson Planning

Selection of Materials

Other Methods

Teaching Methods

Teaching Reading

Readability

Diagnosis

Classroom Evaluation

Marking and Reporting

Guiding Student Learning

The instructor of this course listed 34 objectives in the course syllabus. Two illustrate the magnitude and complexity of the goals held for this course:

> Objective #1: "identify and explain the historical development of our middle and secondary schools"

> Objective #22: "identify and describe the characteristics of and procedures advocated by each of the following techniques: Socratic method, guided discussion, springboard, problem solving, case-study, project method, role-playing, simulation, and community involvement."

Obviously these two objectives alone would be ambitious for one 3-hour course. When thirty other objectives are added it is clear that this course can only be a "mild" intervention for teacher candidates.

This illustration is typical, not an exception. Analyses across syllabi, for instance, show that something called inquiry, discovery, or inductive teaching is covered in over 90 percent of the courses. Yet, the average amount of instructional time devoted to this teaching approach can be estimated as slightly less than 2 hours across courses.

Including so many topics in a single course is understandable. The number of strategies available to teachers has expanded significantly over the past three or four decades as has the knowledge base which informs effective practice. Compare for instance the size and quality of the three *Handbooks on Teaching*, the first published in 1963; the latest in 1986. Special interest groups and accrediting agencies have also required topics to be included in teacher preparation programs, such as mainstreaming, multicultural education and reading methods. Yet, the time allocated for professional training has remained the same.

The net effect of including so many topics in a single course or a series of disconnected courses is about the same as if they were not covered at all. We are sprinkling prospective teachers lightly with ideas they will soon forsake. This approach simply will not break down existing conceptions prospective teachers have about teaching. It certainly will not provide them with sufficient skills to teach in different ways when later confronted with the institutional press of the existing regularities found in schools and classrooms.

# A PROPOSAL FOR CHALLENGING
# THE REGULARITIES OF TEACHING

In this section I illustrate how teacher education programs might be redesigned to challenge recitation teaching and norms supporting teacher autonomy. Space does not permit a detailed description of the various components and details for such a program. Instead, I will provide a sketch of the kind of teacher a redesigned program would aim to educate, an overview of desired programmatic structures, and propose five propositions on which the curriculum and instructional processes of a new program might be constructed.

## The Kind of Teacher We Want

Any professional preparation program has to be built on a conception of what the effective practitioner in the field needs to know, do, and be able to accomplish. Obviously, a program I would design would produce practitioners who could and would challenge existing regularities in teaching in constructive and effective ways. To do this, however, they would need to be effective in all aspects of their work. My view of effective teaching requires as its baseline individuals who are academically able and who care about the well-being of children. It also requires individuals who can produce results, mainly those of student academic achievement and social learning. These characteristics are prerequisites and would become criteria for the selection of candidates into professional preparation programs. They would not have to be addressed in any substantial way in the program itself. There are four higher-level sets of attributes that a program would aim to accomplish:

1. Effective graduates would have control of the knowledge bases on teaching and learning and use this knowledge to guide the science and art of their teaching practice.

2. Effective graduates would have a repertoire of best practices (models, strategies, procedures) and could use these to instruct children in classrooms and to work with adults in the school setting.

3. Effective graduates would have the dispositions and skills to approach all aspects of their work in a reflective, collegial, and problem solving manner.

4. Effective graduates would have the dispositions and organizational skills to work toward school improvement, particularly the desire and abilities to implement pedagogical approaches aimed at challenging recitation teaching and to enter into dialogue with others for the purpose of advancing collegiality.

## Overall Structure of A Redesigned Program

The professional program I have in mind would address the *time issue* directly in two important ways. More time would be required overall for professional preparation in pedagogy as compared to existing practices, and available instructional time would be used to concentrate in depth on a few topics rather than glossing over many areas lightly. Structurally, a redesigned program would require at least four academic semesters. This could be accomplished in two summer sessions and an academic year or in two academic years. Although more time than this might be desirable, this amount pushes the limits of current economic and political realities. Teacher candidates would enter the program only after they had demonstrated sufficient academic preparation in the arts and sciences and in their teaching specialties. Only those with sufficient reflective capabilities would be admitted. The program would be offered at the graduate level. The type of degree offered is perhaps not critical, although I would prefer the work to culminate in a newly created Masters of Teaching (MT) degree similar to the degree now offered at the University of Virginia. Regardless of the exact name of the degree, teacher candidates in the program would already hold a bachelor's degree, would do the majority of their work in pedagogy, and would be prepared to attend school full time. Working with young and often immature undergraduates, or allowing part-time study and the multiple commitments that go with these situations, simply will not afford the energy and time required for serious professional study aimed at challenging existing regularities of teaching and schooling.

## Propositions to Guide Redesign Efforts

Although much more needs to be learned about how to effectively prepare people for professional practice, sufficient knowledge exists today (if used) to move us a long way toward creating more powerful programs and graduates. Several propositions, based on what is currently known about learning to teach, could guide redesign efforts.

*ORGANIZED PROGRAMS AROUND THEMES FOR SCHEMA BUSTING.* A powerful teacher education program would be organized around a set of themes aimed at providing consistency across courses and experiences, and targeted specifically at altering prior conceptions held by teacher candidates. It would provide candidates with alternative and well-organized pedagogical schemata for thinking about teaching and learning. The processes and pedagogy of the program would be modeled by those responsible for the program. Most importantly, a powerful program would give teacher candidates ample opportunities for group work and other activities aimed at providing a basis for understanding, experientially, the importance of professional collegiality.

Chosen themes would challenge directly the existing regularities of teaching. They would also help organize the substantial knowledge base that currently exists on what constitutes effective teaching. Themes would also address the major issues faced by beginning teaching mainly, the nature of learning, schooling, teaching, and learning to teach. Although several clusters of ideas could be good candidates for themes, I offer the following for consideration.

*Theme #1, Learning:* Children and youth construct their own knowledge and knowledge acquisition is influenced heavily by prior knowledge.

I would argue that the constructionists' view that children and youth (adults too) construct their own knowledge and that knowledge acquisition is based on prior knowledge is sufficiently developed today to provide a basis for one important theme in a teacher education program. This conception of learning provides a strong countervailing view to the one that currently supports recitation teaching—a view that knowledge exists as a set of facts, principles, or truths in the teacher's mind for children to acquire.

*Theme #2, Schooling:* The primary goal of schooling is to fight ignorance, although in a complex, multicultural society this means different things to different people.

Goals for formal education in modern democratic societies are likely to reflect the diversity of contemporary multicultural populations. In a general way, there must be a deep understanding and commitment by those who teach about the importance of being able to work toward multiple goals of education while believing every child can learn.

*Theme #3, Teaching:* Effective teachers have control of the knowledge base on teaching and they have command of a repertoire of effective practices which they can employ in a reflective and problem solving fashion.

This theme would address the acts of teaching directly and would be consistent with the previous themes. If students acquire knowledge and construct meaning based on prior knowledge and if the goals for schooling are multifaceted, then effective teachers must have a repertoire of teaching approaches, based on research and the wisdom of practice. They must be able to analyze and reflect on particular teaching situations and match methods appropriately to particular groups of students and particular learning goals. There is no single, best way to teach.

*Theme #4, Learning to Teach:* Learning to teach is a lifelong process of replacing conceptions and ideas based on idiosyncratic experience with ideas and practices based on research and the wisdom of collective practice.

If a constructionist view provides power for understanding how young people learn, it can provide the same kind of power for helping teacher candidates understand the processes of learning to teach. Again, the aim of this theme is for teacher candidates to become cognitively aware of their prior conceptions of teaching, to discover the limitations of these conceptions, and to understand how difficult it is to change knowledge structures, feelings, attitudes, and beliefs about teaching, particularly when they have been so deeply ingrained over such a long period of time. Learning to teach is a life-long process.

## Building Repertoire and Advanced Knowledge Acquisition

A second proposition guiding a powerful teacher education program aims at providing candidates with a repertoire of teaching approaches and advanced knowledge acquisition of carefully selected aspects of the professional knowledge base.

*REPERTOIRE.* Over the past three decades a variety of teaching approaches (models, strategies, methods, and procedures) have been codified and described. Their instructional effects have been tested in a variety of settings and across various subject areas. For instance, in the latest edition of *Models of Teaching* (1986), Joyce and Weil describe 20 different approaches to teaching, most of which vary significantly from recitation teaching. The variety of approaches available to teachers today can be used to accomplish a wide range of important educational goals: to teach concepts and new information, to promote intergroup cooperation, to help students learn self-control, and to help students learn how to learn. Over two decades of research have shown that teachers can be taught to use these approaches effectively if enough time is given and if appropriate training processes are used (see Fullan, 1982; Joyce & Showers, 1988; Joyce & Weil, 1986). There is simply no reason for beginning teachers to rely solely upon recitation teaching except that most training programs today leave them insufficiently prepared to use alternative approaches effectively.

*ADVANCED KNOWLEDGE ACQUISITION.* In a very provocative presentation at the Annual Meeting of the American Educational Research Association, Illinois medical educators Feltovich, Spiro, and Coulson (1989), outlined a model for helping professionals handle the complexity of modern practice. They start with what is known about what experts do (in their case, doctors) in contrast to what novices can do. Expert medical practitioners, according to Feltovich, Spiro, and Coulson, have fast access to a fairly complex knowledge structure, they can recognize families of diverse categories, and they can quickly and accurately cluster logical competitors for theories they may hold. Experts, unlike novices, have the ability to deal with exceptions; that is, they can override rules; they can make crossovers; they can develop new ways to classify overlapping information and procedures.

Based on the research they have been doing, they describe a three-stage process for reaching professional expertise:

Stage 1: Introduction to Professional Knowledge

Stage 2: Advanced Knowledge Acquisition

Stage 3: Expertise

It is impossible, according to Feltovich, Spiro, and Coulson, to get candidates in any field to the expertise stage of development while they are still in formal training, for three important reasons:

(1) Professional schools and professional knowledge are so complex that it is difficult to make all the learning experiences emerge;

(2) Candidates come to training with prior conceptions which produce a set of perceptual biases about knowledge and about what constitutes evidence and explanations. A great deal of training time must go into clearing up these misconceptions; and

(3) True expertise in any field takes years to develop—a time frame that is unrealistic for formal training programs.

It is possible, however, to bring people to Stage 2, "advanced knowledge acquisition." This is a state where the practitioner (1) has complete mastery of content associated with a particular practice; (2) knows how to apply it in routine ways; and (3) can apply it in a limited number of situations which are nonroutine.

To get to advanced knowledge acquisition requires an integrated curriculum and the use of special approaches. Faculty responsible for preparing professionals, regardless of the field, must assemble knowledge so that it applies directly to the specific practices used by practitioners. This knowledge must be presented to candidates in such a way that it not only challenges existing schema but also simplifies the real complexity that exists. Single schema and simple knowledge representations used to introduce a practice are overcome later through multiple knowledge representations and multiple analogies. Each new analogy and each new representation is chosen to counteract the effects of previous ones. This process helps candidates help refine the schema they have about effective professional practice and to apply knowledge in increasingly complex situations.

Feltovich, Spiro, and Coulson emphasize that this process requires an integrated learning environment which is nonlinear and multidimensional, which affords tight connections between concepts and practice, and one where knowledge of the important things are thoroughly explored as contrasted to "sprinkling students with vast volumes of information."

The concept of advanced knowledge acquisition and the processes for training medical students does not differ significantly from what Joyce and Showers (1988) have called developing "executive control," a condition where teachers have thoroughly mastered a particular approach to teaching and can demonstrate its consistent and appropriate use under various conditions. Joyce and Showers have developed processes for working with experienced teachers that are applicable to beginners. There is ample evidence to support the contention that to get "executive control" requires deep understanding of the theory and rationale behind a particular approach, opportunities to see it demonstrated, and ample provisions for practice accompanied by coaching and feedback. Their current rule of thumb for how much time and practice are required to gain executive control of a single teaching approach, such as inquiry teaching or cooperative learning, consists of viewing fifteen to twenty demonstrations over a span of time, and opportunities to practice the approach at least a dozen times in a variety of settings.

For candidates to gain advanced knowledge acquisition and executive control will require faculty to assemble knowledge and the curriculum in such a way that it applies directly to specific practices used by practitioners and to be very parsimonious about what is taught.

## An Illustration: Cooperative Learning

To illustrate these principles, I provide an example of how a teaching approach, such as cooperative learning, might be taught in a redesigned program. Cooperative learning has been chosen as an illustration because of the promises and problems it poses. On the promising side, cooperative learning and associated practices have a long history of use. A substantial knowledge base has been accumulated over the past decade showing its positive effects on student academic and social learning (Johnson & Johnson, 1981; Slavin, 1983; Sharan, et. al. 1984:and Sharan & Sharan, this volume). On the problem side, however, cooperative learning presents the most radical alternative to recitation teaching. As such, it is very difficult for teachers (even experienced teachers) to learn and to implement. (See the situation described by Sharan and Sharan in this volume.) In the discussion that follows I recommend hypothetical instructional processes that would be required to make cooperative learning part of the beginning teacher's repertoire at the level of advanced knowledge acquisition. I also estimate the amount of instructional time required to teach cooperative learning to beginners to illustrate the challenge faced by teacher educators under current time constraints.

*Phase 1: Introducing candidates to cooperative learning.* Cooperative learning would initially be introduced to teacher candidates through carefully prepared presentations, readings and group investigations. Its history, its theoretical stance toward teaching and learning, the knowledge base that supports its use, and the basic environmental requirements for appropriate use would be described thoroughly. This aspect of instruction would be within the context of how cooperative learning differs from recitation teaching. Teacher candidates would be required to read major contemporary theorists. This portion would consume 10 hours of instructional time and 20 hours of outside preparation. Each candidate would be required to show command of the knowledge base on cooperative learning on an essay test, prior to moving on to the next phase of instruction.

*Phase 2: Practice under controlled conditions.* The second phase consists of five practice sessions using peer micro-teaching, a well-developed and re-searched procedure in which candidates plan and conduct lessons for peers in front of a video camera. Structured feedback and critique would be offered by peers and by instructors to promote self-analysis and reflection. Practice sessions would be made increasingly complex and would build on previous sessions. Planning for each lesson would be done by cooperative learning teams. At least half of the lessons would be team taught. This aspect of the course would require a minimum of 20 hours of instructional time and 40 hours of outside preparation.

*Phase 3: Observation and practice in clinical classrooms.* The next phase would consist of observing demonstrations by teachers in clinical classrooms and of practicing cooperative learning lessons with students. These teachers (see Arends & Cohen, 1987; Arends & Winitzky, 1989; Winitzky, 1987) have been trained specifically so they understand the rationale and the knowledge base behind cooperative learning, can demonstrate its use clearly and effectively, and can conduct reflective seminars with teacher candidates assigned to work in their classrooms. This aspect of the course would require 10 hours of observation in clinical classrooms, 10 hours for the actual teaching, plus 20 hours for preparation and reflection.

*Phase 4: Reflection and case analysis.* Experiences during this phase would consist of critiquing cooperative learning using case methods and reflecting on experiences gained in the clinical classrooms. Again, candidates would accomplish these learning activities in cooperative learning teams. This aspect of the courses would require approximately 12 hours of instructional time and 24 hours of preparation by the candidate.

*Phase 5: Studying barriers.* The course on cooperative learning would conclude with an in-depth examination of the features of schools and classrooms which impede a teacher's use of cooperative learning. Candidates would be expected to explore the literature on school culture (Sarason, 1971; 1982, for example) and on school change (Fullan, 1982; Huberman & Miles, 1984). Specific discussions and reflections would consider what to do when the following hypothetical situations arise:

- Other teachers criticize the approach because it doesn't fit their conceptions of recitation teaching.

- Classroom management problems occur because in some instances students are easier to control in whole class instruction as compared to small groups.

- The teacher finds insufficient curriculum materials to support group work and investigation.

- The teacher is starting to feel guilty because he or she is not covering as much material as the teacher next door.

- Parents and students complain about the cooperative task and reward structures (e.g., "why is my grade dependent upon the work of others?")

Teacher candidates would complete this work by making specific plans on how they could reduce impediments they are likely to face in their initial years of teaching. This phase of the course would require 13 hours of instructional time and 26 hours of preparation by the teacher candidates.

## Instructional processes overall

To remain consistent with the cooperative learning approach, the content and procedures would be taught using the model itself. Students would work in learning groups, would practice in the simulated and actual settings in teams, and their grades would be based not only on their individual performance but on the performance of the learning group as a unit. This particular class would be taught by a team of instructors for the purposes of modeling cooperative behavior and for modeling alternative norms to those supporting autonomous teaching.

## Developing A Technical Language and A Common Memory.

Lortie (1975) observed that reform-minded educators have repetitively advanced their own ideology by "discrediting former practices and outlooks" (p. 69). The result of this activity has been that teachers do not develop a sense of what has been tried before and in Lortie's words, "to an astonishing degree the beginner in teaching must start afresh, largely uninformed about prior solutions and alternate approaches to recurring practical problems" (p. 70). It is small wonder, writes Lortie, that "teachers are not inclined to see themselves as sharing in a common `memory' or technical subculture. Since they have not received such instruction, they are forced to fall back upon individual recollections, which in turn are not displaced by new perspectives" (p. 70).

A powerful teacher education program would be constructed on the proposition that teaching requires professionals who possess a common memory and a technical language. Teacher candidates would learn to see the connections between Dewey's democratic classrooms and Slavin's cooperative learning. They would know Ralph Tyler and his influence on the way curriculum is conceived today. They would recognize that there are recurring problems in education and they would know about prior solutions which have been proposed. This memory, however, would not be passed along in a highly academic "history of education" course, the common practice today. Instead, collective memories would be developed using experiential instructional modes connected to the practical world of teaching along with a thorough grounding in the knowledge bases that exist to inform teaching, including an in-depth understanding and appreciation of educational research.

Some find it puzzling that professional schools of education take great pride in their research, yet postpone teaching about research methods and procedures until candidates enter doctoral programs and are essentially in the process of leaving the classroom. Part of helping teachers build a common memory would be developing in them a deep understanding of and commitment to educational research. Candidates would leave with capabilities to read research, provide thoughtful critique of research, and engage in their own classroom research.

Indeed, toward the end of our redesigned program, candidates would be required to conduct action research on their own teaching. Teacher candidates would identify an aspect of their teaching suitable to action research, collect and analyze data on problem, and prepare a formal paper which would be submitted to faculty and peer review. The processes and technology for this type of teacher-initiated research are fairly well advanced and the results from experiments in Australia, Great Britain, and the United States are very positive. (See Hopkins, 1986; Kemmis, 1981; and Oja & Smulyan, 1989.)

*TEACHING EXISTING PATTERNS AND STRATEGIES FOR CHALLENGING THEM.* A fifth proposition guiding a powerful teacher education program would be to teach directly about the behavior regularities existing in schools and classrooms and take a strong stance against those practices in need of reform. Prospective teachers would study, observe, and analyze recitation teaching, for example, in a structured and systematic way. They would be required to thoroughly internalize, that in addition to planning for and delivering instruction to students, teachers are also members of organizations called schools and as such are expected to provide important leadership and organizational functions, most importantly working with other teachers, administrators, and parents in collegial ways. They would come to understand that the way these organizational functions are performed by teachers makes a significant difference in how students behave and what they learn. They would understand how they will be influenced by the individual histories and cultures of the schools in which they work.

These are hard lessons to teach teacher candidates because their primary experiences with schools has been as students. They have yet to experience the school as a place where adults work. Also, most teacher education curricula are not grounded in the "social system" perspective required to get these messages across effectively. However, it seems reasonable that most educated people could understand ideas such as how a school's history and culture (beliefs, norms, and roles) influence the behavior of those who work there. It also seems reasonable that prospective teachers could come to understand that the culture of schools becomes most important, in a practical sense, when they try to change things, such as moving away from recitation teaching or striving to increase collegiality.

*CONNECT KNOWLEDGE-BASED LEARNING WITH CLINICAL PRACTICE.* Finally, a redesigned program would provide opportunities for teacher candidates to participate in ongoing clinical work in schools, but these would differ significantly from current practices associated with early field experience and student teaching.

It is interesting that the one aspect of teacher education programs that has indeed changed over the past 30 years has been the nature of observational and tutorial opportunities for teacher candidates (called early field experiences) and student teaching. Data from the RATE studies (Arends & Galluzzo, 1990) show that over 95% of institutions that prepare secondary and elementary teachers require early field experiences, an activity seldom observed when Conant (1963) studied teacher education in the early 1960s. The typical pattern is for candidates to spend one or two days per week observing and working in schools, most often during the early phase of their program.

All programs require student teaching. On the average this experience consists of awarding 10 credit hours to teacher candidates for spending about 30 to 35 hours per week in two school placements, each lasting from 4 to 10 weeks. A common pattern for those preparing to teach in elementary schools is to have experience in the lower grades for one placement and in the upper grades for the other. Many secondary teacher candidates have experiences in junior high or middle schools and in high schools. Some institutions, particularly in the larger metropolitan areas, try to give students experiences in schools with predominately middle class students as well as schools which draw student populations from the lower socio-economic strata. The time for student teaching, like early field experiences, has expanded somewhat during the past 30 years.

Expanding the amount of time for field experiences has not produced any significant results, if the criterion is preparing candidates who can challenge existing regularities. Without negating the importance of experience for learning to teach, the field experiences (both early and student teaching) as provided today in teacher education programs only serves to perpetuate the regularities of recitation teaching and teacher autonomy. This assertion has been extremely well documented over the past decade. (See, for example, Applegate, 1987; Berliner, 1985; Evertson, et. al., 1985; Griffin et. al, 1983; Lortie, 1975.)

Clinical work in our redesigned program would consist of essentially four types of experiences. The first, focused observation and practice of specific teaching approaches, has already been described. The second, starting at the end of the first year and continuing during the second year, would be work with clinical teachers who have been chosen because they believe in challenging the regularities of teaching and because they work in collegial ways with one another. Candidates would be assigned to these teachers' schools in 2 or 3-member teams. However, candidates would not be allowed to individually "take over" a particular class, now the common student teaching practice. Instead, candidates would join with teams of clinical teachers for the purpose of (1) extended observation across the school; (2) talking and reflecting about teaching; (3) team teaching, and (4) participation in school-wide leadership activities. These would not be full-day experiences and would be tightly connected to the coursework being taken on campus.

During the second year of the program, candidates would also be provided a placement where they would work and study education from the perspective of those who provide leadership and set policy. In larger metropolitan areas this would be quite easy to accomplish because of the numerous public and private organizations or units that exist for this purpose. In rural areas, candidates would be placed in central offices, staff development centers, state departments of education, regional educational laboratories and the like.

Two major reasons are behind this rather dramatic break from tradition. One, it is a strategy to keep teacher candidates from the socializing influences of traditional early field experiences and student teaching. The procedures and processes that currently exist simply undo, in a very short period of time, the effects of prior training. Two, it is a strategy for teacher candidates, in a collegial way, to view and participate in the processes of educational decision-making—an apprenticeship experience they do not get as students growing up in schools.

# BARRIERS AND PROSPECTS FOR RESTRUCTURING TEACHER EDUCATION

Elsewhere I have written (Arends, 1990) how in 1987, Robert Bush, Emeritus Professor at Stanford University, described decade-by-decade attempts to reform teacher education since the 1920s. From a study of this historical record, he concluded that "the first sobering lesson to be learned from the past 50 years of attempted reform of teacher education is that there has been no fundamental reform during that period" (p. 15). I wish I could write with optimism that the current reform will be more successful. That is not the case. Even though myriad remedies abound, many similar to the ones proposed in this chapter, none is close to being implemented. The simple truth is that many barriers exist against helping prospective teachers become sufficiently prepared to challenge the existing behavioral regularities of teaching in any significant way. Cracking the culture of teacher education will be every bit as tough as cracking the culture of the schools.

## Barriers

The culture of colleges and universities where teachers are prepared is, in some ways, significantly different than the culture of schools where beginning teachers start their careers. In other ways they are very similar. These differences and similarities can work for or against a more powerful teacher education program. For instance, academe places a high value on research, reflection, and inquiry. These norms can facilitate tougher, knowledge-based, inquiry-oriented teacher preparation programs. On the other hand, faculty in higher education rely on lecture-recitation teaching just as completely as do K-12 teachers. One cannot expect the regularities of teaching in higher education to change any more quickly than they have elsewhere. This conservatism presents serious problems for faculty who want to teach and model alternative approaches. Similarly, faculty in higher education embrace norms supporting autonomy just as tightly as do their colleagues in K-12 schools, perhaps more. It will be difficult for faculty responsible for teacher education to challenge these norms for the purpose of developing an integrated, thematic-based curriculum and of modeling norms supporting collegiality to those learning to teach.

As with schools, the curriculum of most teacher education programs today are designed to cover a lot of material quickly. As with schools, it will be difficult for faculty, as well as for accreditation agencies, to give up many favorite topics for the purpose of teaching a few things well. For example, courses on individualized instruction, mainstreaming, children's literature, art for teachers, and multicultural education all have strong advocates both inside and outside the walls of academe.

Most members of the teacher education professoriate currently have background and research interests about how students learn and about the way academic subjects are organized for school learning. Many are not keenly aware of the processes associated with learning to teach nor the historical and cultural regularities that govern teacher's work. They do not value, necessarily, the importance of the study of school culture or the necessity of confronting the regularities of teaching in a frontal fashion.

Perhaps the most serious barriers against creating more powerful teacher education programs, however, are those that stem from the norms and structures in higher education that define knowledge production and use. To make teacher education effective requires strong, well-articulated programs connected tightly to the knowledge base on teaching, learning, and schooling. Yet, many of the institutions that prepare teachers have low connections to inquiry. Others, while connected to research and research production, have for the most part disconnected themselves conceptually and structurally from the initial preparation of teachers.

For example, on one end of the continuum a sizeable proportion of the educational professoriate can be found who are not involved with knowledge production. Mainly, these persons work in small liberal arts colleges or medium to large regional public institutions. Conant (1963) criticized the low knowledge production of education faculty as did Joyce and his colleagues in 1977. Clark (1978) reported that the median level of institutional research productivity in education was "zero." This situation has not changed substantially. Data collected from the education professoriate in the RATE studies have shown that over half of educational foundations and secondary methods faculty in smaller liberal arts institutions and in regional state universities have never written an article for publication. These data also show that less than one-third of secondary methods faculty in these institutions read journals such as the American Education Research Journal or the Journal of Educational Psychology, and that only 12 percent belong to the American Educational Research Association.

On the other end of the continuum are the members of the professoriate, particularly in major research universities, who have distanced themselves from the study of teaching and learning in favor of more general social science inquiry. They have abandoned involvement in the programs for the initial preparation of teachers. Like the other end of the continuum, this situation has been known about for a long time. It was described almost a decade ago by Great Britain's Harry Judge (1982). More recently, it was studied and criticized by the Holmes Group (1986) and by Geraldine Clifford and John Guthrie in Ed School (1988). For whatever reasons, faculties in the larger research universities have found other professional activities more engaging and rewarding than the preparation of teachers.

Both situations pose powerful barriers to overcome, because the cornerstone for professional endeavor is, in one way or another, based on technical knowledge that can be brought to bear on problem situations in practice. If the professoriate is not connected to new technical knowledge or abandons the job of making this knowledge available and valued by beginners, then there is little hope of reorienting the culture of schools and the profession of teaching toward alternative methods of instruction and collegial problem solving.

A final barrier to a radically redesigned teacher education program will be the teacher candidates themselves. Traditions associated with what is appropriate to do and not do in teacher education have histories almost as long as do the traditions that define appropriate teaching. Demanding advanced knowledge acquisition is a drastic departure from the rather thin intellectual content and minimum standards that characterize many programs today. Drastically changing the student teaching experience, for instance, will be resisted by candidates who value highly the current 'rite of passage' status accorded this activity. Using cooperative learning strategies and requiring candidates to work in collegial ways will also be resisted. Teacher candidates are fully aware of past practices, and they can be predicted to resist efforts to change, particularly when the new practices will place different and greater demands upon them.

## Prospects

Even though the current reform movements in education carry agenda observed in earlier eras, there does seem to be an new intensity about the need to change public education not felt before. The indictments of schools are severe, as are the indictments of programs that prepare teachers. If we accept the premise that schools cannot be reformed without major changes in those who teach in them, then the demand for restructured teacher training and socialization becomes critical.

Currently, diametrically opposed reforms for changing teacher education are being considered. The first consists of procedures adopted in over twenty states which allow people with bachelor's degrees to enter teaching without special professional preparation and legislation in at least four states that severely limits the number of courses that can be included in a campus-based teacher education program. Advocates of these policies have given up on formal teacher education as we know it. They are seeking alternative routes to teaching. Although the frustration and anger of policy-makers who are advocates of these measures can be fully understood, these alternative routes will not reform schools. Persons who enter teaching without powerful professional training will only perpetuate the inadequate practices and regularities that currently exist. On the other hand, these initiatives challenge directly the legitimacy of the higher education's monopoly for preparing teachers. It may provide a strong motivation for those responsible for university-based teacher education to change their ways.

The second effort, still in an infancy stage, consists of a loosely coupled network of teacher educators across the country, who see the need for a revolution in professional training. They are currently experimenting with several components which may ultimately help form a new paradigm. For instance, knowledge-based, thematic programs have been devised and implemented on an experimental basis, particularly at Michigan State University and the University of Maryland. Some teacher education programs (Universities of Pennsylvania, Virginia, Houston, New Hampshire, Maryland and Catholic University) are experimenting with alternative strategies for helping teacher candidates to be reflective about their teaching and to recognize the influences classroom cultures and existing regularities have on teaching. Experiments are also underway to find out how to get teacher candidates to understand and value research, and to engage teacher candidates in "action research" so they have the means to uncover the hidden dimensions of their own work. Different "internship" arrangements which provide opportunities for teacher candidates to experience school-wide activities (working with colleagues, working with parents) rather than just activities which occur within the four walls of the classroom can also be found.

Similarly, the efforts of the 90-plus members of the Holmes Group, a consortium of major research universities who have joined together for the purpose of reform in teacher education and of schools, may produce new structures and processes for the preparation of teachers. It is too early to know the outcomes of this group's work. However, if the group maintains its commitments to post-baccalaureate teacher education, to develop radically redesigned programs, and to work more closely with schools, these actions could provide creative and powerful models in the future.

Conceptually, ideas about effective teaching and teacher education now exist with sufficient clarity to guide serious change. Getting there will be the problem. Implementation of new programs will remain a very tough and complex process.

## SUMMARY

Heroic efforts have gone on for the better part of this century to change schools and the regularities of teaching deemed undesirable by many. In the process of trying to improve schools, we have learned a great deal about the regularities of teaching. Most important, they simply cannot be changed in any significant or lasting way by direct intervention into schools themselves, except in rare instances. Our best hope for changing the regularities of teaching, is through the initial preparation of teachers at the present time. Current professional preparation programs for teachers, however, are totally inadequate for accomplishing this task. Programs are needed that confront the dysfunctional regularities of teaching as well as challenge the intuitive approaches to teaching learned by teacher candidates through their years of apprenticeship-of-observation. The knowledge and technology exist today to design such programs. Changing the regularities of teacher education, however, will be every bit as tough as changing the regularities of teaching. It remains to be seen if this challenge can be met.

# REFERENCES

American Association of Colleges for Teacher Education. (1976). *Educating a profession*. Washington, D.C. Author.

American Association of Colleges for Teacher Education. (1987). *Teaching Teachers: Facts and Figures. RATE I*. Washington, D.C. Author.

American Association of Colleges for Teacher Education. (1988). *Teaching Teachers: Facts and Figures. RATE II*. Washington, D.C. Author.

American Association of Colleges for Teacher Education. (1989). *Teaching teachers: Facts and Figures. RATE III*. Washington, D.C. Author.

Applegate, J.H. (1987). Early field experiences: Three viewpoints. In M. Haberman & J.M. Backus (Eds.) *Advance in Teacher Education*, Volume III. Norwood, NJ: Ablex.

Arends, R.I. (1989). Analysis of content in teacher education programs: A working paper. College Park, MD: University of Maryland.

Arends, R.I. (1990). Connecting the university and the school. In Joyce, B. (Ed.) *Changing School Culture through Staff Development*. Alexandria, VA: Association for Supervision and Curriculum Development.

Arends, R.I., & Cohen, L. (1987). Using research in teacher education: The role of clinical teachers. Paper presented at the Annual Meeting of the American Association of Colleges of Teacher Education. New Orleans.

Arends, R.I. & Galluzzo, G. (1990). Clinical, laboratory, early field experiences and student teaching: Institutional structures and practices. Paper presented at Annual Meeting of the American Educational Research Association, Boston.

Arends, R.I. & Winitzky, N. (1989). Moving research into practice: The effects of various forms of training and clinical experiences on preservice students' knowledge, skill, and reflectiveness. Paper presented at Annual Meeting of the American Educational Research Association, San Francisco.

Berliner, D.C. (1985). Laboratory settings and the study of teacher education. *Journal of Teacher Education*, 36, 2-8.

Carnegie Forum on Education and the Economy. (1986). *A Nation Prepared: Teachers for the 21st Century*. New York: Author.

Cazden, C. (1986). Classroom discourse. In M.C. Wittrock (Ed.) *Handbook of Research on Teaching*. (3rd ed.). New York: Macmillan.

Cazden, C.B. & Mehan, H. (1989). Principles from sociology and anthropology: Context, code, classroom and culture. In M. Reynolds (Ed.) *Knowledge Base for the Beginning Teacher*. New York: Pergamon Press.

Christensen, P. (1990). Content analysis of teacher education course syllabi. Paper presented at Annual Meeting of the American Association of College for Teacher Education. Chicago.

Clifford, G. & Guthrie, J. (1988). *Ed School*. Chicago: University of Chicago Press

Conant, J.B. (1963). *The Education of American Teachers*. New York: McGraw-Hill.

Counts, G. (1932). *Dare the School Build a New Social Order?* New York: John Day, Inc.

Cuban, L. (1984). *How Teacher Taught: Constancy and Change in American Classrooms: 1900-1980*. New York: Longman.

Cuban, L. (1981). Persistent instruction: The high school classroom, 1900-1980. *Phi Delta Kappan*, 64, 113-118.

Evertson, C., Hawley, W. & Zlotnik, M. (1985). Making a difference in education quality through teacher education. *Journal of Teacher Education*, 36, 2-12.

Feiman-Nemser, S., & Floden, R.E. (1986). The cultures of teaching. In M.C. Wittrock (Ed.) *Handbook of Research on Teaching* (3rd ed.). New York: Macmillan.

Feltovich, P., Spiro, R., & Coulson, R. (1989). Professional cognition: Management of complexity. Invited presentation at the Annual Meeting of the American Educational Research Association. San Francisco.

Fullan, M. (1982). *The Meaning of Educational Change*. New York: Teachers College Press.

Galluzzo, G., & Arends, R.I. (1989). The RATE Project: A profile of teacher education institutions. *Journal of Teacher Education*, 40, 56-58.

Goodlad, J. (1984). *A Place Called School*. New York: McGraw-Hill.

Holmes Group. (1986). *Tomorrow's Teachers*. East Lansing, MI: Author.

Hopkins, D. (1985). *A Teacher's Guide to Classroom Research*. Philadelphia: Open University Press.

Howey, K.R. (1989). Research about teacher education: Programs of teacher preparation. *Journal of Teacher Education*, 40, 23-26.

Huberman, M., & Miles, M. (1984). *Innovation up close*. New York: Plenum.

Johnson, W.R. (1989). Teachers and teacher training in the twentieth century. In D. Warren (Ed.) *American Teachers: Histories of a Profession at Work*. New York: Macmillan.

Johnson, D.W. & Johnson, R.T. (1986). *Learning Together and Alone: Cooperative, Competition, and Individualism* (2nd ed.). Englewood Cliffs, NJ: Prentice-Hall.

Joyce, B., Hersh, R., & McKibbon, M. (1983). *The Structure of School Improvement*. New York: Longman.

Joyce, B., & Showers, B. (1988). *Student Achievement through Staff Development*. New York: Longman.

Joyce, B., & Weil, M. (1986). *Models of Teaching,* (3rd ed.). Englewood Cliffs, NJ: Prentice Hall.

Joyce, B., Yarger, S. and Howey, K. (1977). *Preservice Teacher Education*. Palo Alto, CA: Consolidated Publications.

Judge, H. (1982). *American Graduate Schools of Education: A View from Abroad*. New York: Ford Foundation.

Kemmis, S. (1983). Action research. In T. Husen & T. Postlehwaite (Eds.) *International Encyclopedia of Education: Research and Strategies.* Oxford: Pergamon.

Kerr, D. (1983). Teaching competence and teacher education in the United States. In L. S. Shulman and G. Sykes (Eds.) *Handbook of Teaching and Policy*. New York: Longman.

Lanier, J.E., & Little, J.W. Research on teacher education. In M.C. Wittrock (Ed.) *Handbook of Research on Teaching,* (3rd ed.). New York: Macmillian.

Lieberman, A. & Miller, L. (1984). *Teachers, Their World, and Their Work.* Alexandria, VA: Association of Supervision and Curriculum Development.

Lortie, D. (1975). *School teacher: A Sociological Study*. Chicago: University of Chicago Press.

Palincsar, A.S. & Brown, A.L. (1984). Reciprocal teaching. *Cognition and Instruction*, 1 (2), 171-175.

Resnick, L.B. (1987). *Education and Learning to Think*. Washington, DC: National Academy Press.

Sarason, S. (1971). *The Culture of School and the Problem of Change*. Boston: Allyn and Bacon.

Sarason, S. (1982). *The Culture of School and the Problem of Change,* (2nd ed.). Boston: Allyn and Bacon.

Schlechty, P.C., & Vance, V.S. (1981). Do academically able teachers leave education? The North Carolina case. *Phi Delta Kappan*, 63, 106-112.

Schmuck, R.A. & Schmuck, P.A. (1989). Adolescents' attitudes toward school and teachers: From 1963 to 1989. Mimeographed. Eugene, OR: University of Oregon.

Sharan, S., Kussell, P., Hertz-Lazarowitz, R., Bejarano, Y., Raviv, S. & Sharan, Y. (1984). *Cooperative Learning in the Classroom: Research in Desegregated Schools*. Hillsdale, NJ: Eribaum.

Slavin, R. (1983). *Cooperative Learning*. New York: Longman.

Thelen, H.A. (1954). *Dynamics of Groups at Work*. Chicago: University of Chicago Press.

Thelen, H.A. (1960). *Education and the Human Quest*. New York: Harper and Row.

Waller, W. (1932). *The Sociology of Teaching*. New York: Russell and Russell.

Weinstein, C.S. (1988). Preservice teachers' expectations about the first year of teaching. *Teaching and Teacher Education*, 4, 31-40.

Weinstein, C.S. (1989). Teacher education students' preconceptions of teaching. *Journal of Teacher Education*, 40, 53-60.

Welsh, P. (1989). Why Johnny can't teach: It's lonely, thankless work that few can do well and fewer still can master. *The Washington Post*, November 26, C1; C4.

Winitzky, N. (1987). Applying schema theory to educational demonstrations of cooperative learning in preservice teacher education. Doctoral dissertation. University of Maryland, College Park.

Zimpher, N.L. (1989). The RATE project: A profile of teacher education students. *Journal of Teacher Education*, 40, 27-30.

# Reflections on Cultures in Postmodernism

# Chapter 14
# Decentering Culture: Postmodernism, Resistance, and Critical Pedagogy

*by Peter McLaren, Miami University [Ohio]*

## INTRODUCTION

This essay is intended to provide teachers with an introduction to the topic of culture written from a post-structuralist theoretical perspective. In particular, it is an attempt to explore some of the themes which have resulted from recent debates within social theory over the status and meaning of the term "culture" and to apply some of the findings to my long-standing project of formulating a critical pedagogy of liberation.

In trying to rethink the topic of culture, school culture in particular, in post-structuralist terms, I have drawn upon what may be for some readers relatively unfamiliar terminology and concepts. Post-structuralist discourse can be highly complex and when working within its boundaries it is often difficult to apply what some might consider a 'normative' standard of accessibility for readers. I must confess that I find post-structuralist discourse less troublesome than many of my colleagues and find myself in sympathy with the recent observation of Richard Wolff, that to write in a manner which some consider inaccessible is not necessarily to show disrespect for one's readership. As Wolff puts it, "major shifts in ways of thinking usually interact complexly with related shifts in ways of speaking and writing" (1989: 138). In fact, Wolff suggests that it is quite justifiable to make the claim that, in an age of television journalism, writing in an easy and accessible language may (but not necessarily) signal the abandonment by many critics of "the tough work of convincing readers of politically unpopular truths" (1989: 139).

Why is it, then, that critical social theorists speak in what often appears to be a dense and arcane—and I dare say alienating—language? Why can't the social theorist just adopt the language and reasoning of the social actors he or she is attempting to study?

Certainly, the critical social theorist must acknowledge the fact that the social actor understands a great deal about the world by his or her participation in social life; thus, the critical social theorist must include the actor's own rationalization of his or her behavior in any critical analysis. On the other hand, as Anthony Giddens (1979: 250) points out, "the rationalization of action is always bounded, in every sort of historical context; and it is in exploring the nature and persistence of these bounds that the tasks of social science are to be found." While, as Giddens notes, we cannot dismiss in our analysis ordinary language and the world of natural attitude, by the same token we need to avoid the "paralysis of the critical will" which has been brought about by the rediscovery within social critique of ordinary language and common sense. To engage critically in forms of social life is to participate in that life. It also means understanding how what is taken to be "common sense" is socially organized through tacit presuppositions which form the background of every discursive formation. Giddens suggests that this involves making a distinction between "mutual knowledge" and "common sense." Mutual knowledge mediates frames of meanings and brackets the factual status of tacit and discursive understandings. It is applied in often tacit and routine ways. Common sense, on the other hand, refers to the "un-bracketing of mutual knowledge" and a consideration of the status of its belief claims. The critical assessment of common sense beliefs does not logically presume drawing upon mutual knowledge and, of course, the reverse is also true.

Following Giddens, the critical discourse which I am trying to develop respects the mutual knowledge that participants share in every day life, yet such an appreciation does not serve as an obstacle to a critical assessment or "un-bracketing" of such knowledge.

Making the challenge of sharing insights from a post-structuralist perspective even more difficult is that such insights have rarely been applied to educational theory and research on schooling. Consequently, this paper is to be understood as exploratory and its conclusions regarded as provisional and in some respects even quite tentative.

To assist the reader, I have tried to ground my "post-structuralist" reading of the culture of schooling in concrete examples to assist those unfamiliar with post-structuralist discourse. The reader may still feel a bit discursively stranded in unfamiliar territory. Yet I believe that such unfamiliar terms as "discourse," the "decentering of the subject" and the current theoretical trajectories which inform their use will, in time, come to realize a broad application in critical studies of schooling. In fact, I believe that such a debate has ushered in a whole new range of categories, formulations, and perspectives that can assist teachers in politicizing and radically reshaping their understanding of what is at stake in the current struggle over the future of education in the United States.

More specifically, I intend to sketch out some of the more general implications that the recent post-structuralist formulations of culture have for the way teachers view their role as cultural agents. This will entail advancing some suggestions for politicizing the role of teachers as individuals engaged in a form of cultural politics and for rearticulating the purpose of schooling as a transformative cultural practice leading towards the establishment of more reciprocal social relations based on the principles of freedom and social justice. In further accomplishing this task, I will address five interrelated moments in the debate over culture: culture and the age of postmodernism; culture as a form of discourse; culture as plurivocal; culture as resistance; and cultural politics as the discourse of the other. Each of these moments rearticulates a number of common assumptions about the nature of the cultural field and the problematic and often contradictory sociocultural positioning of individuals within such a field. Focusing on these particular strands of the debate will enable me to establish at least a provisional cultural agenda for rethinking pedagogy as a form of cultural politics. The essay will conclude with a general description of a postmodernist discourse of liberation for teachers.

## RETHINKING CULTURE

An important new debate over culture is currently surfacing in the social sciences with respect to how contemporary social life is to be understood and the various roles which individuals have been consigned to play (both wittingly and unwittingly) in it. In the United States, this debate has spilled beyond the insular borders of mainstream sociology and anthropology to include new post-structuralist approaches, largely European in origin and formed within a decidedly radical political framework. Appropriating these new disciplinary frameworks into analyses of contemporary social, cultural, and political life, constitutes, in Rosaldo's (1989: 198) terms, the veritable "remaking of social analysis." This debate has profound implications both for the manner in which contemporary schooling is understood and for the possibilities of reconceiving the transformation of schooling.

I shall draw on such perspectives in the following essay to advance the argument that culture does not simply consist of isolated, bounded, and cohesive meaning systems, but a multiplicity of voices reflecting a wide array of conflicting and competing discourses. I take the position that what have been commonly referred to as "cultures" (cf. Geertz, 1973) within mainstream educational and anthropological studies are never self-authenticating or self-legitimating; they do not determine their own effects on the people who live "inside" them. That is, cultures do not speak their own truth in that they are present to themselves apart from the discourses and relations of power which inform them. As systems of meaning, cultures can never be ontologically separated from economies of privilege and politics. For teachers, this means that cultures do not exist as metaphysical entities which *impose* themselves on schools; neither do they occur as uniform standards of behavior and beliefs. Cultures occur to the extent that students and teachers *live them*. It is as important to pay attention to the contradictions and disharmonies within cultures as it is to their appearances of uniformity and consensus.

Correlatively, I take the position that the cultural field is never a monadic site of harmony and control but rather a site of disjuncture, rupture, and contradiction. It is better understood as a *contested terrain* that serves as the loci of multivalent voices and powers. It is, in short, an arena of conflict in which a politics of difference is played out. I suggest that teachers need to bring a critical astringency to their understanding of culture which can come about only if they are willing to situate their own practices within larger structures of power and privilege. Furthermore, as researchers, teachers must be willing to acknowledge the interests served by their own ideological predilections, rather than purge the cultural field of difference through the universal calculus of putatively disinterested, objective analysis.

Given the language of efficiency that has colonized the disciplinary domain of education in recent years, and the current stress on management techniques and accountability schemes, which strips schooling from any substantial concern with justice, equality, or democracy, it is hardly surprising that this debate over culture has only just begun to spill beyond the cramped and insulated boundaries of mainstream educational research. In particular, white Anglo-Saxon educators have been generally incautious about their pretenses to occupying a privileged cultural vantage point with respect to other cultures; they have, for the most part, remained loyal to a view of culture which permits them to anchor their meanings in a bedrock of their own prejudices. In so doing they have failed to disturb the popular assurance of received orthodoxies about the cultural fields that inform the classrooms where they teach. The discourse of technocracy, which has insinuated its disturbing presence into school policy and practice over the last decade, and which has been seriously invasive of democratic life, has proliferated largely due to the lack of attention to the way culture has been defined and understood by educators and researchers. Such a lack of understanding has rendered them ill-equipped to resist and transform the recent assault on education in the United States by the New Right—and to strive for a greater role for schools to play in the struggle for democracy.

## CULTURE AND THE AGE OF POSTMODERNISM

One of the central strands of the debate over culture within contemporary research on schooling centers around the question of the role of schools in shaping student identity. That is, the way schooling provides students with opportunities for understanding the meaning and purpose of living in a world where democratic practices have become subverted, originary values simulated, and emancipatory symbols and their affective power commodified.

I do not wish to draw out all the implications of this debate for educators except to note that it has generated a great deal of concern with respect to the increasing alienation of our youth brought about by what Angela McRobbie (1986: 55) has called "the frenzied expansion of the mass media," what Voss and Schutze (1989: 133) refer to as "a world blanketed with signs and texts, image and media of all kinds, and which has brought forth a culture... based on an overproduction of sensations that dulls our sensory faculties."

The postmodern condition signals the undecidability, plurality, or "throwness" of culture rather than its homogeneity or consensual nature. Postmodern culture organizes life not only ideologically, but also in relation to affective structures: structures of desire, emotion, mood, pleasure, etc., which are assuming increasingly powerful determining moments in culture and everyday life. Grossberg (1988: 40) writes:

> Postmodernity... points to a crisis in our ability to locate any meaning as a possible and appropriate source for an impassioned commitment. It is a crisis, not of faith, but the relationship between faith and common sense, a dissolution of what we might call the "anchoring effect" that

articulates meaning and affect. It is not that nothing matters—for something has to matter—but that we can find no way of choosing or of finding something to warrant our investment. It is as if one had to live two lives, one defined by the meanings and values available to us to make sense of our lives and the other defined by the affective sense that life can no longer be made sense of.

## Culture as Discourse

One of the most significant contributions made by postmodernist social theorists has been the insight that culture is a construction that is not always immediately present to itself. A radical reconceptualization of culture as a field of discourse or text (cf. Clifford and Marcus, 1986) has helped to make our common understanding of culture quite uncommon and allows us to explore the complexity of the meaning of this term and the process to which it refers. By discourse, I follow E. Ann Kaplan's definition as "any social relation involving language or other sign systems as a form of exchange between participants, real or imaginary, particular or collective . . . which defines the terms of what can or cannot be said and extends beyond verbal language to a range of fields in which meaning is culturally organized" (1987: 187). The point I wish to underscore is that all discourses are competitive and as such embody particular interests, "establish paradigms, set limits, and construct [human] subjects" (Collins 1989: 12). Frow (1986: 225) writes that discourse "constitutes the guarantee and the limit of our understanding of otherness." Furthermore, it unites us with the past through what Frow (1986, p. 225) calls "the self-evidentiality and unconsciousness of institutionally regulated meanings." In Green's (1986: 9) terms, discourse refers to "the *means* to meaning, the mechanisms in and by which the social production of ...`knowledge' [and] `truth' takes place." To speak of culture as a discourse is to situate discourses in what Foucault calls a *discursive field*. Chris Weedon (1987: 35) describes discursive fields as "competing ways of giving meaning to the world and organizing social institutions and processes... [offering]... the individual a range of modes of subjectivity."

In other words, reality within this perspective is always constructed, made rather than invented, always being produced within a multiplicity of contexts; furthermore, the only grounds for deciding "how deeply and precisely one has cut into the body of the real" are political and historical (Grossberg, 1989, p. 143).

When surveying any discursive field, it is important to recognize that not all discourses will carry equal weight or power. For instance, in education there are competing discourses which, when considered in their varying contexts of articulation, influence how teachers plan curricula, organize the classroom space, undertake disciplinary measures, grade papers, evaluate student progress, etc. Some of these classroom discourses are drawn from competing discourses in educational psychology, critical social theory, learning theory, and the like. Discourses which contest the organization and selective interests of dominant forms of pedagogy—such as Marxist social theory—are likely to be marginal and generally dismissed by most teachers, whereas other discourses, such as behaviorism, are likely to enjoy widespread use. In other words, teachers give meaning to the material and social relations which constitute their identities and which structure their classroom practices, according to the range and social power of existing discourses, their access to them, and the political strengths of the interests which they represent.

Discourses, according to Foucault, refer to a system of rules and structures of language rooted in relations of power which are embodied in specialized institutions and languages (Connor 1989: 203). Bahktin argues that *power operates to centralize and unify discourses, and serves as a regulating force in which eccentric, unorthodox, and marginalized voices are excluded* (p. 203). Foucault's work can help teachers direct attention to the analysis of discursive formations within the classroom and school in terms of "the concrete mechanisms through which power is exercised and the contexts of historical events and strategies that condition that exercise" (Grossberg 1982: 95). For instance, schools are organized into separate tracks according to a student's presumed ability in various subjects, where certain tracks are "college bound" and certain tracks are "vocationally bound." In this case, the power arrangements which are reproduced in each of these tracks bear a striking similarity to those in the world of work: certain types of knowledge (which is always bound up with cultural capital and social practices) are accorded a higher status than others and the knowledge considered to possess the most status remains the privileged preserve of the higher tracks.

The abstract theoretical knowledge taught in the higher tracks is the kind of knowledge which the middle-class white student from an affluent home background can master more successfully than, say, a minority student from a disadvantaged ethnic home precisely because it is reproduced within the social, ethnic, and linguistic relations of the home. Practically oriented and vocational educational skills are geared for students from economically disadvantaged homes. This is the knowledge that is required for the entry level jobs that require few skills. In this way, it is the working-class students who remain, in the words of Aronowitz and Giroux (1985: 64) "a conceptually illiterate population whose skills extend to the technical plane ...[and who are]... able to follow orders under the direction of managements that are responsive to bureaucracies and capital, but unable to examine critically public and private life, to determine how and what should be produced and by whom, and to make the public choices that become policy."

In this case, power operates from a particular vantage point in producing systems of instruction, modes of evaluation, and hierarchically organized bodies of knowledge in each track. These provide the knowledges, social practices, and skills necessary to maintain the class-based division of labor in the larger society. Many students accept this state of affairs as natural and necessary, because it is presumably based on their innate abilities. This is helped along by the fact that society has produced certain myths of minority cultural and intellectual inferiority.

In addition, both teachers and students often come to believe and accept that the rules, regulations, systems of moral scruples, and social practices that undergird and inform everyday life in schools are necessary if learning is to be successfully accomplished. They fail to recognize that tradition has provided this condition, not because it is based on some "metaphysical truth" or wisdom but because these regulations have been "discursively won" through a long series of historical and cultural struggles over whose knowledge counts, what knowledge is most worthwhile, and who is to benefit most from things remaining the way they are. For instance, the fact that white students outnumber black students in classes for gifted learning or that black students outnumber white students in classes for behavioral 'disorders' is not based on any empirical or metaphysical truth claims, but *is the result of a dominant discursive trend which understands blacks to be intellectually inferior to whites and which helps to institutionally regulate this understanding through curricular forms, classroom practices, and institutional apparatuses.*

## Culture as Plurivocal

Postmodern social theory has given us a differentiated view of culture as distinct from the unitary one which informs most mainstream discourses of teaching. Culture has come to be understood as more distinctly multiplex and political than its usual conception as the proliferation of historically produced artifacts forged within a neutral arena of social relations. Conceived from the postmodernist perspective, culture is both the medium and the outcome of discourses which "establish the limits of the sayable" (Frow 1986: 78) and a constituent aspect of subjectivity forged within asymmetrical relations of power and privilege.

In a recent paper, Richard Quantz (1988) summarizes some of the prevailing conceptions of culture in order to set the stage for a drastic rethinking of the concept. He argues that traditional scholarship has defined culture as a social construction created by an interrelated network of people, a consensual entity created in the intersubjective reality of an identifiably bordered group. Whether researchers or educators happen to be speaking about the "culture of poverty" or "Appalachian culture," or the culture of a particular school, these cultures are usually understood as relatively homogeneous entities consisting of shared patterns of symbols and cultural practices. Quantz argues that this traditional conception of culture as shared patterns of beliefs and customs is wrong because it fails to take into account how such beliefs, values, and customs are historically and ideologically constituted.

Drawing from work done at the Birmingham Centre for Contemporary Cultural Studies, Quantz argues that culture needs to be understood with reference to the level at which social groups develop distinct patterns of life and also the meanings and expressive forms which these groups give to those *structures of lived experience.* But as Henry Giroux (1988c), Quantz, and others have pointed out, this emphasis on shared meanings and understandings will not suffice because culture is fundamentally a struggle *over* meanings and *about* meanings. Furthermore, it is a struggle over events, representations, and interpretations. From this perspective, it is important to recognize that there is not simply one monolithic, unitary, seamless culture, but a multiplicity of cultures, subcultures, oppositional cultures, and alternative cultures. Culture in this view can be seen as an arena of socially educative discourses that produces an array of knowledge positions for subjects (Belsey 1980) which sets limits to the possible. Those who possess the power and legitimacy to define the possible generally work within discourses which privilege the interests of the dominant class.

This view coheres with a remark by James Clifford (1988: 273) who writes, "we should attempt to think of cultures not as organically unified or traditionally continuous but rather as negotiated, present processes." We should constantly remind ourselves that such processes do not occur in a vacuum, whether it be ideological or material, but rather take place within arenas of power. Within such a cultural frontier, some groups occupy positions of dominance and privilege with respect to shaping discourses and hence defining human subjects (i.e., defining what are appropriate values and actions) while others are subordinate to them. Sometimes groups are positioned differentially within relations of both subordination and dominance.

Drawing on the work of the Soviet sociolinguist Mikhail Bahktin, Quantz argues that culture must be understood as "multivoiced" or "polyphonic." He writes:

> Culture is better understood to be the expressions and silences of the multiplicity of voices found in a group membership's given political, social, and material power relations. Rather than seeking the commonalities [and] uniform intersubjectivities, we should be seeking the tensions and conflicts of a group. It is in the disagreements, the interstices of community that we can understand the potentially regenerative themes. It is by giving expression to the silenced and legitimacy to their struggles that we advance the possibility for social transformation.

Here Quantz warns against the expression of polyphonic cultures as monophonic entities, which tends to misrepresent the concrete and lived experience of subordinate groups. For instance, by presenting black teenage parents as a monophonic culture, as many news reports have done recently in the U.S. media, the ideological illusion is created that these teenagers frequently choose to uniformly victimize themselves by making selfish choices at inopportune moments in their lives. In other words, blacks are presented as uniformly and willfully negligent and irresponsible parents. This view can only be unproblematically asserted by those who choose to ignore the complexity and specificity of material constraints and ideological apparatuses which position black women and men at an extreme disadvantage within the larger social order. Quantz also argues that the black community can better empower itself by recognizing and transforming the corporate industrial social relations which promote racist ideologies.

I would agree with Quantz that social class should not be considered the primary referent for the formation of subjectivity but rather we should recognize race, gender, sexual orientation, and religion also as constructing the ideological dimensions that inform identity. While I generally support the move towards a conception of culture as heterogeneous, one which stresses difference and conflict, I also share with Daniel Cottom (1989: 101) the cautionary stance that concepts like heterogeneity may become the basis of a new essentialism or formalism. Quantz and O'Connor (1988: 96) suggest that "this one-sided emphasis could lead to a kind of relativism where cultural differences are viewed as mutually exclusive, self-sufficient sets of patterns of mind." This position bears a conceptual affinity to Cottom's warning that the stress on the provisionality and partiality of culture, as well as on its heteroglossia, could indeed slide the concept of culture into another form of cultural relativism. Cultural relativism should not lead us to pay homage to the system of meaning proper to every culture but rather

> to question this boundary of culture. It should lead us to question the strange idea that there ever existed a situation of "ethnocentrism." It should concentrate our attention on the people whose nonexistent, demeaned, isolated, or repressed subjectivity, as this has been established by "culture," has enabled culture to seem to be (Cottom 1989: 100, my emphasis).

Of course, the issue of cultural relativism is one which is liable to become more problematic given the growth of urban diversity over recent decades and the multiplicity of cultures one can find in almost any inner-city school setting.

Perhaps the reader is wondering at this moment: What has this reformulation of culture to do with teaching? I would suggest that the view of culture I advocate teachers adopt helps, for instance, to underscore the folly of any national curriculum which claims to represent the values, knowledges, and interests of all groups in American society. Undoubtedly, there are groups who benefit more than others from the inclusion or exclusion of particular subject matter and particular practices. For instance, it would not be difficult to see which groups would benefit most from a history curriculum that excludes the contributions of women and minorities, or writers from Latin America or Eastern Europe.

But at another level, certain interests are also at work in curricula which fail to bring critical perspectives to bear on specific subject matter. It is important for students to be able to engage ideas critically, regardless of what the content might be. In many instances, it is not so much the inclusion or exclusion of specific content, because whatever the content happens to be, it can be worked to critical advantage by competent and creative teachers to help students understand the logic of oppression in the world and the meaning of freedom. That is to say, if Shakespeare becomes required reading to the exclusion of, say, contemporary black feminist writers, questions related to gender, class, and racial oppression could still be addressed by questioning the accepted view of what constitutes high status knowledge and why it happens that black women writers, other minorities, and marginalized groups rarely fit into mainstream literature courses. The point is to underscore the idea that before teachers can solve the issue of curriculum content, they need to understand the relationship between knowledge and power and the interests such knowledge serves.

With such considerations in mind, it is more accurate to view the classroom or school as a terrain upon which battles are continuously waged in terms of technologies and strategies of power. Culture in this view becomes a contested, conflictual terrain, not a harmoniously integrated complex of discourses and discursive practices. It bears a stronger affinity to jostlement than to harmony. It is decidedly *not* a strutwork of rules of how people behave; rather, the concept draws attention to the sheer range of discourses, indeterminacy, and semiotic rupture that constitutes most cultural terrains. Culture is decidedly not simply about uniformity and cohesion but also about splintering effects and reversal, about discourses of hope and possibility, those which attempt to administer our ways of thinking and doing so as to institute a premature closure on the open-endedness of social life.

## Culture and Resistance

The making of cultures is not controlled by passive, compliant individuals or groups. Except in rare instances, a culture is not seamless or all of one piece. For instance, if we look at the culture of patriarchy, we notice it is not monolithically repressive. Not everything about patriarchy is oppressive, since cultural spaces do open up where oppressive discourses can and have been contested by women. This is evident in the women's movement and in the development of various strands of feminist theory and practice. Discourses *are* struggled over and resisted.

The importance of the concept of resistance has been taken up over the last decade, most notably by Paul Willis and Henry Giroux. Henry Giroux points out that "the idea that people do make history, including its constraints, has been neglected" (1983: 259). Schools are seen as "sites" for ideological struggle and class conflict, in which subordinate cultures partake of moments of self-production as well as reproduction. In reference to the classroom, Giroux maintains that students do not constantly submit to the dictates of the legitimation and socialization of the educational systems. In his view, "schools represent contested terrains marked not only by structural and ideological contradictions, but also by collectively informed student resistance" (1983: 268). There are numerous examples of alternative pedagogies being practiced by politically informed teachers, such as the work being done at Pedro Albizu Campos Puerto Rican High School in Chicago. Kathleen Weiler's book, *Women Teaching for Change*, documents some important work being done by feminist teachers to counter the expansive hegemony of dominant social and cultural arrangements.

A more recent ethnographical study by Fagan (1989) focuses on Irish early school-leavers from lower socioeconomic backgrounds. It gives voice to their perspective on schooling and to their reasons for leaving without educational qualifications. The young people involved in this research are obviously those for whom schooling fails to benefit, those for whom its power relations serve to oppress. They struggle within the school system, giving reasons for their resistance, while also locating their conflict with schooling in its cultural context. This study gives a clear example, that is particularly relevant to teachers, of a struggle over competing discourses. The principal discourse that underpins the formal educational system is that of meritocracy: Young people who don't achieve educational qualifications and who drop out of school are deemed 'failures' and their lack of success is related to a lack of intellectual ability. Fagan's study shows that this individualization of failure is resisted by the early school-leavers. They articulate their non-participation to the virtual exclusion of the notion of lack of intelligence or failure. In fact, their culture supports early school leaving and non-participation as a form of "standing up for themselves." Resistance to this individualization of failure is to allocate responsibility for their educational under-achievement to the schooling system itself. Thus the meritocratic ideology is contested and struggled over by those whom it oppresses most.

In my study of Azorean students in a Toronto Catholic school (McLaren, 1986) and in my work with Italian and West Indian students in a Toronto elementary school (McLaren, 1989), an attempt was made to extend the concept of resistance to include forms of political consciousness which often take forms alien to the researcher, and which do not always fit dominant, active conceptions of political struggle. One of the areas which I investigated was the political economy of the body—"a phallocentric economy of the flesh" (1989a) and how body logic among males was linked to the production of desire in a culture of capitalist consumerism. The classroom was revealed to repress the symbolic economy of the body and resistance was linked to a form of "corporeal unlearning" of the gestures and body postures connected to the ideology of "becoming a worker." Student resistance often took the form of certain types of laughter, of dress, of moving, and of speaking which reflected life on the streets and control over the entire symbolic economy of identity production (what to wear, how to talk, what ways to move and interact). Resistance was a symbolic drama that tried to bring the symbolic economy of the streets directly into the classroom.

Research on resistance in schools and its uncovering of cultural struggle in the classroom presents educators with educational data that could assist teachers to politicize their own understanding of the schooling system. Teachers would do well to use resistance theory as a means to understand how to transform classroom resistance to an emancipatory struggle towards empowerment.

## Culture and the Construction of the Individual Subject

It is now commonplace in critical educational studies which attempt to move beyond some of the theoretical parameters of resistance theory to give serious consideration to the relationship among schooling, culture, and subjectivity. I am using the term "subjectivity" after Weedon (1987: 32) to refer to "the conscious and unconscious thoughts and emotions of the individual, her sense of herself and her ways of understanding her relation to the world." In recent years, radical educators have paid close attention to the semiotic basis of cultural activity, in particular the social and cultural production of student subjectivity with respect to race, class, and gender. In so doing, they have employed the term *"subjectivity"* rather than *"identity"* in order to highlight the decentered aspect of the self which post-structuralist theorists argue is more fluid, plural, discontinuous, and contingent than the model of the self bequeathed by the Cartesian or humanistic tradition associated with conservative and liberal conceptions of the subject. Much of the recent work in feminist versions of postmodern social theory has also taken up the idea that subjectivity is contradictory and multiplex, a view which runs counter to various traditions of humanist social theory. Within this perspective, the subject is always partial and often defined in contradictory ways as the effects of multiple determinations which may be affective, ideological, material, or gendered.

Feminist post-structuralists have made the important realization that human subjects are constantly traversed by contradiction within their respective discursive fields. Individuals are *always already installed* by available discourses into contexts that have been historically constructed and therefore position individuals ideologically. Yet it is important to emphasize that the positioning of social agents (e.g., teachers and students) within the cultural field (e.g., classroom, school) is *relational*, as students enter the struggle over subjectivity from different historically given levels of material, social, and cultural endowments. It is also important to see the subject as never irrevocably determined but also determining (making culture and not just the product of it). We are not suspended placelessly outside of history nor lodged immovably within discursive positions. The human agent can never indeterminately float outside of historical and cultural determinations, antiseptically removed or extracted from the larger social formation; at the same time it is true that the human agent is never irrevocably determined by the social structures out of which it has been formed.

Human agents exist as a tangle of discourses, crossed by dialectical lines of force, often with no central narrative to coordinate the play of differences of every competing human text (Collins 1969: 64). The different contexts in which various discourses intersect will determine which discourses will prevail in providing the subject with his or her primary subject position. For instance, a teacher may reflect a "contradictory" subjectivity in the sense that he or she takes a pro-life stand with respect to the issue of abortion, yet at the same time maintains an aggressive stance in favor of the death penalty. Or he or she may work with students using a student-centered pedagogy, yet as a parent adopt a strict and perhaps even abusive disciplinarian approach to child-rearing. It is the context of the specific situation, the discourses available, as well as the individual's own history, race, and gender, and socioeconomic status that will shed some determinative light on the subject positions which are "taken up" on a daily basis. A progressive teacher may, for instance, hold radical views on issues related to race, gender, and class, and yet assume a pedagogical discourse which exhibits forms of racism, sexism, and classism. In this case, personal and pedagogical discourses may contradict each other.

By now it should be relatively clear that ideological struggle often consists of attempting to "win" some new sets of meanings—some new discourses—from which we can position ourselves as subjects. Thus, it should be more evident how culture functions not as a frozen, pressed, cast-iron set of meanings and practices, but rather as a field of discourses in a decentered power struggle in which they are vying for decidedly heterogeneous audiences and groups (Collins, 1989, p. 101).

## Cultural Politics as the Discourse of the Other

I have been arguing that it is important to understand culture as a process which involves both the disjunctive patterning of identities and the mutual constitution of the political and the pedagogical. Consequently, it is difficult to offer any definition of culture that allows culture to maintain an immunity to politics; that is, that allows it to remain unimplicated in the process of ideological production. This is so because any cultural discourse, as a linguistic creation, is always historically and socially contingent. In other words, any discourse of culture is bounded by the historical, cultural, and political conditions and also the epistemological resources available to articulate its meaning.

Rosaldo draws attention to the way in which the discourse of culture reproduces itself through ideological constructs of the "Other," that is, with respect to its fictions of the marginal, the deviant, the disaffected, and the underclass. The questions that we must raise as analysts of the discourse of culture in our classrooms and in society at large is: "What is left out?" and "What is the unsaid?" "Whose voices are silenced in our classroom through exclusion?" "Whose voices are barbarized and demonized through our fictions of what constitutes cultural difference?"

Rosaldo (1989) points out that "zones of cultural visibility and invisibility" play a distinct part in the location of these groups in the social hierarchy in which "full citizenship and cultural visibility appear to be inversely related." (p. 198) Here Rosaldo is introducing the important idea of precultural, cultural, and postcultural identities. He suggests that within the social order certain groups are classified into those who have culture and those who are civilized. For instance, within the nation-state, cultural distinctiveness "derives from a lengthy historical process of colonial domination" (p. 199). Rosaldo is quick to point out that cultural differences are "relative to the cultural practices of ethnographers and their readers" (p. 202). This common form of ethnographic practice sees difference generally from the North American upper-middle-class professional perspective, in which "the `other' becomes more culturally visible [as] the `self' becomes correspondingly less so" (p. 202).

Cultural visibility or having more culture is associated with being less rational or civilized than the white citizen who is considered "postcultural." Viewed from this perspective, the process of schooling is geared to creating a postcultural citizenry and often involves what Rosaldo calls a form of "cultural stripping." Cultural stripping takes place when individuals are stripped of their former cultures, "enabling them to become American citizens—transparent, just like you and me, "people without culture." In this view, social mobility and cultural loss become conflated, for to become middle class in North America is purportedly to become part of the culturally invisible mainstream (Rosaldo 1989). White culture loses its ethnicity and passes unobserved into the rhythms of daily life. Being white is an entitlement, not to preferred racial attributes, but to a raceless subjectivity. That is, being white becomes the invisible norm for how the dominant culture measures its own civility.

Blacks are stereotypically portrayed as being more physical and emotional (less rational) and therefore betraying more culture. The same is true of the French Canadians in Canada. And in both cases these 'cultural' minorities are denied full participation in the economic, social, and political life of the nation-state. To be cultural in Rosaldo's terms is to be more visible and to get less. Educators must be wary, therefore, of labeling certain minority groups as those in possession of a surplus of "authentic" culture because such a perspective tends to celebrate the distance middle-class whites have evolved (e.g. have become more 'rational' and less 'cultural').

Educators, like ethnographers, often err by regarding "authentic" culture as something frozen and static—if it exists at all. Rosaldo claims that such a position has, in fact, become a "useful fiction" in developing research strategies "that exclude social struggles revolving around issues of class, race, gender and sexual orientation" (p. 220). The "other," in this case, becomes a cultural fiction that allows educators and researchers to ignore the partiality of their own perspectives which assigns cultural "otherness" to certain groups. The process of constructing the "other" also helps to conceal how the pedagogies used by teachers who work with visible minorities are actually exercises in forms of cultural repression and ideological violence and a means of indulging in the will to dominate. Furthermore, such pedagogical practices conceal the possibilities for democratic and empowering social relations available through assuming multiple cultural positions from which individuals are able to speak, act, and contribute to pluralistic society.

Within the discourse of cultural authenticity, individuals are seen as representatives of self-contained, unified, and homogeneous groups rather than as "complex sites of cultural production" (p. 217). However, within the discourse of cultural multiplicity (discontinuity), individuals are encouraged to assume multiple subject positions (which are always already cultural positions). In other words, educators need to reject the discourse of cultural authenticity (what Rosaldo calls the "authenticity of cultural purity") lest they make their own interests hidden in the process of creating the "other" in order to subjugate the other. This process of cultural invisibility becomes an effacement of the complicity of educators in constructing their own subjectivity against that of the "other" which is, in reality, a creature of their own struggle for power. This is a process of identity construction which takes as its goal stability and self-identity across contexts. In essence, it becomes the (postcultural) referent (rationality) by which the "other" can be culturally designated. What I am arguing is that the culture of authenticity as we have been describing it is discriminatory in both senses of the word. It discriminates in the sense of distinguishing the "other" from the mainstream and in marginalizing certain groups on the basis of a perception of cultural endowment. Speaking to the issue of cultural identity, Rosaldo raises the question: "What cultural politics erase the 'self' only to highlight the 'other?' (p. 198).

I believe that we need to move beyond the perspective that James Clifford (1987: 122) refers to as "salvage ethnography" (recording the language and lore of disappearing peoples) represented by the works of Boas, Kroeber, and others, which attempts to "rescue authenticity out of destructive historical change." Such a perspective allows human difference to be "redistributed as separate, functioning cultures" (p. 122). The 'ethnographic present' which is constructed by western researchers, largely white males, as a point of reference for judging the worth of varying degrees of "primitiveness," keeps ethnic groups buried in the past and "marginal to the advancing world system" (p. 122). The lowly knowledge of the ethnic minority becomes, in this view, helpful to us only in terms of "aesthetic appreciation." Clifford's insights have implications for the way teachers view minority cultures in their classrooms.

As educators, we must cease to attribute to certain groups "mythical consciousness" while we reserve "historical consciousness" for ourselves. We should look to the day when the dominance of modernist dichotomies of literate/non-literate, developed/underdeveloped have substantially ebbed. It is necessary that we cease to characterize ourselves as "dynamic and oriented towards change" and those from nonwestern societies as constantly "seek[ing] equilibrium and the reproduction of inherited forms" (p. 125).

Clifford notes in this regard that "culture is a migration as well as rooting—within and between groups, within and between individual persons... New definitions of authenticity (cultural, personal, artistic) are making themselves felt, definitions no longer centered on a salvaged past. Rather, authenticity is reconceived as hybrid, creative activity in a local present-becoming future" (p. 126). This definition of culture is implicit in the pointed reminder by Trinh T. Minh-ha (1989: 75) that "'authenticity' is always produced, never salvaged, any clear-cut opposition between authenticity and inauthenticity is bound to be reductive and atrophic. "We must also be cautious, however, in thinking that as white, western educators, we are in a position to "define reality for others, including those of westernization, authenticity and, of course, racism" (Minh-ha, 1987: 139). Minh-ha is worth quoting at length:

> Even in this age of "decolonization" one frequently encounters situations where the white man still arrogates the privilege to tell Third World individuals, without any hesitation or consideration, they should be taught to be dewesternized. Or that they are nostalgic or naive toward their own culture, or even that they are racist toward other Third World people. For, according to this logic, acculturation means that they are more whitewashed than their illiterate peers; or reciprocally, illiteracy means ignorance, and therefore those who suffer such a lack are easy prey to westernisms. Divide and conquer.

To assume, as members of the dominant culture, a privileged position as 'postcultural' subjects with respect to the attitudes and practices of the "other" is to participate in a procession of colonial modes of thought, in the advance guard of a dominative pedagogy. As Michael Rogin (1990: 108) has argued, the United States is a "settler society" which began in European imperialism against people of color, continued with the "subjugation, dispossession, and extermination of Indian tribes" to the more recent "racial bias of American expansion carried forward into the Philippines, the Caribbean, Latin America, and eventually the Asian mainland with full consciousness (since forgotten) of the continuity between the triumph of civilization over savagery at home and the white man's burden abroad." The attitudes shared by many teachers towards the "other" often constitutes participation in what Rogin calls "historical amnesia" or "motivated forgetting." This occurs when the dominant culture encourages (through teacher discourses, teacher education programs, etc.) teachers to conveniently forget how current educational opportunities for students of color are historically and culturally linked to the organization of American politics around racial domination (the invasion of Grenada and Panama being the two most recent examples).

Of course, I am not arguing that educators from the dominant culture cannot take a strong ethical and political stand on issues of racism and cultural injustice. But it does mean that such educators must act *with* the oppressed, not *over them* or *on behalf of them*. Critical pedagogy must be *organic to* and not *administered upon* struggling peoples.

As educators, we need to provide the conditions which enable the oppressed to name their reality and, through dialogue, to transform their present historical and cultural conditions. By the same token, students must refuse inducements by teachers, whether well-intentioned or otherwise, to rewrite themselves into a white, patriarchal or Eurocentric narrative. We need to work towards what Nancy Fraser (1989: 182) calls "interpretations... reached by means of communicative processes that most closely approximate ideals of democracy, equality, and fairness" while at the same time "comparing alternative distributive outcomes of rival interpretations."

## Towards a Postmodernist Discourse of Liberation

Teachers must attempt to recognize their own subjective cultural status and in doing so refrain from reserving a noncultural status (a status that creates subject positions which carry civic power and self-interest) for those most like "them," that is, most like educators from the dominant middle-class culture. The importance of this insight for educators as well as anthropologists lies in the recognition that by defining groups as differentially endowed with "culture," the gate-keepers of the status quo are able to erase (suffocate) the normative interests which inform their own cultural politics. By remaining unreflective about the interests which inform their own cultural politics, teachers fail to notice how their pedagogies, curricula, and research practices may be employed at the expense of the "other." Our pedagogies often produce and represent difference as "other" by hiding (naturalizing) the interests which inform them. That is, the cult of (postcultural) rationality that undergirds the discourse of cultural authenticity renders these interests invisible. I would additionally argue that this conceptualization has obvious implications for curriculum in respect to what is put in and left out and the grounds upon which this is justified or rationalized.

Another way of putting this would be to argue that critical pedagogy must always be directed against the indissolubility of the self, that is, against a concept of the self that is static, unchanging, and unified. The postcultural self to which white culture adheres must therefore be recognized as only one reality within a multiplicity of realities. In this way educators can avoid the privileging of patriarchal and bourgeois assumptions which inform the postcultural self and a subjugation of all other interests to them. The postcultural self must not assume a definitive ascendancy as a privileged position from which to construct the "other." The "other" is constructed by systems of meanings which have been "durably installed" and which become other-destructive when they remain buried by tradition and transformed into weapons of stigmatization.

Cottom (1989: 100) offers us a way of avoiding both the identity-in-difference of cultural relativism and the identification with a monolithic culture by "working to identify the differences between the imaginary law of culture and the life that escapes it." The pedantic rationality of assuming a `proper' cultural decorum and possessing the requisite cultural "facts" turns culture into a mausoleum of dead historical relics and history into a junkyard. Educators need to reject the view that education simply involves the transmission of collected information in favor of the more critical practice of disentangling the codes, ideologies, and social practices that make social life meaningful and understanding how these meanings have been constructed and how they remain implicated within domains of power.

Teachers should avoid both the authoritarianism that accompanies an ethnocentric perspective of culture and the relativism which goes hand-in-hand with the concept of a liberal cultural pluralism. A critical pedagogy should speak against the notion that all cultural realities need to follow one dominant narrative or that all diverse cultural realities need to be given voice, since it is obvious that many of these realities harbor racist, classist, and sexist assumptions. The key here isn't to insist simply on cultural diversity, transforming culture into a living museum of contemporary choices (e.g., pluralism) but a *critical diversity*. A critical diversity means that choices need to be seen as social practices which are themselves historically and socially constructed and teachers need to distinguish cultural choices as liberating or oppressive. Choices under the name of democracy or totalitarianism all occupy specifiable locations in relations of power. This perspective of culture slices up its presumed uniformity into diverse pieces of shifting perspectives and untold possibilities. This should signal the importance of redefining the educator's role as the "authority." As Chock and Wyman (1986: 11) remark: "An ambiguous and multivocal world demands an interpreter, a translator, a reader, or chronicler to replace the realist and the monophonic voice that spoke in ethnographic realism." It is in this spirit that we must ask who has access to and power over the discourses which define, order, and classify the social world for students.

If we follow Rosaldo in understanding culture as "multiple border zones" and as an "intertextual arena" in which social practices do not have or possess norms but continually remake cultural norms (which are remade again and again) then one of the challenges of a critical pedagogy becomes clear. It becomes the challenge of softening the certainty and, in some cases, rupturing the discursive authority of social texts which circumscribe and command both the classroom and the larger arena of social life. It becomes, in the words of John Frow (1986: 81), "the possibility of disruption of discursive authority, and the integration of this disruption into general political struggle."

If reality does not exist as a social fact, it need not exist the way it presently does. Freedom, therefore, becomes something that must be won *within discourse*, and not sought outside of the social practices which anchor it, as though freedom can somehow be found outside the materiality of the social world, as in some metaphysical meadow. We must remember that just as there are multiple forms of power, there are also multiple forms of resistance. Students living in subordinate social positions need not accept those positions and consequently they often struggle against the dominant articulations of groups in power. Teachers must decide which discourses are to be hacked out from a thicket of possibilities, and which are to be discarded, which discourses need to be denaturalized and democratized, and which need to be opened up as potential points of resistance and political struggle. Established knowledges and social relations can be revised. New pedagogical discourses can be constructed which allow women, minorities, and working-class students to struggle for voice, for new subject positions which will allow them to speak and act *both in and on the world*. In this way educators can play a part in the regenerative processes of cultural change.

Teachers need to recognize that too often in their classroom practices the "other" (blacks, women, Hispanics, working class people) have been demonized as a result of a monogamous identification between the self of discourse and the rules, strictures, codes, and social practices which normatively ground the surrounding culture (Lankshear 1989). What is needed is an informed resistance to such monological identification, a commitment to the sounding of multiple voices, and participation in a dialogue with self and other, while always recognizing our divided selves, realizing the alien voice ringing in discourse itself, and how such a voice has been worked and traversed by contradictions.

Giroux (1988) points out that difference and pluralism in this view do not mean reducing the struggle for democracy to the celebration of diverse interests. What must be argued for, notes Giroux, is a discourse in which different voices and traditions exist *to the degree that they listen to the voices of others, engage in an ongoing attempt to eliminate the forms of subjective and objective suffering, and maintain those conditions which extend rather than restrict the creation of democratic public spheres*. This is an understanding based on the need for those designated as "others" to reclaim their subjugated histories, voices, and visions as part of a broader struggle within the public sphere to transform their lived subjugation.

The challenge for teachers in the postmodern age is to identify within curricular forms and pedagogical practices the centralizing principles of power at work with respect to race, class, and gender, self, nation, and aesthetic form "in order to determine what these centres push to their silent or invisible peripheries" (Connor 1989: 227). Teachers need to ask themselves what effects of race, class, and gender arrangements lie beneath the naturalizing facades that make up various forms of schooling. In other words, how do the curriculum forms, institutional practices, and pedagogical processes at work in schooling silence those whom they address in their regimes of representation?

I refer here to much more than a form of critical demystification, decoding, or deconstruction. I suggest that critical pedagogy must seek to simultaneously *release and explore* the multiplicity of "otherness" which those who are served by the dominant discourses regard as threatening and thus act to delegitimize and marginalize (Spanos, forthcoming). Otherness has a radical potentiality which needs to be addressed. The emergence of otherness across the landscape of generative cultures necessitates, it seems to me, the fashioning of a pedagogy that is able to contest the contradictions which inhere in the current historical juncture with respect to politics, identity, power, and the struggle for democracy. This means, of course, denaturalizing cultural production by dismantling the "regimes of truth" (sovereign or imperial discourses of culture) which inform our understanding of difference and otherness. This means that we must become aware of the ideological conflicts concealed and carried in our pedagogical agendas.

We must become aware how the historically specific terms we use to construct the "other" often result in disabling ideological effects. For instance, any white male teacher seeking to undertake a critique of patriarchy and class oppression from a Eurocentric subject position without subjecting this position to critical scrutiny does violence to rather than contributes to the project of decolonization and liberation (cf. Spanos, forthcoming).

In short, we must not attempt to fit the multiplicity of otherness into an imperial, sovereign "whole." To deny "otherness" its historical and contextual specificity is to undermine difference in the service of protecting the authority and power of universalized whiteness and maleness. Viewed in this way, we can see the dominant purpose of the culture of the school is to inscribe the "other" (blacks, Latinos, women, gays, working-class youth) with certified identities by differentially relegating their "otherness" to the domain of cultural evolution (cultural lack or cultural surplus). This is why a truly critical pedagogy for the postmodern age must constantly unveil reality in such a way as to serve both as a delegitimization of the oppressive hegemonic discourses of the dominant cultural order and a decolonization (liberation) of classroom knowledge which the discourses of schooling have purified by systematically concealing and repressing oppositional voices and practices.

The conceptual frameworks of critical pedagogy which purport to uncover and transform the constructions of subjectivity—including feminine constructions—need to be purged of their phallocentrism, Eurocentrism, and masculinist ideologies. A major task for the development of critical pedagogy is to de-authorize and rewrite the master narratives of liberal post-industrial democracy and the humanist, individualist, and patriarchal discourses which underwrite it while at the same time undermining and reconstructing the idealized and romantic conception of the subject which is shaped by Eurocentric and androcentric discursive power relations. We need to construct a de-Cartesianized, nonhumanist ethical paradigm that does not link the ideal of autonomy to the subordination of women (Fraser, 1989).

Michel Plecheux provides us with a typology for understanding how discourses are engaged by various groups in contemporary social life. To *identify* with a discourse means to live within the terms generated by that discourse; to *counteridentify* with a discourse means to live within its governing structure of ideas but to reverse its terms; to *disidentify* with a discourse means to go beyond the structure of oppositions and sanctioned negations which it supplies (Conner 1989: 236-37). Applied to schooling, to identify with the dominant curriculum discourse means to accept terms of reference that privilege the economies of power which sanction the values of white, middle-class males. To counteridentify with this discourse means to bring the margins into the center by making the interests of the disadvantaged and excluded heard in the classroom and by including them in mainstream curricula. To disidentify means to refuse the very frames of reference which splits off the marginalized from the dominators and to create new vocabularies of resistance which do not separate curriculum from gender politics, values from aesthetics, pedagogy from power.

While disidentification seems the most urgent option for critical educators, we don't want to set the stage for rejecting the notion of universality outright. Totality and universality should not be rejected in all situations, but only when they are used unjustly and oppressively as global, all-encompassing and all-embracing warrants for thought and action in order to secure an oppressive regime of truth. We need to retain some kind of moral, ethical, and political ground—albeit a provisional one—from which to negotiate among multiple interests. We could establish pedagogies and curricula which fall prey to the very error which critical educators seek to correct, which duplicate the original silencing of the Other, which replicate the concepts and systems of power they seek to revoke, and which relegitimize those very terms they seek to reject.

By repudiating domination without at the same time establishing some ethical "bearings" for a universal struggle for freedom, critical pedagogy could recover such domination in different forms. We need to ask the question: Are our pedagogies built upon a normative backdrop which privileges Eurocentric and patriarchal representations and interests? Are our multicultural and feminist pedagogies mortgaged to theoretical formulations which, however ruthlessly deconstructed, still reaffirm the primacy of Western individualism, patriarchy, and class privilege?

Within the tension produced by these questions we affirm a *solidarity in difference*, a common ground where we can work together to reconceptualize the principles of freedom and social justice, recognizing the partiality of all perspectives, and the role that criticism and the concept of difference play in creating the rhetorical ground upon which we can give voice to our call for liberation.

One step we can take as oppositional educators in this age of postmodernism is to work towards the cultivation in ourselves and our students, what Richard Kearney refers to as the development of an *ethical imagination*, the recognition of the ethical existence of the other as *other*. Kearney calls this "the inalienable right to be recognized as a particular person whose very otherness refuses to be reduced to a mimicry of sameness" (p. 361). Before you ask the epistemological question *"Who* are you?" Kearney argues you must first ask the ethical question *"Where* are you?". Kearney claims that this entails a priority of praxis over theory. Kearney is worthwhile quoting at length:

> Ethics has primacy over epistemology and ontology. Or, to put it less technically, the good comes before the question of truth and being. At the most basic level of pre-reflective lived experience, the ethical face discloses a relationship to an other before knowledge and beyond being... When a naked face cries 'Where are you?' we do not ask for identity papers. We reply, first and foremost, 'Here I am' (p. 362).

To act ethically means to act with a certain *narrative identity*. A narrative identity is "a self which remembers its commitments to the other (both in its personal and collective history) and recalls that these commitments have *not yet* been fulfilled" (p. 395). The narrative self is contingent, partial, and "must be ceaselessly reinterpreted by imagination" (p. 395). It is decidedly not egological (permanent sameness) but rather is constantly under revision, and therefore is self-rectifying. It is an identity in which the self and the collective mutuality dialectically constitute each other. Personal history takes the form of a political project by extending ethical responsibility to include a collective history. The narrative self is forever in crisis because it refuses to reduce the Other to any representation form. Its political project, notes Kearney, is to imagine alternative forms of cultural and political practice.

By uncovering those discourses in our classrooms that feed the economy of privilege, we take a major step in contesting the reproduction in our classrooms of the historical configuration of oppression. Yet this task is replete with challenges and difficulties. How can we construct narratives of cultural difference which affirm and empower while at the same time manage not to undercut the efforts of other social groups to win self-definition? In what ways are our own discourses and those of our students disguised by self-interest and defined by the exclusion of the voices of others? In what ways must we rewrite the stories that guide our so-called liberating praxis, and our interpretations of these stories in relation to shifting cultural boundaries and new political configurations? How can we redefine knowledge so that it no longer describes the discourses and practices of white males who putatively speak on behalf of everyone else? How can we affirm students' stories while at the time recognizing the inevitable partiality of these stories, and our own, and the *always already* contingency of the outcomes? How do we position the Other in the semantic field of our research so that he or she does not become a "silent predicate" that gives birth to Western, patriarchical assumptions of what constitutes truth and justice? How can we, as educators, both unlearn our privileged positions as narrators of other people's lives and still be able to exercise moral and political leadership in the struggle for social change and political transformation?

We must continue to seek multiple discourses (black pedagogy, Marxist pedagogy, feminist pedagogy, etc.) but such non-totalizing alternatives to humanist discourse must not reject the dream of totality outright. While there may be a number of public spheres from which to wage an oppositional politics, and while the micropolitical interests of groups that fleck the horizon of the postmodern scene may have overwhelmingly separate and distinct agendas, I believe that we should—all of us—work together towards a provisional and perhaps even *ephemeral totality* to which we can all aspire, as paradoxical as this may seem. It is imperative that we break away from this insider-outsider position that sets up critical pedagogy to either be complicitous with domination (another form of oppression) or else unremittingly revolutionary and contestatory.

In closing, while educators need to decenter the universality of individualism[3] which sees individuals individuate themselves *beyond* society, they need to still insist on the universality of individuals to differentiate themselves *within* society around the principles of freedom and social justice. While it may be true that we will always be decentered as human subjects, at some unconscious level at least, we nevertheless need to struggle to free ourselves from the bondage of discursive determinations and produce ourselves through the act of imagining other "selves" we could become. We need a plurality of possibilities of what we might become by recovering who we once were, what we are at present, and how we might position ourselves and (through what discourses) to become otherwise. Yet we must be clear that we need to achieve more than merely an alteration of our ideological standpoints on social and pedagogical issues; rather, we must develop the historically specific tools which will result in the transformation of our society. That is, *we need to change reality rather than simply change our conception of reality*, although the latter is certainly a prerequisite to the former.

We should no longer remain prey to the force of history but instead engage history in order to emerge from it and transform it. The critical pedagogy which I have been espousing in this essay adopts the position that the task ahead calls for both students and teachers to assume the role of active citizens for social change, and to produce history rather than yield to it. Critical knowledge does not speak its own essence but aligns itself with certain interests and powers. Our goal as educators working within a discourse of social intervention is to ensure that those interests and powers are put into the service of the oppressed.

In psychoanalytic terms, we might fear that our own ignorance of the contradictions which inform us as human subjects may lead to a "return of the repressed." For as Constance Penley (1989: 52) notes, "we only know repression through its failures; if repression were total, nothing would remain to make us aware of what had been repressed or the act of repression itself." On this basis, we may never know (or know that we know) ourselves well enough to understand in which direction we should be looking to recreate ourselves, both individually and collectively. This, however, should never prevent us from struggling to establish the conditions which make such a pursuit possible.

## ACKNOWLEDGEMENTS

Thanks to Nancy B. Wyner for her sensitive reading of this essay, and for her excellent comments for revision. I would also like to thank G. Honor Fagan for her contribution to the discussion on resistance. Also, a special note of thanks to Colin Lankshear for his helpful comments on this article, and also for his generous editorial assistance. I would also like to express my gratitude to Henry Giroux, Richard Quantz, and Martin O'Neill for their helpful suggestions.

## NOTES

1. For one of the few comprehensive accounts of North American educators engaging the concept of postmodernism and pedagogy, see the special issue of *Journal of Education* (Boston University) guest-edited by Henry Giroux (Vol. 170, no. 3, 1988). Giroux's essays in this volume contain an excellent introduction to many of the issues surrounding the debates over postmodernism. I want to make it clear at the outset that I am interested in sharing with educators some of the insights from those postmodernist perspectives which call for the development of "research as praxis" (Lather 1986), a "critical postmodernist pedagogy of liberation" (McLaren and Hammer, in press), or a "border pedagogy" (Giroux 1989; Giroux, in press) which are calling for new forms of resistance to the postmodern condition and the development of new forms of democratic social relations both in our schools and in the larger social arena.

2. MacCannell (1984) makes the important point that discourses structure our unconscious and bear a relation to macrostructural social arrangements. In his lecture on Freud, Lacan remarks that the unconscious is located at that point where between cause and effect there is always something wrong. The unconscious reveals a gap through which the neuroses recreate a harmony with the real (MacCannell 1984: 43). MacCannell points to the important connection between macrosocial arrangements and the realization of a collective unconscious desire by offering the example of U.S. leaders making Free Enterprise "an abstract totalization which justifies violent territorial and political adventures in the Third World and a bizarre foreign policy which in many instances comes down to nothing more than the principle that being a leftist is a capital offense" (p. 38).

3. See Richard Litchman, *The Production of Desire.*

# REFERENCES

Belsey, C. (1980). *Critical Practice.* London: Methuen.

Berman, R. A. (1989). *Modern Culture and Critical Theory.* Madison: University of Wisconsin Press.

Chock, P., & Wyman, J. R. (1986). Introduction: Discourse and the social life of meaning. In P.P. Chock and J.R. Wyman (eds.), *Discourse and the Social Life of Meaning* (pp. 1-20), Washington, D.C.: Smithsonian Institution Press.

Clifford, J. (1988). *The Predicament of Culture: Twentieth Century Ethnography, Literature and Art.* Cambridge, MA: Harvard University Press.

Clifford, J. (1987). Of other peoples: Beyond the 'salvage' paradigm. In H. Foster (Ed.), *Discussions in Contemporary Culture, Number One* (pp. 121-130). Seattle: Bay Press.

Clifford, J., and Marcus, G. E. (1986). *Writing Culture: The Poetics and Politics of Ethnography.* Berkeley: University of California Press.

Collins, J. (1989). *Uncommon Cultures: Popular Culture and Postmodernism.* London: Routledge.

Connor, S. (1989). *Postmodern Culture.* Oxford: Basil Blackwell.

Cottom, D. (1989). *Text and Culture: The Politics of Interpretation.* Minneapolis: University of Minnesota Press.

Dallmayr, F. R. (1986). Democracy and post-modernism. *Huma, 10,* 143-70.

Donahue, Patricia (1989). Teaching commonsense: Barthes and the rhetoric culture. In P. Donahue and E. Quandahl (eds.), *Reclaiming Pedagogy* (pp. 72-82). Carbondale and Edwardville: Southern Illinois University Press.

Fagan, H. G. (1989). Resisting school: The educational experience of Irish early school-learners from lower socio-economic background. Unpublished. Kildare, Ireland: St. Patrick's College.

Fraser, N. (1989) *Unruly Practices.* Minneapolis: University of Minnesota Press.

Frow, J. (1986). *Marxism and Literary History.* Cambridge, MA: Harvard University Press.

Geertz, C. (1973). *The Interpretation of Cultures: Selected Essays.* New York: Basic Books.

Giddens, A. (1979). *Central Problems in Social Theory.* Berkeley: University of California Press.

Gilligan, C. (1982). *In a Different Voice*. Cambridge, MA: Harvard University Press.

Giroux, H. A. (1988a). Postmodernism and the discourse of educational criticism. *Journal of Education, 170*(3), 5-30.

Giroux, H. A. (1988b). Border pedagogy in the age of postmodernism. *Journal of Education, 170*(3): 162-81.

Giroux, H. A. (1988c). *Schooling and the Struggle for Public Life*. Minneapolis: University of Minnesota Press.

Giroux, H. A. (1983). *Theory and Resistance in Education: A Pedagogy for the Opposition*. London: Heinemann Education Books.

Giroux, H. & Simon, R. (1989). Popular culture as a pedagogy of pleasure and meaning. In H. Giroux and R. Simon (eds.), *Popular Culture, Schooling, and Everyday Life* (pp. 1-29). South Hadley, MA: Bergin and Garvey.

Green, B. (1986). Reading reproduction theory. *Discourse, 6*, 2 (April), 1-31.

Grossberg, L. (1989). Formations of cultural studies: An American in Birmingham. *Strategies*, No. 2, 115-149.

Grossberg, L. (1988). *It's a Sin: Postmodernism, Politics, and Culture*. Sydney, Australia: Power Publications.

Grossberg, L. (1982). Experience, signification, and reality: The boundaries of cultural semiotics. *Semiotica, 41*(1/4), 73-106.

Grossberg, L. & Nelson, C. (1988). Introduction: The territory of Marxism. In C. Nelson and L. Grossberg (eds.), *Marxism and the Interpretation of Culture* (pp. 1-13). Urbana and Chicago: University of Illinois Press.

Harvey, D. (1989). *The Condition of Postmodernity*. London: Basil Blackwell.

Johnson, R. (1986). The story so far: And further transformations? In D. Punter (ed.), *Introduction to Contemporary Cultural Studies* (pp. 277-313). New York and London: Longman.

Kaplan, E. A. (1987). *Rocking Around the Clock: Music Television, Postmodernism, and Consumer Culture*. New York: Methuen.

Kearney, R. (1988). *The Wake of Imagination*. Minneapolis: University of Minnesota Press.

Lankshear, C. (1987). *Literacy, Schooling, and Revolution*. Philadelphia, PA: The Falmer Press.

Lash, S. & Urry, J. (1987). *The End of Organized Capitalism*. Madison: University of Wisconsin Press.

Lather, P. (1987). Educational research and practice in a postmodern era. Paper presented at the Ninth Conference on Curriculum Theory and Classroom Practice, Dayton, Ohio, October 1987.

Lichtman, R. (1982). *The Production of Desire*. New York: The Free Press.

MacCannell, Dean (1984). Baltimore in the morning... after: On the forms of post-nuclear leadership. *Diacritics*, 33-46.

McLaren, P. (1989). On ideology and education: Critical pedagogy and the politics of resistance. In H. Giroux and P. McLaren (eds.), *Critical Pedagogy, the State and Cultural Struggle* (pp. 174-202). Albany, NY: State University of New York Press.

McLaren, P. (1988). Schooling the postmodern body: Critical pedagogy and the politics of enfleshment. *Journal of Education, 170*(3): 53-83.

McLaren, P. (1986). *Schooling as a Ritual Performance*. London: Routledge and Kegan Paul.

McRobbie, A. (1986). Postmodernism and popular culture. *Postmodernism: ICA Documents 4* (pp. 54-6). London: Institute of Contemporary Arts.

Minh-ha, T. T. (1987). Of other peoples: Beyond the 'salvage' paradigm. In Hal Foster (Ed.), *Discussions in Contemporary Culture Number One* (pp. 138-141). Seattle: Bay Press.

Minh-ha, T.T. (1989). Introduction. *Discourse, 11*, 5-17.

Penley, C. (1989). *The Future of an Illusion*. Minneapolis: University of Minnesota Press.

Pfohl, S. & Cordon, A. (1987). Criminological displacements: A sociological deconstruction. In A. Kroker and M. Kroker (eds.), *Body Invaders: Panic Sex in America* (pp. 224-54). New York: St. Martin's Press.

Quantz, R. (1988). *Culture: A Critical Perspective*. A paper presented at the American Education Studies Association, Toronto, Canada, November 1989.

Quantz, R., & O'Connor, T. (1988) Writing critical ethnography: Dialogue, multivoicedness and carnival in cultural texts. *Educational Theory, 38* (1), 95-109.

Rosaldo, R. (1989). *Culture and Truth: The Remaking of Social Analysis*. Boston: Beacon Press.

Smith, P. (1989). Writing, general knowledge, and postmodern anthropology. *Discourse, 11*(2), 160-70.

Spanos, W. V. (forthcoming). *The End of Education: Towards a Posthumanist Padeia*. Minneapolis: University of Minnesota Press.

Voss, D., & Schutze, J.C. (1989). Postmodernism in context perspectives of structural changes in society, literature, and literary criticism. *New German Critique, 147*, 119-42.

Walkerdine, V. (1986). Video replay: Families, films, and fantasy. In V. Burgin, J. Donald, and C. Kaplan (eds.), *Formations of Fantasy* (pp. 167-99). London: Methuen.

Weedon, C.(1987). *Feminist Practice and Poststructuralist Theory*. London: Basil Blackwell.

Willis, P. (1977). *Learning to Labour*. Farnboraugh: Saxon House.

Wolff, R. (1989). Review of *The Last Intellectuals* by Russell Jacoby.

# Index

AACTE, RATE II & III (American Association for the Colleges of Teacher Education), 210, 211
Apple, M.A., 125
Apple, M.W., 92
Applegate, J., 84, 91, 222
Arends, R.I., 211, 223
Arends, R.I., & Cohen, L., 219
Arends, R.I., & Galluzzo, G., 221
Arends, R.I., & Winitsky, N., 219
Argyris, C., 146, 151, 153
Argyris, C., & Schon, D.A., 92
Arnot, M., & Weiner, G., 48
Astin, A.W., 110

Bakhtin, M.M., 47, 236, 238
Bandura, A., 80, 90
Barone, T.E., 91
Barthes, R., 102
Bateson, G., 9
Beckum, L.C., Othegyt, R., Garcia, O., Zimny, A., Perry, P., Lord, E., & Rollett, B., 128
Bell, A.P., 91
Bellah, R., Madsen, R., Sullivan, W., Swidler, A., & Tipton, 5., 56
Berliner, D.C., 222
Berman, P., & McLaughlin, M., 143, 149
Bernard, C., 34
Bernstein, B., 56, 125
Bird, T., 185
Bird, T., & Alspaugh, D., 186
Birmingham Centre for Contemporary Cultural Studies, 237
black culture, misrepresentation of, 238
black visibility in multi-ethnic high school, 65
  positive invisibility, 70-73
  positive visibility, areas of, 67-70
  Riverview High School, 66, 67
    historical development, 72
  unity of school and town, 66
  visibility outside of school, 74
Bloom's taxonomy, 6, 7
Blumenfeld, P.C., & Meece, J.L., 135
Book, C., Byers, J., & Freeman, D., 91
Boyd, R., 13, 27

Boyd, R., & Richerson, P.J., 91
Boyer, E., 109, 111, 113
Breakfast Club, 45, 46, 57, 58, 59
Bright Prospects School, 45, 48, 51, 52, 53, 59
  implausible endings, 58
  plausible endings, 45
  setting & research methodology, 48
  success stories, first & second impressions, 52, 53
  teenage mothers & fictions of school success, 45
  theoretical background of study, 47
Burlingame, , 15, 23
Bushell, D., & Rappaport, D., 143

Campbell, D.T., 23, 91
Carnegie Forum on Education & the Economy, 204
Cavalli-Sforza, L.L., & Feldman, M.W., 89
Cazden, C.B., 204
changing instructional methods, 143, 147
  components related to instruction, 147
  impact of project, 154, 157
  Israeli schools, 143
  resistance to, 149, 161
    coping with, 151
  teachers' reactions to change project, 153
    innovators, resisters, 153, 155
Children's Defense Fund booklets, 55
Chock, P., & Wyman, J.R., 247
Chodorow, N., 60
Christensen, P., 211
Clifford, G., & Guthrie, J., 224
Clifford, J., 238, 245
Clifford, J., & Marcus, G.E., 235
Cole, M., & Griffin, p., 134, 137
Cole, M., & Scribner, 5., 124
Collins, J., 235, 242, 243
Collins, P.H., 57
Combs, A.W., 88, 89, 92
Combs, A.W., Richards, A.C., & Richards, F., 89
Conant, J.B., 211, 222, 224
Conner, 5., 236, 249, 250
cooperative learning, 143, 162
  adoption of, proposed stages, 159

Israeli schools, 143

Corbett, H.D., Dawson, J., & Firestone, W., 146, 149, 153

Cottom, D., 239, 247

Counts, G., 206

Cuban, L., 205, 207

cultural approach to school reform, 85
  strategies of change, 86

cultural politics, 243

cultural relativism, 239

cultural visibility vs. stripping, 243
  authenticity, 244, 247
  counteridentify vs. disidentify, 250

culture & age of postmodernism, 232, 234
  discourse of liberation, 246

culture and resistance, 240
  capitalist consumerism, 241
  meritocratic ideology, 241
  patriarchy, 240

culture as discourse, 235

culture as plurivocal, 237

culture, decentering, 231
  culture of schooling, 232
  culture, rethinking of, 233
  post-structuralist discourse, 231

culture of teaching in higher education, 109, 113, 119, 120
  rewards of teaching career, 113

cultures of teaching
  alienation, 99
  bilingual education, 95
  challenges, 103
  communication, failures in, 101
  differences in origins, 97
  diversity, 95
  emerging research, 96
  myths, 102
  social changes, 97

cultures of teaching: stability & change, 79, 81
  culture & social learning, 80
  life cycle of teacher, 83
  selection, 82, 85

Cummins, J., 124

Cusick, P.A., 9

D'Andrade, R.G., 2

Darling-Hammond, L., 165

DeStefano, J., & Pepinsky, H., 133

Dewey, J., 204, 205, 206, 220

Dyer, W.G., Jr., 92

Eisner, E.W., 8, 90

Ellison, R. , 65, 67

Elmore, R., 198

Erickson, F., iii, 4, 95, 96, 124, 126

Erickson, F., Cazden, C., Carresco, R., & Gozman, A., 133

Erickson, F., & Mohatt, G., 133

Evertson, C., Hawley, W., & Zlotnick, M., 222

Faculty Council to Study Reorganization, 113

Fagan, H.G., 240, 253

Fanon, F., 9

Farber, S.L., 111, 112

Feiman-Nemser, 5., & Floden, R.L., 1, 92, 96, 112, 113, 114, 206, 207

Feistritzer, C.E., 91

Feltovich, P., Spiro, R., & Coulson, R., 216, 216

Fisher, R.L., & Feldman, M.E., 91

Flinders, D., 191

Foucault, M., 53, 54, 236

Fraser, N., 246, 250

Freshman Year Program, University of Lowell, 109, 116, 119, 120
  focus & purpose, 109
  freshman centers, 116
  computing & tutoring programs, 117

Frow, J., 237, 248

Fullan, M., 2, 104, 117, 119, 120, 149, 151, 153, 185, 188 198, 216, 219

Fullan, M., & Connelly, F.M., 197

Fullan, M., & Hargreaves, A., 198

Fullan, M., & pomfret, A., 182, 188

Fullan, M., Rolheiser-Bennett, C., & Bennett, B., 192, 193

Fuller, F., & Brown, 0., 155

Galluzzo, G., & Arends, R.I., 208

Gamson, 2., 109, 114

Gay, G., 134

Gee, J.P., 47

Geertz, C., 3, 47, 106, 233

Giddens, A., 231, 232

Ginsburg, H.P., 124

Giroux, H.A., 3, 9, 132, 137, 237, 240, 248, 253

Goodenough, W.H., 3, 89

Goodlad, J.I., 2, 80, 90, 92, 111, 144, 146, 204, 205

Gordon, L., 48

Green, B., 235

Green, M., 127, 133, 137

Greenfield, T.B., 32, 34
Grossberg, L., 234, 235
Gumperz, J.J., 133
Gusfield, J.R., 53
Guttmacher Institute, 49, 55
Gwaltney, J.L., 65, 73

Hall, G., George, A., & Rutherford, W., 159
Hargreaves, A., 191, 192, 198
Hargreaves, A., & Dawe, R., 192, 198
Harris, L., & Associatec, 92
Harris, M., 89
Hart, A., 186
Heckman, P., 90, 92, 144
Henriques, J., Hollway, W., Urwin, C., Venn,
    C., & Walkerdine, V., 47, 53
Hertz-Lazarowitz, R., & Shacher, H., 156
Holmes Group, 204, 211, 224, 226
Hopkins, D., 221
Howe, F., 48
Howey, K.R., 208
Huberman, M., 197
Huberman, M., & Miles, M., 145, 150, 151, 159,
    160, 182, 186, 188, 207, 219
Huling-Austin, L., 185
Hymes, D.H., 4

Israel Center for Educational Television, 143

Jackson, P., 132, 137
Johnson, D.W., & Johnson, R.T., 218
Johnson, M., 65
Johnson, W., 207
Jordan, C., 134
Joyce, B., McKibbon, M., & Hersh, R., 206, 207
Joyce, B., Murphy, C., Showers, B., & Murphy,
    J., 184, 187, 197
Joyce, B., & Showers, B., 186, 188, 216, 217
Joyce, B., & Weil, M., 216
Joyce, B., Yarger, 5., & Howey, K., 211
Judge, H., 224

Kantor, R., 117, 119
Kaplan, E.A., 235
Kearney, R., 251
Kellogg, J.B., 97
Kemmis, 5., 221
Kerr, D., 211
Kerr, H., & Bruun, 5., 156
Kilcher, A., 185

Kirp, D., 46
Kochman, T., 68, 73
Kroeber, A.L., & Kluckhohn, C., 1

Labelle, T.J., 126
Labov, W., 68
Lakoff, G., 65
Laman, A.E., & Reeves, D.E., 91
Lanier, J.E., & Little, J.W., 90, 207
Lanier, P.E., & Henderson, J.E., 91
Lankshear, C., 248, 253
Latane, B., Williams, K., & Harkin, 5., 156
Lather, P., 253
leadership & school district culture, 29
    Felicia Singer, Hispanic superintendent,
        29
    game plan, 30
    personnel changes, 32
    school board & community, 31
    school district image, 34
    school site administration, 37
    selection of cabinet team, 35
    student performance improvement, 32
    superintendent/principal relationship, 37
    superintendent/school board relationship,
        40
    superintendent's role, 34
    teachers, impact of, 39
Learning Consortium, 192, 197
    purposes, 193
    staff development, 197
Lee, R.A., & Nishio, A.T., 111
Lesko, N., 46, 47, 50, 52, 56
Levi-Strauss, C., 47
Lieberman, A., 2, 104
Lieberman, A., & Miller, L., 165, 206
Lieberman, A., & Rosenholtz, 5., 146
Litchman, R., 254
Little, J.W. , 165, 168, 178, 181, 185, 188, 190,
    192, 192, 198
Little, J., Sparks, D., & Loucks-Horsley, 5., 181
Lortie, D., 91, 146, 155, 165, 191, 204, 206, 207,
    209, 220, 227
Lumsden, C., & Wilson, E.O., 90
Lutz, F.W., & Wang, L.Y., 32

MacConnell, D., 253
McDermott, R., & Goldman, 5., 3
McKeachie, W.J., 113
McLaren, p., ii, 47, 241

McNeil, L.M., 90
McRobbie, A., 234
March, J.G., 33, 35, 36, 37
Markus, H., 81, 90
Martin, J.R., 48, 56, 60
Massachusetts Board of Regents, 118
mentor teacher program, 185
  coaching, 186, 188, 189
  mentoring, 187, 188, 189
Metz., M.H., 90
Mezirow, J., & Associates, 106
Miles, M., 151, 187
Miles, M.B., Saxl, E.R., James, J., & Lieberman, A., 165, 174
Miller, N.K., 45
Minha-ha, T.T., 245
Montero-Sieburth, M., & Perez, M., 101
mythical vs. historical consciousness, 245

National Center for Education Information, 85
Nias, J., 197, 198
Nichols, P.C., 105

O'Brien, C., 115
Ogbu, J., 124
Olson, L., 92
O'Neill, M., 253
Ost, D.H. , 90, 97

Palincsar, A.S., & Brown, A.L., 204
Paris, C., 181, 198
Penley, C., 252
Pink, W., 181, 184, 185
politics of conflicting forces, 20
politics of state & federal relationships, 16
politics of survival, 14, 26
  rules of survival, 15
power of superintendency, 23
  balancing act, 25

Quantz, R., 237, 253
Quantz, R., & O'Connor, T., 239

Rains, P.M., 46
Resnick, L.B., 204
Rich, A., 48
Richardson, V., 105
Rist, R., 65, 66, 67, 125
Robinson, L., 72

Rodman, B., 92
Rogin M., 246
Roman, L., Christian-Smith, L., & Ellsworth, E., 48
Rosaldo, M.Z., & Lamphere, L., 60
Rosaldo, R., 233, 243, 244, 245
Rosenholtz, S.J., 165, 168, 188, 193
Rosenthal, T.L., & Zimmerman, B.J., 81, 90
Russo, M. , 49, 55

St. John, N.H., 71
Sarason, S.B., i, ii, 1, 80, 90, 96, 120, 143, 144, 145, 146, 151, 188, 206, 219
Sarason, S.B., Davidson, K.S., & Blatt, B., 96
Saxl, E.R., Miles, M.B., & Lieberman, A., 169
Schein, E.H., 92
Schlechty, P.C., & Vance, V.S., 208
Schmuck, R., & Schmuck, P., 205
Schon, D., 102
school board and community, 31
school culture, 1, 29, 143
  coaching, 189
  changing instructional methods, 143
  conceptions of, overview, 1
  examples of, 5
school culture in multicultural settings, 123
  culture, definition of, 124
  culture in the classroom, 125
    two dimensions, 127
  focus of research, 123
  important role of, 125
school cultures, behavioral regularities, 145, 148
  organizational flexibility, 145
school cultures, conceptions of, 1
  conceptual structures, 3, 10
  knowledge bits, 2, 8, 10
  political struggle, 10
  social structure/culture intertwined, 3
  sociocognitive task structure, 6
Schuster, J., 112
Scribner, 5., & Cole, M., 124
Seeley, D.S., 133
Seller, W., & Hannay, L., 189
Sharan, 5., & Hertz-Lazarowitz, R., 143, 151, 153, 155
Sharan, 5., & Hertz-Lazarowitz, R., & Ackerman, Z., 157
Sharan, 5., & Hertz-Lazarowitz, R., & Hare, P., 147

Sharan, 5., & Kussell, P., Hertz-Lazarowitz, R., Bejarono, Y., Raviv, 5., & Sharan, Y., 143, 204, 218
Sharan, 5., & Rich, Y., 143
Sharan, 5., & Shachar, H., 143, 147, 218
Sharan, 5., & Sharan, Y., 105, 143
Shulman, L.S., 91, 112
Sidel, R., 48, 57
Sivan, E., 127
Slavin, R., 205, 218
Smith, 5., 45, 53, 54, 56
Smylie, M., 197, 198
Smylie, M., & Denny, J., 198
sociocognitive task structure, 6
  controversial beliefs, 7
Solomon, D., Watson, M., Schaps, E., Battis-tich, V., & Solomon, J., 161
Spanos, W.V., 249
Spindler, G.D., 90
Spindler, G.D., & Spindler, L., 90
Sprinthall, R.C., & Sprinthall, N.A., 126
staff development, innovation, & institutional development, 181
  definition of, 181
  innovation perspectives, 181
  staff development & implementation, link between, 182
    barriers to, 184
  teacher as learner, 195
Student Life Committee Report, 113
successful teachers of multicultural children, 128
  institutions in Austrian, English, & U.S. schools, 128
  qualitative observations, 131
  research design, 4 categories, 129, 130
  teachers, 128
superintendency & politics, 13, 19
  comments of superintendents, 17
  political dilemma of nonelected public official, 13
  superintendent as politician, 21
Sykes, 89, 93

teacher as "intercultural broker," 126
teacher as learner, 195, 196
  four aspects, 195
teacher leadership ideology & practice, 165
  as learner, 177
  as professional model, 178

building colleagueship, 168
entry characteristics, 166
on-the-job learning, 167
Parkridge Elementary School, 176
teacher/leader skills, 165
  three approaches, 166
Urban High School, 174
teacher training, implications, 134
teaching through teacher education, 203
  barriers & prospects, 223
  cooperative learning, 218
  patterns of teaching, 204
    recitation, 204, 205, 207, 211, 223
    teacher autonomy, 204, 206
  proposal for challenging, 213
  redesigned program, structure of, 213
    guidelines, 214
Thelen, H., 144, 205
Time Magazine, 46, 49, 50, 52, 35
Truebe, H.T., 124
Turner, V., 47
Twain, M., 89

underprepared students, changing faculty beliefs, 109, 115
  interaction with students, 113
University of Lowell, 110
  background, 110
  faculty culture, 112
  Strategic Plan, 111
  students, demography, 111
  teaching culture, 119, 120

Vandement, W., 112
Varenne, H., 47
Vetter, B., 111
Voss, D., & Schutze, J.C., 234
Vygotsky, L.S., 124, 127

Walkerdine, V., 45, 47, 53, 56
Waller, W., 206
Weedon, C., 53, 235, 241
Wehlage, G., Rutter, R., Smith, G., Lesko, N., & Fernandez, R., 46, 53
Weinstein, C.S., 209, 210
Welsh, P. 206
Wertsch, J.V., 124
Wexler, P., 47
Whitson, J.A., 45, 47, 53
Willis, P., 3, 9, 240

Willow Creek Unified School District, 29, 30, 36, 38, 42

Willower, D.J., & Smith, J., 29

Wise, A.E., Darling-Hammond, L., & Berry, B., 92

Wittgenstein, L., 1

Wolff, R., 231

Wyner, N.B., 95, 253

Zaltman, G., Florio, D., & Sikorski, L., 159

Zimpher, N.L., 208

Zinn, M.B., 57